Clarissa Tossin

Clarissa Tossin
to take root among the stars

Edited by Georgia Erger

Frye Art Museum 2023

Foreword

"A threat is harder to ignore when it's closer to home, or literally happening in your backyard," writer and educator Reuben Merringer wrote in consideration of Clarissa Tossin's work.[1] Tossin's practice, which spans mediums—installation, film, performance, sculpture, and photography—and scales to interrogate material cultural production and the exchange of its related resources, will undoubtedly resonate around the globe. Merringer made his observation in relation to an exhibition of Tossin's work in Los Angeles, where she resides. Yet his sentiment feels particularly apt in this moment, the occasion of the artist's first solo exhibition in Seattle. In conceiving of this exhibition, Associate Curator Georgia Erger astutely brings to the Frye Art Museum artwork that offers a particular level of insight to our community, an epicenter of diffuse multinational companies.

In some respects, it can be more difficult to apply a critical eye to our own surroundings—to see the threats among us—as the extraordinary becomes normalized. It is routine to witness contemporary corporate leaders offering up grandiose, utopic visions, ranging from the mission statement of Mark Zuckerberg's Meta, "to give people the power to build community and bring the world closer together," to the "billionaire space race" entrepreneurship effort among Jeff Bezos, Richard Branson, and Elon Musk. As the home of Amazon's and Microsoft's headquarters, as well as offices for Adobe, Google, Meta, and others, Seattle is a hub of "big tech," yet many of its citizens are rarely in contact with the global ramifications of these companies' practices on the resources—natural, human, economic, and beyond—that are often at the heart of Tossin's art and the critical perspective it offers. The artist spent her childhood in Brasília, the federal capital of Brazil conceived as a modernist utopia in the mid-twentieth century—a place whose lasting legacies and shortcomings the artist at times references for potent comparisons to the present.

"Humankind is nothing if not optimistic, even to the point of blindness," wrote Nathaniel Rich,[2] in the context of the many opportunities and decades we have had—and failed—to stop climate change, a subject particularly relevant to Tossin's work. To overcome this blindness is among the great quandaries of our time. In order to lead us past the false visions of the present and the fences of our own backyards toward a wider, more global perspective, Tossin offers viewers a lens of highly specific material culture. Thanks in no small part to the insightful introduction by Georgia Erger and illuminating essays by Vic Brooks and Leslie Dick, this catalogue begins to unpack the deeply layered meanings found within the architecture, the appropriations, the sneakers, and the Amazon boxes, woven together—both physically and metaphorically—within this artist's rich oeuvre. Given the stakes of the threats we are facing, here in Seattle and among the global community of which we are a part, there is truly no time like the present to better understand the more honest visions of the world that Tossin's work urges us to see.

I am grateful to the many people who collaborated on this important exhibition and accompanying publication. Profound thanks are due to Clarissa Tossin, not only for her incisive and powerful work, but also for her generous partnership, without which this project would not have been possible. I thank Georgia Erger for her foresight in bringing this thought-provoking art to Seattle and for her tireless efforts realizing the exhibition and publication. We express our immense appreciation to Vic Brooks and Leslie Dick for contributing richly developed research and writings that are invaluable at this juncture of Tossin's career.

I extend my gratitude to the Frye's staff for its dedication and contributions to the museum's exhibitions and publications, and I thank the board of trustees for its unwavering commitment to the museum's mission and work. We are also grateful to the exhibition's media sponsor, Encore Media Group, and to the Frye Foundation and Frye Art Museum members for their support.

Commonwealth and Council in Los Angeles played a crucial role in realizing this exhibition and publication. We are grateful to Breanne Bradley, Young Chung, and Kibum Kim for lending works, and to Brenda Reyes-Chavez and the rest of the gallery staff for their gracious support. Our deep appreciation goes to the individual lenders to the exhibition, Janice Niemi and Dennis Braddock and the Mohn Family Trust, and to our colleagues at the Los Angeles County Museum of Art for their support in lending *Future Fossil*:

Rita Gonzalez, Michael Govan, and Megan Smith. We are also grateful to Luisa Strina and her staff at Galeria Luisa Strina in São Paulo: Flávia França, Kiki Mazzucchelli, and Cristiana Thompson.

It is an honor to present—for the first time in an exhibition—Tossin's film *Mojo'q che b'ixan ri ixkanulab' / Antes de que los volcanes canten / Before the Volcanoes Sing* (2022), which was commissioned by EMPAC—the Curtis R. Priem Experimental Media and Performing Arts Center at Rensselaer Polytechnic Institute in Troy, New York. Much gratitude is owed to Vic Brooks, EMPAC's associate director of arts and senior curator of time-based visual art, for curating this remarkably ambitious four-year project and guiding it through the challenges of a global pandemic. We would like to thank two of the film's collaborators—Ixil Maya artist Tohil Fidel Brito Bernal and K'iche'-Kaqchikel poet Rosa Chávez—for graciously allowing us to reproduce works they contributed to the film: Brito Bernal's contemporary glyphs—created from his knowledge of Classic Maya hieroglyphics—that translate as "before the volcanoes sing" and Chávez's poem "Dame permiso espíritu del camino (Give me permission spirit of the path)," which inspired the film's title. We would also like to acknowledge other collaborators on the film: cinematographer Jeremy Glaholt, archaeologist/anthropologist Jared Katz, flautist Alethia Lozano Birrueta, and composer Michelle Agnes Magalhães. Thanks also go to the incredible EMPAC production team, especially project manager Ian Hamelin, video engineer Ryan Jenkins, and audio engineer Jeff Svatek.

Heartfelt thanks are due to the staff at Marquand Books for their invaluable partnership and top-notch work on this book, including Leah Finger, Jeremy Linden, Adrian Lucia, Julia Powers, and Kestrel Rundle. I am particularly grateful to Tom Eykemans for the book's stellar design, which thoughtfully builds on the framework created by Purtill Family Business for the series. I extend my thanks to copy editor Kathleen Garrett for her assiduous editorial work and to Janice Lee for her meticulous proofreading.

I would also like to thank the Frye's manager of exhibitions and publications, Laura Landau, for her thoughtful oversight of this publication and Erin Langner, assistant editor and exhibitions coordinator, for her astute editorial contributions and sourcing of the book's images and related rights

The individuals and institutions that grant reproduction permissions are key to any book, and we express gratitude to Michael Carnes, Blanton Museum of Art, University of Texas at Austin; Sara Cordes, California State Library, Sacramento; Samuel

Freeman Gallery, Los Angeles; Instituto Inhotim, Brumadinho, Brazil; Mélanie Kiry, La Kunsthalle Mulhouse, France; Miranda Lash, Museum of Contemporary Art Denver; Rosemary Lennox, Ezra and Cecile Zilkha Gallery, Center for the Arts, Wesleyan University, Middletown, Connecticut; Micah Musheno, Whitney Museum of American Art, New York; Erin Rolfs, Moody Center for the Arts at Rice University, Houston; and Meg Rotzel, Harvard Radcliffe Institute for Advanced Study, Johnson-Kulukundis Family Gallery, Cambridge, Massachusetts.

Finally, we acknowledge that none of what we do at the Frye Art Museum would be possible if not for the Coast Salish peoples, who have since time immemorial stewarded the lands and waters of this place we now call Seattle. We offer our gratitude and respect to their elders past and present, as well as to future generations for their continued stewardship.

AMANDA DONNAN
CHIEF CURATOR AND DIRECTOR OF EXHIBITIONS
FRYE ART MUSEUM

Notes

1. Reuben Merringer, "Clarissa Tossin at Commonwealth and Council," *Contemporary Art Review Los Angeles* (June 11, 2022). https://contemporaryartreview.la/clarissa-tossin-at-commonwealth-and-council/.
2. Nathaniel Rich, "Losing Earth: The Decade We Almost Stopped Climate Change," *New York Times*, August 1, 2018. https://www.nytimes.com/interactive/2018/08/01/magazine/climate-change-losing-earth.html.

Introduction: Encounter Zones

Georgia Erger

The black and beige waters of the Negro and Amazon Rivers meet but do not mix at Brazil's Port of Manaus, a site of multifaceted ecological, cultural, and economic confluence in the heart of the Amazon rainforest. Global industries that have developed in the region and local Indigenous communities alike rely on the rivers and forests for survival. Manaus was declared a free-trade zone in 1967; consequently, tons of electronic and organic goods are manufactured and exported downstream for international consumption. Meanwhile, local communities contend with the ruinous effects of extractive capitalism while continuing to maintain and develop cultural traditions, as they have since the region was first colonized at the turn of the sixteenth century.

The late nineteenth-century demand for rubber turned Manaus into the most industrialized city in Brazil until 1912, when the British Empire assumed control of the world market by creating rubber plantations in its colonies in Southeast Asia and Africa. In the 1930s, Henry Ford purchased land in the interior of the rainforest with significant tax breaks and established industry towns to harvest latex from rubber trees to produce automobile tires.[1] These industrial outposts in the Amazon exemplify how colonial frontiers function as encounter zones between foreign capital and nature, wherein nature is not only destroyed, but put to work, as cheaply as possible. As Raj Patel and Jason Moore succinctly state, "capitalism not only has frontiers; it exists only through frontiers."[2]

This long history of the Amazon and its meanings in the popular imagination have led to the present, where the playful yet jarringly dislocated name of the Seattle-based company looms large. The name also well represents artist Clarissa Tossin's sustained, nuanced explorations of the intersections and geopolitical causes of climate change and capitalism's frontier mythologies. Tossin, who was born in Porto Alegre, was raised in Brasília, and is now based in Los Angeles, first began repurposing Amazon delivery boxes as sculptural material while investigating colonial histories of—and resistance to—exploitative natural resource extraction in Manaus. Her sculptural work *Nova gramática de formas #2 (New Grammar of Forms #2)* (2018; pl. 21), for example, features terracotta replicas of electronics cradled in baskets woven from strips of recycled Amazon delivery boxes and satellite images of the Negro and Amazon Rivers. Tossin found inspiration in Amazonian basket-making traditions to devise her paper-weaving technique (fig. 1). The laborious weaving process disrupts associations of expeditious commodity chains conjured by the immediately recognizable barcodes and smiling arrow logos of the Amazon boxes. Tossin is mining overlooked frontiers of cultural knowledge to present potential futures that could reconcile, or survive, capitalist-driven ecological destruction.

Tossin's use of Amazon boxes—ubiquitous detritus of our rampant consumerist culture—points to our simultaneously significant and insignificant role in climate change, and to the overwhelming scale of the crisis itself. Climate change is so massively distributed in time and space that we can see only pieces of it (the single cardboard box delivered overnight to our doorstep, for example) at once.[3] Further, much of our anxiety about a climate

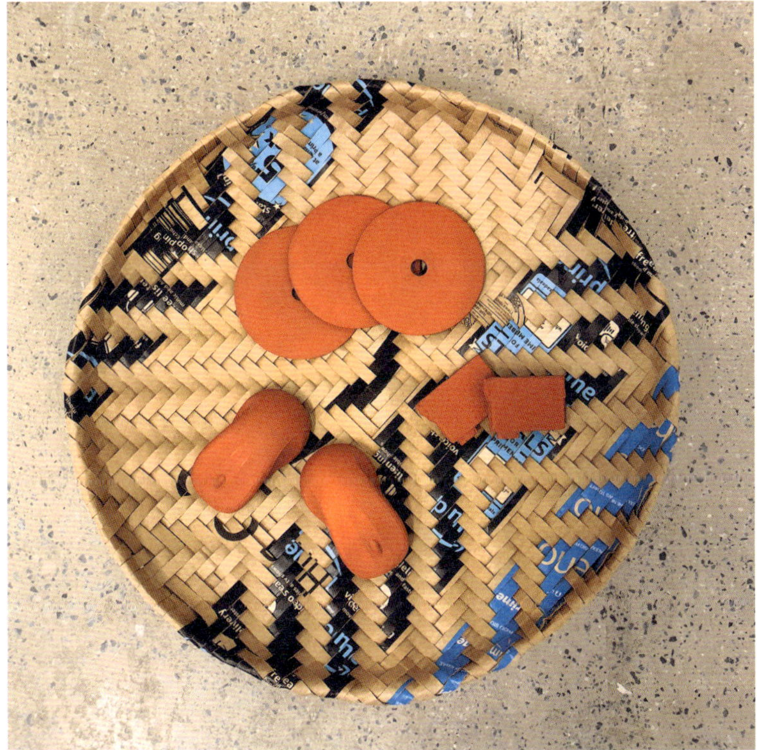

Fig. 1. *Nova gramática de formas #1 (New Grammar of Forms #1)* (detail), 2018. Terracotta objects, baskets woven from used Amazon.com delivery boxes, thread, wood, fishing net. Dimensions variable. Private collection. Installation view, *Azul Maia*, Galeria Luisa Strina, São Paulo, November 18–December 21, 2018. Courtesy of the artist and Galeria Luisa Strina. Photo: Edouard Fraipont

apocalypse stems from our inability to identify whether it is imminent or if we have already reached that terrifying frontier.

Tossin troubles capitalism's unwavering faith in progress, a culturally situated "way of knowing," and instead engages ideas of difference and repetition, cycles and transformation, and circular time. *Clarissa Tossin: to take root among the stars* brings together works across mediums from the last decade of Tossin's practice, including newly commissioned weavings and drawings, to speculate on uncertain futures and networks of interconnectedness across time and geographies.

The exhibition begins with the translucent corporeal form of a deceased tree. Hanging upside down in the Frye Art Museum's rotunda, *Rising Temperature Casualty (Prunus persica, home garden, Los Angeles)* (2022; pl. 10) is a silicone cast of a peach tree from the artist's garden that perished due to heat waves and drought in Los Angeles. The subtitle of the artwork serves to indexically archive the consequences of climate change; however, this rational, scientific treatment is betrayed by the ghostly, skinlike materiality of the sculpture, which viscerally points to the fragility of life on our planet. The silicone cast retains bark from the imprinted tree. This seamless melding of synthetic and organic materials is prevalent across Tossin's practice and embodies the tension between extractive approaches to Earth's natural resources and Indigenous ways of knowing and being in reciprocity with the land.

Rising Temperature Casualty—and the death it memorializes—points to how climate apocalypse might be not a single event, but a series of seemingly insignificant, intimate, interconnected moments that unfold right outside our back door. As Timothy Morton states, "the end of the world is not a sudden punctuation point, but rather it is a matter of deep time. Twenty-four thousand years into the future, no one will be related to me. Yet everything will be influenced by the tiniest decisions I make right now."[4] While Morton directly implicates us, Tossin more subtly identifies endemic exhaustion—of natural, physical, and emotional resources—across "deep time." And indeed, the limply hanging branches of the cast tree physically express this sense of depletion and ephemerality.

A series of clay imprints, *Becoming Mineral* (2021; pls. 3–4 and fig. 7, p. 31), captures Tossin's face, eyes closed and in a state of partial disappearance. They evoke death masks, or "memento mori," and "grapple with the death of a certain way of being human, a certain way of inhabiting this planet, a certain way of being a collective body that's now being put into question due to technological

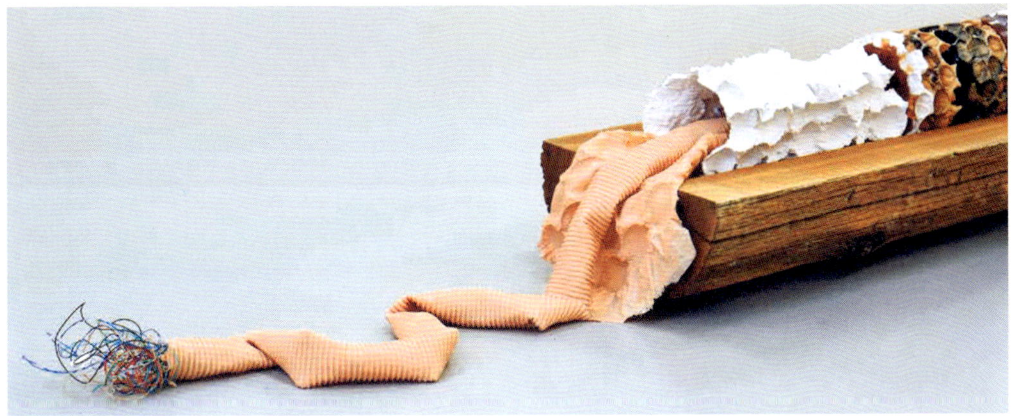

Fig. 2. *Future Fossil* (detail), 2018. Cedar tree trunk, rocks, roots, leaves, bark, soil, sand, plaster, cement, silicone, foam, resin, aluminum foil, electronic waste, recycled plastics (PET, HDPE, LDPE, PP, and PS). 14 × 240 × 17 in. Los Angeles County Museum of Art, Purchased with funds provided by AHAN: Studio Forum, 2019 Art Here and Now purchase. Installation view, *Future Fossil*, Harvard Radcliffe Institute for Advanced Study, Johnson-Kulukundis Family Gallery, January 31–March 16, 2019. Image courtesy Harvard Radcliffe Institute for Advanced Study. Photo: Stewart Clements

advances."[5] The masks were made during the pandemic lockdown with leftover clay from the artist's studio; the striking marbling effect reflects the haphazard combination of different-toned clays, including porcelain. Tossin consistently uses recycled and waste materials in her sculptures and of her motives states, "I'm very interested in the idea of degrowth, and slowing down the hectic cycles of production and consumption. My own pressing dilemma is: How do I maintain a sustainable art practice aligned with degrowth ideas, while also engaging in material production?"[6]

If not a solution to this dilemma per se, *Future Fossil* (2018; pls. 25–26), a melted composite of the artist's own plastic waste, reflects our contradictory relationship with the environment. Tossin's imagined "core sample" of a future geological record is preserved for a speculative, even post-human landscape. Composed of melted plastics, electronic waste (a bundle of wires hangs from the end of the sample), silicone, plaster, cement, and organic matter, and embedded in a fallen cedar tree trunk, this twenty-foot "future fossil" visualizes the entanglement of human consumption and the environments that necessarily adapt and react to our overwhelming presence (fig. 2). The future geological strata of our present era, alternatively dubbed the Anthropocene, Capitalocene, or Wasteocene,[7] will no doubt include layers of manmade "minerals" and materials such as concrete and plastic. Tossin describes *Future Fossil* as sprinkled with sci-fi content.[8] Indeed, the sculpture can be interpreted as a fictionalized readymade: found, incidentally aesthetic, neither industrially manufactured nor geologically created. The swirling colors of the composite core set this "sample" apart from the familiar visual language of fossils, but the materiality of plastic—bright, cheap, sterile—is deeply integrated into the cultural imagination of advanced capitalist societies. It is therefore darkly humorous, or perhaps wonderfully optimistic, to imagine a future in which plastic might be unfamiliar.

Such a scenario is imagined in Octavia E. Butler's Xenogenesis trilogy (1987–89), which chronicles the survival of the human race after a nuclear apocalypse. Humans endure through a partnership with an alien species who select the Amazon rainforest as the site for a new civilization of alien-human hybrids. Akin, a hybrid, is made nauseous when he tastes a found piece of plastic: "It was . . . more poison packed tight together in one place than I've ever known." He asks, "Did Humans make it that way on purpose?" His human companion, who experienced pre-apocalyptic life on Earth, replies, "It just worked out that way. Hell, maybe that's why the stuff is still here. Maybe it's so poisonous—or so useless—that not even the microbes would eat it."[9]

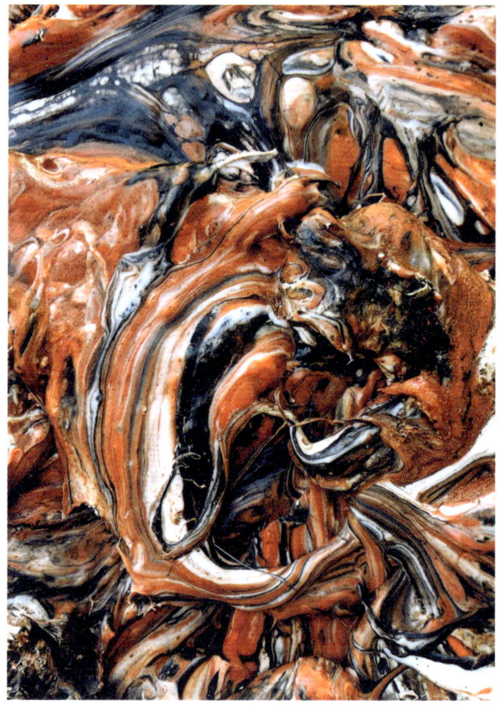

Fig. 3. *#AmazonisPlanitia2* (detail), 2018. Archival inkjet prints on glossy photo paper, recycled plastic from artist's own waste. 20¾ × 29⅞ in. and 11¼ × 19⅝ in. Courtesy of the artist and Commonwealth and Council, Los Angeles. Image courtesy Harvard Radcliffe Institute for Advanced Study. Photo: Stewart Clements

A 2019 series of related sculptures, such as *The Only Lasting Truth Is Change* (2019; pl. 27), is composed of melted layers of recycled synthetic materials and forms a constellation of planets. The series's titles are derived from three "Earthseed" verses in Butler's later novel *Parable of the Sower* (1993): "All that you touch / You Change / All that you Change / Changes You / The only lasting truth / Is Change."[10] Earthseed, the religion and eventual community founded by protagonist Lauren Olamina, proclaims the inevitability of change and humankind's capacity to adapt to those changes. Tossin's planetary sculptures underscore our agency in determining Earth's ecological future, manifesting in their very materiality the central themes of change—of malleability and *plasticity*. The prominently reddish hues of the sculptures' sedimentary strata allude to Earthseed's destiny, "to take root among the stars,"[11] and specifically a young Olamina's fascination with Mars, "a whole other world," which she presciently describes as "too close within the reach of the people who've made such a hell of life here on Earth."[12]

Mars has already felt the destructive impact of humans: it is littered with more than 15,000 pounds of trash from robotic exploration. In *#AmazonisPlanitia2* (2018; pl. 28 and fig. 3), Tossin melts her own plastic waste on photographic prints of the planet's vividly red surface. The name of one of Mars's smoothest and most desolate plains, Amazonis Planitia, paradoxically evokes the lush abundance of Earth's Amazon forest, fueling colonial fantasies of terraforming. The series *Valuable Element* (2022; pl. 30) similarly maps human intervention on a celestial body. Here, Tossin's artistic process evokes strip-mining the Moon. She incrementally effaces a photographic print of the Moon's surface by repeatedly folding and then scraping away the ink on the paper. The extracted ink, visually akin to moondust, is collected in a glass vial, representative of the valuable lunar resources proposed as ripe for the taking and necessary for sustained human life on Earth and beyond.

Frontier mythologies, constructed and enacted with alarming ease by global capitalism, are further examined by Tossin in the series *Future Geography* (2021–ongoing; pls. 11–16). Reproductions of NASA satellite images of the Moon, Mars, and star clusters are interwoven with strips of Amazon delivery boxes, recalling the Amazonian weaving traditions referenced in *Nova gramática de formas #2* (2018; pl. 21). Tossin focuses on sites in space that are targeted for future exploration and resource extraction. For example, *Future Geography: Shackleton Crater, Moon* (fig. 4) centers the

Fig. 4. *Future Geography: Shackleton Crater, Moon*, 2021. Used Amazon.com delivery boxes, archival inkjet print with matte lamination, wood. 60 × 84 × 1½ in. Courtesy of the artist and Commonwealth and Council, Los Angeles. Photo: Paul Salveson

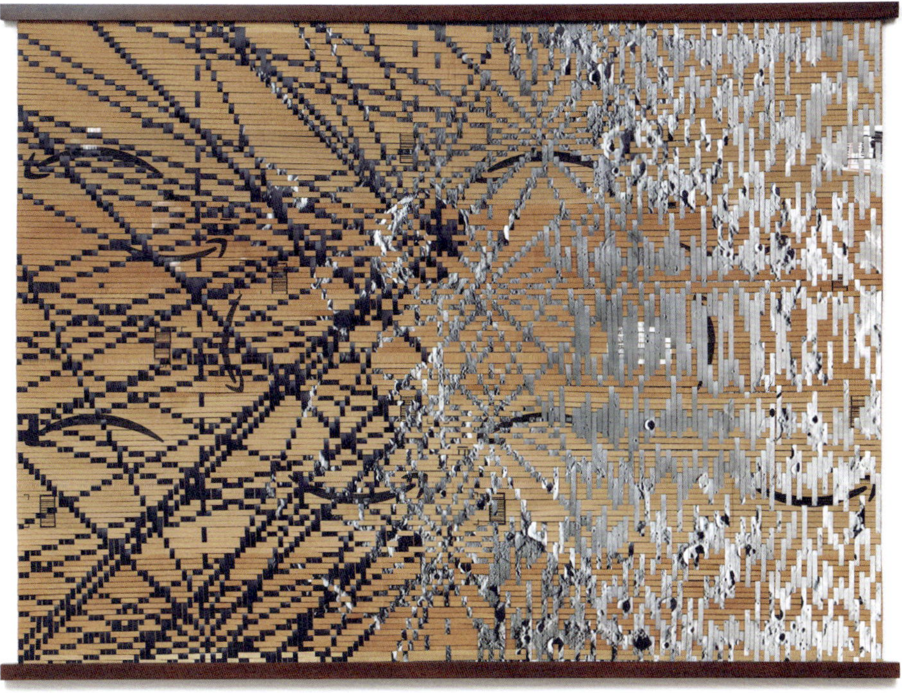

proposed site of the first lunar ice-mining facility. Shackleton crater's floor exists in permanent darkness and is thus conducive to ice deposits, while portions of the rim are in perpetual sunlight, which is ideal for harvesting solar energy to power the machinery necessary for ice extraction. This ice water is crucial for producing hydrogen rocket fuel for NASA's Artemis exploration program. It is both "poetic and disturbing," Tossin notes, that our presence on the Moon will begin with water and sunlight, the two elements that fostered biological life on Earth.[13] Tossin identifies the same cycles of resource extraction that have accelerated environmental disaster on Earth playing out in twenty-first-century space exploration. Once considered a "global commons," a demilitarized zone for free exploration and use by all nations, the Moon has seen its protections eroded to make way for private enterprise. Recent laws, including a 2020 executive order by President Trump, have not only legalized space mining, but "encouraged" American private interests to claim and profit from the sale of resources in space.[14]

Tossin has created new works in the *Future Geography* series for the Frye exhibition that feature images of star and galaxy clusters captured by NASA's James Webb Space Telescope and published in July of 2022. *Future Geography: Cosmic Cliffs* (2023; pls. 12–13) focuses on the star-forming region NGC 3324, specifically the "Cosmic Cliffs," in the Carina Nebula (fig. 5). The "cliffs," sculpted by high-energy radiation from hot, young stars within

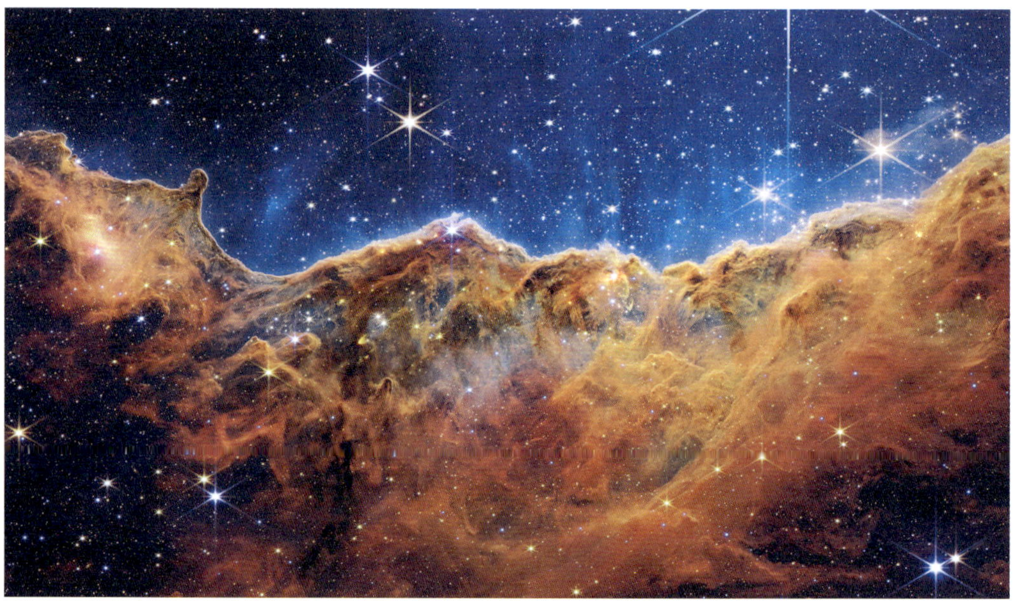

Fig. 5. "Cosmic Cliffs" in the Carina Nebula (NIRCam Image), captured by NASA's James Webb Space Telescope, released July 12, 2022. Image: NASA, ESA, CSA, STScI

the nebula, evoke the spectacular mountain vistas of the much-romanticized Western frontier as captured by nineteenth-century photographers, in particular Carleton E. Watkins's photographs of the Yosemite Valley, which he produced on assignment from mining companies who sought powerful images to attract investors for their new ventures (fig. 6). Watkins's images responded to the prevailing taste for sublime visions of nature, an aesthetic at odds with his commercial motivations. The Cosmic Cliffs visualize the "emptiness" of a next frontier as perceived through a settler colonial lens. This understanding of a pristine wilderness, "a vast expanse of land" acquired by colonists from "a scattering of benighted peoples who were hardly using it,"[15] is rooted in the founding myth of the United States, enshrined to law by the doctrine of terra nullius. While flirting with the uncanny, the Cosmic Cliffs seem especially beautiful because we can assign familiar imagery of a "pristine wilderness" to them: in fact, the accompanying NASA image caption describes the cloud of dust and gas as resembling "craggy mountains on a moonlit evening."[16]

Tossin reflects on the intricate weaving patterns in *Future Geography*: "I was very much thinking about trajectories of spaceships and rockets crisscrossing the sky and getting to other planets, other celestial bodies and maps of journeys that are yet to be made."[17] The abstracted patterns bring to mind the playful scribbles of Christopher Columbus's 1492–93 drawing (and the first

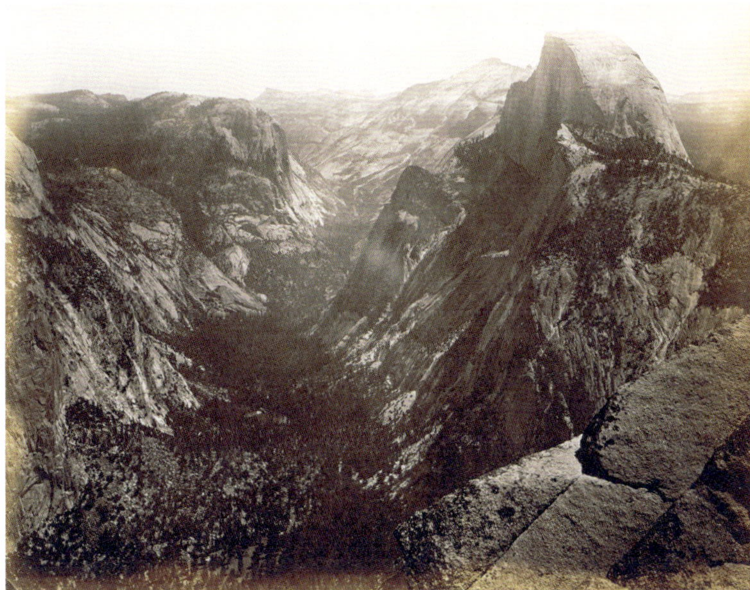

Fig. 6. Carleton Watkins. [*Half Dome from Glacier Point*], 1865–66. Albumen silver print. 15½ × 20½ in. The J. Paul Getty Museum, Los Angeles, 84.XP.220.32

European map) of the land he would name Insula Hispana (today, Hispaniola). *Unmapping the World* (2011; pl. 31) challenges the fixity of the modern map as an organizing principle. Tossin drew Earth's continents on balled-up sheets of tracing paper and then re-flattened the paper to reveal a fragmented world map. Tossin's new work, *Maritime Arrivals* (2023; pl. 32), further explores how colonial fantasies of discovery are enacted through mapping and naming as technologies of conquest. Employing the visual language of portolan charts (fifteenth-century nautical maps) (fig. 7), Tossin drew and named sites from the Moon on the surfaces of recycled Amazon delivery envelopes. Craters—dubbed *mare*, Latin (singular) for "sea," by early astronomers who mistook them for actual bodies of water—are identified alongside landing sites of twentieth-century American and Russian lunar missions, including the Apollo and Luna programs. Rhumb lines, scale bars, and compass roses intersect with barcodes and QR codes—the contemporary navigational tools of the Amazon envelope—to collapse time and space. Tao Leigh Goffe notes that "if mapping is about knowing and surveying, then unmapping is about unknowing and uncharting the territory."[18]

Tossin continues to complicate static, linear ways of knowing across geographies, languages, and time in her monumental film *Mojo'q che b'ixan ri ixkanulab' / Antes de que los volcanes canten / Before the Volcanoes Sing* (2022; pls. 41–54). The title, translated from Mayan K'iche' into Spanish and English, is borrowed from a poem by one of the film's protagonists, poet Rosa Chávez, who is in the process of recovering her ancestral language of K'iche'. In the same way that language maps meaning to sounds in the form of words, music also carries with it cultural knowledge and connections.

In *Mojo'q che b'ixan ri ixkanulab'*, Tossin uses Maya wind instruments to recenter sound as space. The flutes and ocarinas played in the film and presented in the exhibition are 3D-scanned and 3D-printed replicas of instruments in United States and Guatemalan museums.[19] While the original instruments are now static artifacts within pre-Columbian collections in museums, the intended functionality of the instruments is restored to their replicas. When the instrument is played, wind travels through its architectonic chamber to create its sound. Every flute or ocarina has its own pitch and frequency, and even different iterations of a single 3D print file have variances.[20] This understanding of the instrument as architecture is an extension of Tossin's explorations of built and imagined spaces—from Henry Ford's industry towns and

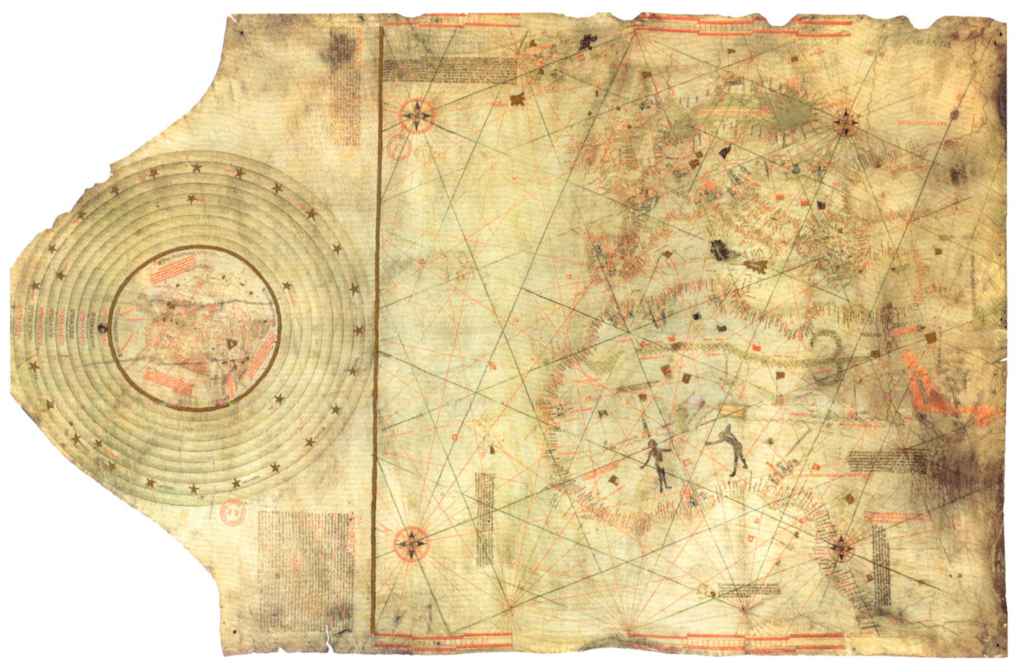

Fig. 7. Reproduction of the "Columbus Mappa Mundi" portolan chart attributed to Christopher Columbus, ca. 1492. Barry Lawrence Ruderman Antique Maps

contemporary manufacturing plants in the Amazon to star-forming galaxies nearly 300 million light-years away and speculative future landscapes.

The textures of the replica wind instruments, precisely rendered in the 3D-printing process, mirror the textures in 1920s and 1930s Mayan Revival architecture—specifically the hand-cast concrete "textile blocks," themselves neocolonial translations of Maya hand-carved stone blocks. Indigenous cultural motifs were appropriated, translated, and reinscribed by Western architects in these buildings, including the Sowden House and the Mayan Theater in Los Angeles, where much of the film was shot.[21] Tossin's collaborators and filmic protagonists animate these Mayan Revival buildings with ritualistic actions, reclaiming connections to lineages beyond the modernist tradition: flautist Alethia Lozano Birrueta performs on the Mayan Theater's stage with a replica monkey flute from the Guatemalan Highlands region, and artist Tohil Fidel Brito Bernal transcribes the days of the Cholq'ij Maya sacred calendar onto the Sowden House's glass doors.

At one point in the film, a starry sky, replete with bright blue-and-purple interstellar dust and shooting stars, spins with tantalizingly accelerated speed above the Sowden House's courtyard. The sky is framed by the silhouetted pyramidal façade of the building,

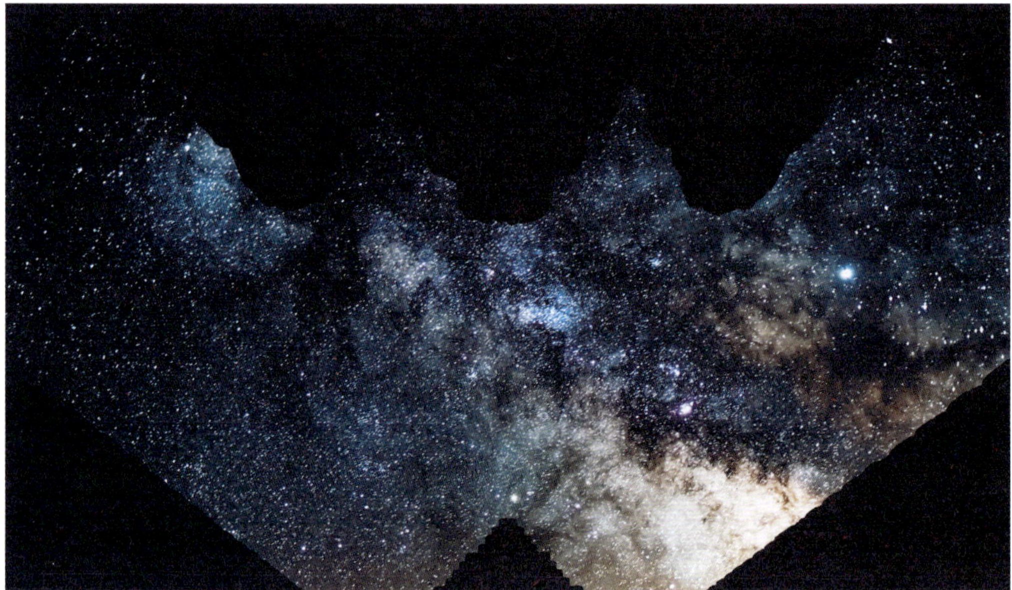

Fig. 8. *Mojo'q che b'ixan ri ixkanulab' / Antes de que los volcanes canten / Before the Volcanoes Sing* (still), 2022. Digital video (color, sound); 64:17 min. Courtesy of the artist, Galeria Luisa Strina, São Paulo, and Commonwealth and Council, Los Angeles

symbolically bringing the disparate geographies and temporalities into a vast cosmology (fig. 8). Here, and across the works in the exhibition, Tossin negotiates seemingly irreconcilable frontiers, from culturally situated ways of knowing to climate apocalypse and the future of humans on Earth and beyond. These constructed and mythologized frontiers are rarely as clearly defined as borders on maps or chronological timelines. Tossin brings these frontiers into an organically networked conversation that is necessarily meandering and dauntingly precarious.

Notes

1. Tossin has several early projects that visualize the global reach of Henry Ford's capitalist vision. Fordlândia was the name of Ford's first industrial town in the Amazon rainforest, in which he decentralized the distinct stages of automobile production to extract cheap resources and labor. The sculptural topographical maps in *Fordlândia Fieldwork* (2012), for example, combine satellite images of the abandoned Fordlândia rubber plantation and post-industrial American cities, including Detroit, where Ford started his business.
2. Raj Patel and Jason Moore, *A History of the World in Seven Cheap Things: A Guide to Capitalism, Nature, and the Future of the Planet* (Berkeley: University of California Press, 2017), 19.
3. These are defining characteristics of what Timothy Morton terms a "hyperobject"; Timothy Morton, *Hyperobjects: Philosophy and Ecology after the End of the World* (Minneapolis: University of Minnesota Press, 2013), 70.
4. Morton, *Hyperobjects*, 122.
5. Clarissa Tossin, "Circumnavigation Towards Exhaustion," interview by Sandrine Wymann, La Kunsthalle Mulhouse exhibition publication no. 51 (July 2021): 16, http://kunsthallemulhouse.com/wp-content/uploads/2021/06/journal-digital-clarissa-tossin.pdf.

6. Tossin, "Circumnavigation Towards Exhaustion," 17–18.
7. Jason Moore, "The Rise of Cheap Nature," in *Anthropocene or Capitalocene? Nature, History, and the Crisis of Capitalism*, ed. Jason Moore (Oakland: PM Press, 2016), 78–115; and Marco Armiero and Massimo De Angelis, "Anthropocene: Victims, Narrators, and Revolutionaries," *South Atlantic Quarterly* 116, no. 2 (2017): 345–62.
8. Clarissa Tossin, "Future Fossil," interview by Meg Rotzel, Harvard Radcliffe Institute for Advanced Study, Johnson-Kulukundis Family Gallery exhibition publication, 2019.
9. Octavia E. Butler, *Adulthood Rites*, rev. ed. (New York: Warner Books, 1988; repr., New York: Grand Central Publishing, 2021), 155–56. Citations refer to the Grand Central Publishing edition. Akin is the first human-"Oankali" alien hybrid (or "construct") in the post-apocalyptic world of Octavia E. Butler's Xenogenesis series. Akin is a male son born of the human protagonists Lilith and Joseph through the intervention of Nikanj, an "ooloi" alien shapeshifter. Ooloi, who use the pronoun "it," are a third-gender alien species of the Oankali that are able to gather and manipulate genetic materials from others. Tossin cites Butler as an influence throughout her work, and particularly the constructs and ooloi, whom she interprets as shaman-like figures, given their capacity to store genetic information within their bodies (we see Akin made sick when he attempts to ingest a synthetic rather than organic sample) and heal others (an ooloi notably cures Lilith's cancer).
10. Octavia E. Butler, *Parable of the Sower*, rev. ed. (New York: Four Walls Eight Windows, 1993; repr., New York: Grand Central Publishing, 2019), 3. Citations refer to the Grand Central Publishing edition.
11. Butler, *Parable of the Sower*, 77.
12. Butler, *Parable of the Sower*, 21.
13. Clarissa Tossin, "In Houston, Artist Clarissa Tossin Ponders the Colonial Implications of the 21st-Century Space Race," interview by Betse Huete, *ARTnews*, March 18, 2022. https://www.artnews.com/art-news/artists/clarissa-tossin-moody-center-houston-exhibition-interview-1234622226/.
14. In 2015, President Obama signed into law the "U.S. Commercial Space Launch Competitiveness Act," and in 2020 President Trump signed Executive Order 13914 on "Encouraging International Support for the Recovery and Use of Space Resources."
15. Roxanne Dunbar-Ortiz, *An Indigenous Peoples' History of the United States* (Boston: Beacon Press, 2014), 46.
16. "'Cosmic Cliffs' in the Carina Nebula (NIRCam Image)," Webb Space Telescope, accessed November 2022, https://webbtelescope.org/contents/media/images/2022/031/01G77PKB8NKR7S8Z6HBXMYATGJ.
17. Clarissa Tossin, MCA Denver audio guide, *Clarissa Tossin: Falling From Earth*, 2022, 1:21, https://mcadenver.org/exhibitions/clarissa-tossin/future-geography.
18. Tao Leigh Goffe, "Unmapping the Caribbean: Toward a Digital Praxis of Archipelagic Sounding," *archipelagos* no. 5 (December 2020), http://archipelagosjournal.org/issue05/goffe-unmapping.html.
19. Although we often associate 3D-printed objects with plastic, Tossin's replica flutes and ocarinas are printed with a porcelain mix and dipped into a terracotta ceramic slip. They visually and materially recall the handmade replica terracotta electronics in *Nova gramática de formas #2*.
20. Alethia Lozano Birrueta, "In Collaboration," in *Clarissa Tossin: Mojo'q che b'ixan ri ixkanulab' / Antes de que los volcanes canten / Before the Volcanoes Sing* program book, interview by Mariana Fernández (Troy: Rensselaer Polytechnic Institute, 2022), 35.
21. The Sowden House was designed in 1926 by architect Lloyd Wright, son and protégé of Frank Lloyd Wright; the Mayan Theater was designed in 1927 by architect Stiles O. Clements.

Clarissa Tossin: Becoming Mineral

Leslie Dick

It's almost accidental that Amazon.com was called Amazon. In the origin story, Jeff Bezos named his online bookstore Cadabra, Inc., as in the incantation *abracadabra*, because online shopping for books would seem like magic: effortless. Then a lawyer misheard the word as *cadaver* and it was clear that invoking a corpse would not sell books. The next try was also discarded: Relentless, Inc.—the opposite of effortless, this business would be *relentless* in seeking out the books you might want. But in 1994, there were so few websites they could still be listed in a directory, and Bezos wanted his business near the top. The word Amazon not only refers to the world's largest river, but also to a location, Amazônia, that holds the greatest biodiversity of flora and fauna on the planet. By implication, the website holds everything you may want or need, delivering it without impediment, like a river flowing. Coincidentally, the word contains another buried reference: to the woman warrior, who is, perhaps, relentless, rebellious, untamed. A gigantic, immeasurable river, a place of infinite diversity, a woman who will fight to the death: these powerful images are intertwined, woven together in the name of what is now the third-largest business organization in the world.

Further: the spelling of "Amazon" has an echo of a more everyday word within it—"amazing"—just as the English mispronunciation of IKEA recalls the word "idea." And Amazon's letters contain the implied promise of *A* to *Z*—a claim of completeness, totality—another accident that was eventually exploited in Amazon's logo. Rolled out in the year 2000, this takes the form of a stroke of the pen underlining the word Amazon, linking the *A* to the *Z*. It is a line that is at once a curved arrow (directional, motivated) and a penis (relentless!) and a smile (signifier of our satisfaction, or their delight in providing it).[1] It may even resemble the wave of a magic wand, after all.

Amazon boxes are everywhere: the arrow-penis-smile logo identifies them instantly. In everyday speech, Amazon (the business) displaces Amazon (the location), in a kind of overlay, the company label glued over our mental maps, interrupting the imaginary and actual connection to a part of the planet where the climate catastrophe is measured in hundreds of thousands of square miles of devastated rainforest. It goes without saying that Amazon (the business) exacerbates that global catastrophe, as the delivery of consumer goods generates emissions from various modes of transportation, as trees are cut down to make the apparently endless boxes, each marked with the smile that points towards our end.[2] Amazon is globalization in a cardboard box.

In recent bodies of work, Clarissa Tossin takes possession of the overlap of Amazon and the Amazon through weaving laser-cut cardboard strips of used Amazon boxes into patterns of her own devising, that echo, repeat, and deconstruct certain traditional basket-weaving practices of Amazônia. With her wall piece, *Disorientation Towards Collapse* (2020; pls. 17–18), woven Amazon boxes reorient the logo's "smiles": these arrows point in all directions, chaotic, as if pulling the world apart, while disrupted and fragmented barcodes, instantly recognizable commercial coding, are subjected to another kind of patterning. Tossin is fascinated by the generative potential of the overlay; in her artwork, she finds ways to put disparate elements together, juxtapositions and superimpositions that bring out the formal, conceptual, and political contradictions that constitute our shared realities. Combination and comparison provide a method, as her work enacts an interweaving of dissimilar elements, interrupting the singular form in a dissonance that informs, reverberates, and unsettles.

With her *Future Geography* series (2021–ongoing; pls. 11–16), Tossin alternates sliced strips of used Amazon boxes, their broken smiles repeating across the weave, with cut-up ribbons of inkjet prints, silvery images of space, the "final frontier."[3] In these works, the large-scale photographic print, itself a kind of fetish object, is woven through the monochromatic strips of an ordinary cardboard box, disrupting both the image's capacity to convey information and its power to seduce. The weave pattern designed by the artist is structured to reveal parts of the photographs, glimpses of brilliant, distant stars, bright moments that punctuate the surface, creating another level of pattern-making. In *Future Geography: The Five Galaxies of Stephan's Quintet* (2022; pl. 11), the lines inscribed in the textured weave recall radiating diagonal lines that cross rectangular maps: possible pathways of travel, or satellite routes maybe, angles of measurement and orientation, or proposed locations, destinations that are demarcated in ways that take hold of our unruly world, while at the same time shattering it into a starburst pattern.

These works take time, as their fabrication requires a set of repetitive gestures typical of traditional crafts. Following the geometric patterns across the surface, there's an implied choreography of body movements, in contrast to the rigors of mechanical production, or the relentless repetitions of the algorithm. (It may be important here to remember that a woven basket is one of the few everyday objects that cannot be manufactured by a machine.) There's an implied touch, a sensing of both the hand of the artist, slowly manipulating the cardboard and paper across the expanse of the work, and the imagined touch of the viewer, an embodied absorption of these textured surfaces. Tossin moves the spectacular photograph of the ultimate "elsewhere" into the zone of the tactile, taking it out of the instant into another temporality, one marked by contemplation and repetition (fig. 1).

Considering the power of the interrupted, woven photograph, I bump up against the recognition that any image of outer space is an enhanced graphic representation, a fictional construct, informed by memories of the epic and unforgettable credit sequences of *Star Trek: Voyager*, *Deep Space Nine*, and *The Next Generation*. The

Fig. 1. *Future Geography: Hyades Star Cluster* (detail), 2021. Used Amazon.com delivery boxes, archival inkjet print with matte lamination, wood. 60 × 84 × 1½ in. Courtesy of the artist and Commonwealth and Council, Los Angeles. Photo: Paul Salveson

Amazon box is, by contrast, much more coherent, an ordinary object with clear boundaries, although it is perhaps less an individual object than an archetype, a function, eradicating difference and distance in the fulfillment of our wishes. One of hundreds of millions of almost identical delivery boxes, it makes sense in our world, a blank container for other things, for "everything."[4] These "photographs" of space, on the other hand, derive from NASA telescopes, orbiting the earth, that capture data with infrared and ultraviolet sensors; the images these distant telescopes provide are visual propositions, computer generated, with color and other visual effects contrived by human beings. Such images of distant nebulae seem designed to make me fall in love with the future, or make me believe in those brilliant scientists somewhere far, far away—surely they must know everything, accessing a truth I can't even name. Above all, these images of space offer a beautiful, sublime alternative to the measureless heaps of wet cardboard and discarded IKEA furniture soaking into the landfills—all those LACK tables! These bright stars shine in counterpoint to the unrelenting droughts, to the skies full of toxic smoke from wildfires out of control. Utopian promises, the images show the pure potential of nowhere.

Tossin's woven works, interposing slices of Amazon boxes with slices of space, foreground the ways that these cardboard boxes are part of the problem (a problem almost too big to grasp, as big as the planet itself) and also the ways that the imaginary seductions of "space" are part of the very same problem, as these images promise a future beyond our planet, yet more worlds to conquer.[5] At a formal level, the work underlines the ways that the material structure of weaving, both baskets and textiles, forms the most ancient example of human systems of distinction and classification—either/or, this/that. In basket weaving, vertical elements support and are interrupted by horizontal strands, back and forth, making something like a grid, a form that recalls the x/y axis of difference and distinction. Textiles and loom-weaving are similarly structured in a grid form, with the possibility of elaborated pattern-making through differentiated threads, textures, and colors, making stripes, checks, and tartans. Jacquard tapestry looms, patented in 1804, were controlled by a sequence of perforated cards; fine silk threads in alternating binary combinations could produce figurative images so detailed that they are easily mistaken for etchings, or even black-and-white photographic prints. Expanding her inquiry into weaving in relation to digital-image production, Tossin made jacquard tapestries in her work *The 8th Continent* (2021; pl. 29 and fig. 2), depicting different

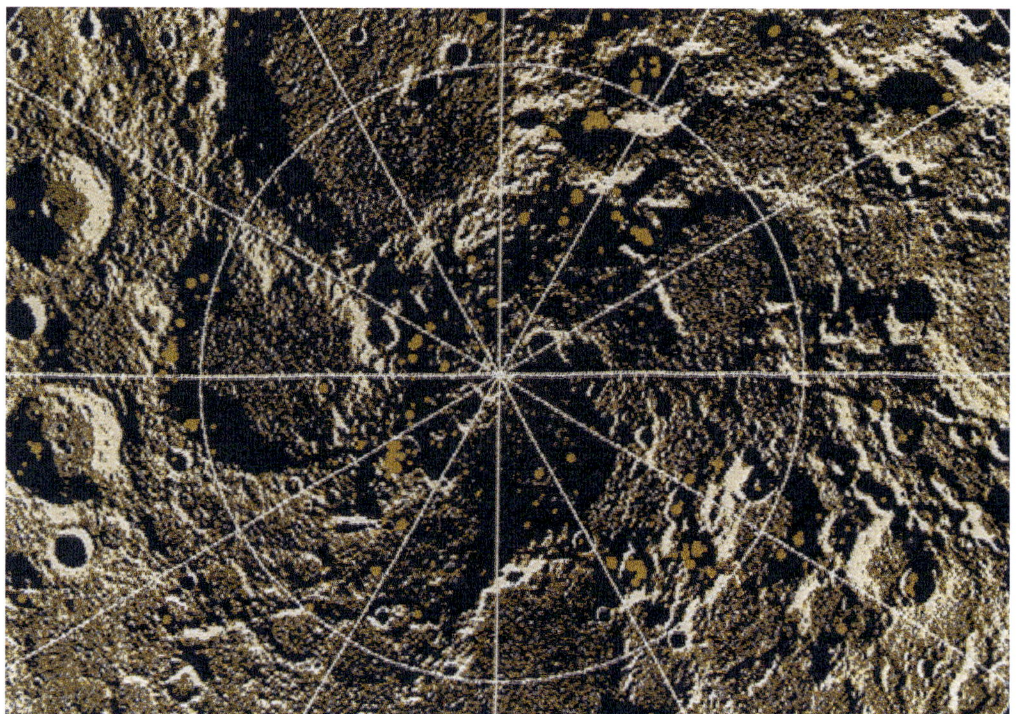

Fig. 2. *The 8th Continent* (detail), 2021. Digital loom jacquard tapestries with metallic thread. Three panels, 9 × 5 ft. each. Courtesy of the artist, Galeria Luisa Strina, São Paulo, and Commonwealth and Council, Los Angeles. Courtesy of the Moody Center for the Arts. Photo: Nash Baker

locations on the Moon, and a view of Earth from space.[6] Tapestry produces images in the weave of the fabric itself, with a positive and a negative, front and back. Embroidery, by contrast, superimposes pattern and image on a textile that performs like a painting's canvas, a "support" for color and motif. Weaving pattern and image into the basket, the textile, or the tapestry, a hierarchy of image and support cannot be distinguished: they are one and the same. The different elements, warp and weft, support each other, and it is through that interdependency that they generate meaning.

People tend to use whatever organic material is easily at hand to make their baskets; in different places, palm leaves, willow stems, cane, or marsh reeds are plentiful, cheap, and within reach. In Los Angeles (where Tossin resides), and many other places today, the equivalent material would be discarded Amazon boxes. The geometric patterns in the artist's woven works enter into a coded dance with recognizable visual elements in the Amazon boxes (such as "Prime" labels, barcodes, and the "smile") and the images of space.[7] In these works, the quotidian, already-used, discarded cardboard box is interlaced with a picture of somewhere, some time, that we can barely imagine. It is a place that we will never visit, another time as well as another place, possibly light-years distant from our planet and in some sense not a place at all.

These artworks revolve around the different ways that forms produce and contain meaning, as well as the ways that the patterned surfaces of the containers we use (boxes or bags or baskets) may themselves function as a language. Tossin's *Monument to Sacolândia* (fig. 3) presents a scale model of the presidential palace, the first Oscar Niemeyer building that was completed in Brasília. Sacolândia, or "Bagland," was a shantytown where some of the thousands of workers who came to build Brasília lived. Shelters were built out of the heavy paper cement bags that were everywhere, discarded by-products of the construction of the public buildings, broad avenues, and open vistas of the city. When their work was done, the shacks were demolished, the workers once again displaced, and an ornamental lake was built on the site where they had lived. Tossin's architectural model, just over six feet long, is made out of cement bags, printed with their colorful brands. In video and photographs, the miniature palace floats on the lake, a small and temporary memorial to another time and place, now invisible. *Monument to Sacolândia* connects to Tossin's later investigations using Amazon

Fig. 3. *Monument to Sacolândia* (still), 2010. Cement-bag architectural model, unlimited edition postcard, and digital video (color, sound); 3:15 min. Dimensions variable. Courtesy of the artist, Galeria Luisa Strina, São Paulo, and Commonwealth and Council, Los Angeles

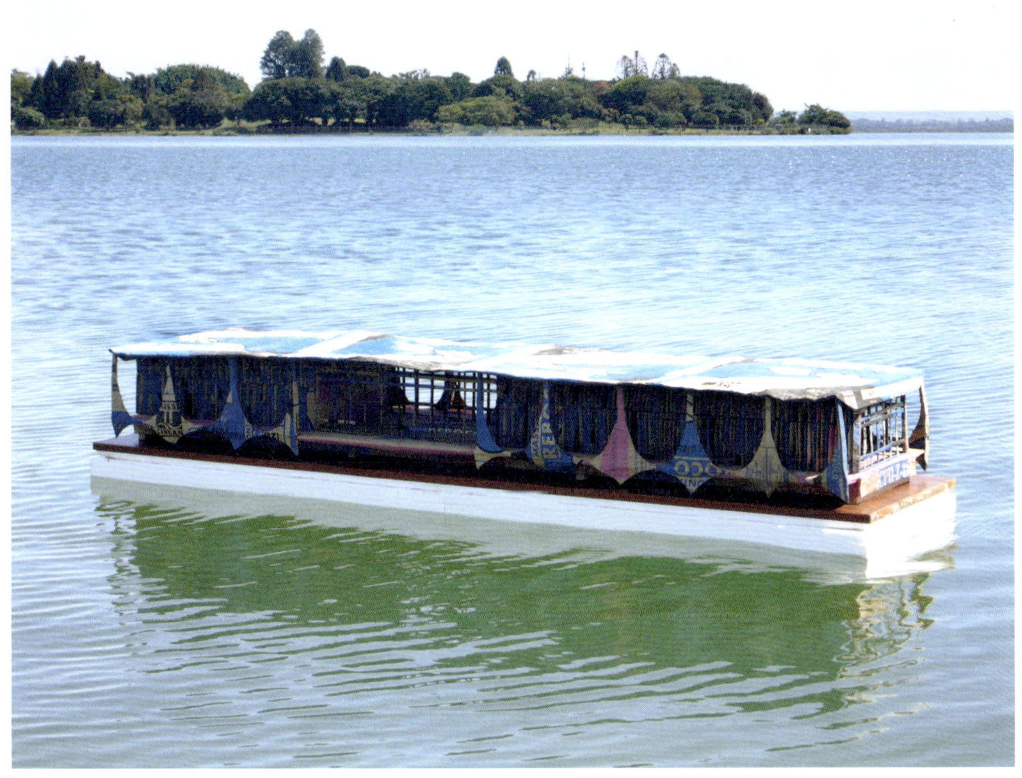

boxes: in each case, she's working with a discarded container (a box, a cement bag) that has a certain material resiliency (capacity for re-use) and a decorative surface (logos). The printed branding and labeling of the paper cement bags, bright blue and deep pink, work with and against the purism of Niemeyer's Palácio da Alvorada, to undo (at a formal level) some of the ideological implications of that utopian project.

Within the series *Future Geography*, Tossin also uses images of the surface of the Moon and Mars in her cardboard weavings, changing the emphasis from remote fantastical nebulae to our near neighbors in space, places that human beings have mapped and explored, if only with robots. These locations are specific: the Shackleton crater on the Moon may provide ice, precious H_2O, which could theoretically fuel further exploration and conquest, and Jezero crater on Mars, where a mechanical rover explored the bed of a dried-up lake, searching for ancient signs of life. Turning three-dimensional spaces into two-dimensional maps or photographs is a key component of the process of exploration, a reduction and simplification that makes conquest and extraction possible. The three-dimensional Amazon box unfolds, flattening to become a woven surface, while the three-dimensional landscape on the surface of the Moon or Mars is transformed by mapping software, translated into a two-dimensional image, making a fixed representation that denies the unfolding of time, even as it brings remote places within reach. Tossin's work links strategies of mapping and appropriation to the underlying logic of the colonial project, defining it as a cultural space of fantasy and desire, a space of wishful thinking.[8] Her work invites our imagination to roam around this territory, experiencing the ways that human representations of time and space have always distorted reality and at the same time delivered something precious to us, something we really, really want: the promise of a future, and the promise of control.

Weaving is a structural device, a fundamental form that builds strength and meaning through combination and overlay. In other projects by Tossin, the palimpsest, an overlay of past and present, draws formal connections between her woven works and her use of video and architecture. In *Ch'u Mayaa* (2017; pls. 33–36), the choreographer and performer Crystal Sepúlveda moves through the Hollyhock House, Frank Lloyd Wright's Mayan Revival mansion built in 1919–21. Sepúlveda's body is multiplied in post-production, so that what appears to be multiple dancers animate and punctuate the façade of the building, while the bright blue sneakers and jaguar-patterned bodysuit underscore how alive and ironic this visual proposition is (fig. 4).[9] There is no claim of authenticity, rather a bright collision of disparate historical moments: now, when you can easily acquire the inexpensive, synthetic jaguar-patterned outfit in the Fashion District of Los Angeles nearby; and then, around 1920, when this extraordinary setting was an exciting new development in contemporary architecture; and the other then, the ancient Maya times, a period that lasted thousands of years. Here, a palimpsest of different historical moments demonstrates the ways in which the architectural site itself is, so to speak, up for grabs: by superimposing the dancer's gestures, derived from ancient Maya ceramics and murals, Tossin takes temporary possession of the Hollyhock House, through strategies of (re)appropriation and (mis)translation.[10] The dancer folds pleasure into this process: her embodied interactions with the surfaces of the building seem propelled by curiosity and delight. There are multiple echoes of violence, the music grating as the dancer repeatedly tumbles down the stairs, yet these are balanced by the last views of her, ghostly in the shadows, as if she will be haunting this place forever.

In Tossin's recent film *Mojo'q che b'ixan ri ixkanulab' / Antes de que los volcanes canten / Before the Volcanoes Sing* (2022; pls. 41–54), the Ixil Maya artist Tohil Fidel Brito Bernal writes the Maya calendar with a colored marker on the glass grid of windows looking out over the courtyard of the Sowden House, built in 1926

Fig. 4. *Ch'u Mayaa* (still), 2017. Digital video (color, sound); 17:56 min. Choreographer/ Performer: Crystal Sepúlveda. Courtesy of the artist, Galeria Luisa Strina, São Paulo, and Commonwealth and Council, Los Angeles

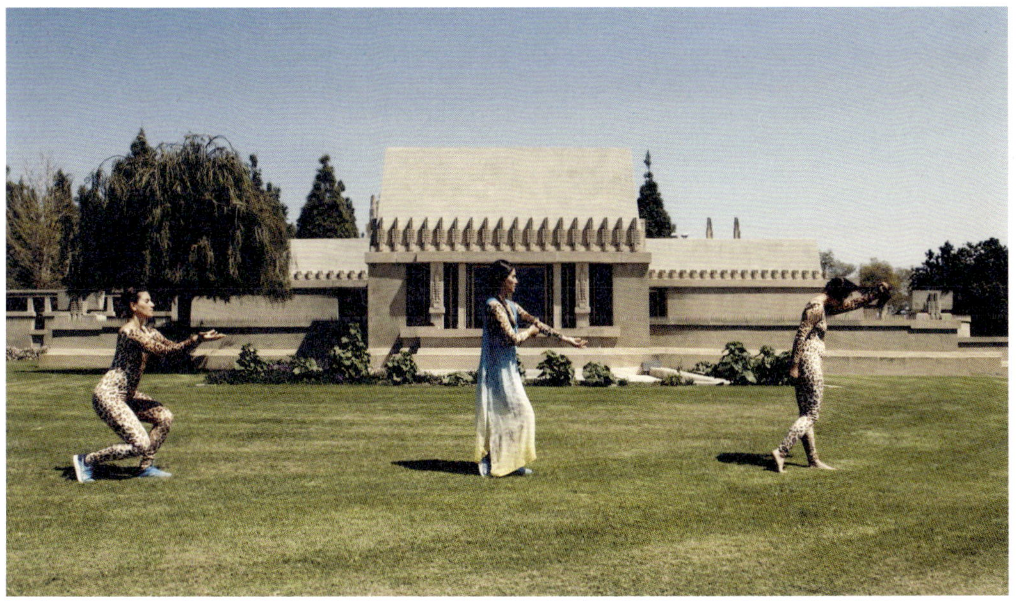

by Wright's son, Lloyd Wright, in a continuation and elaboration of the Mayan Revival style. These architects' twentieth-century appropriation of Maya motifs is here repurposed, reanimated, and repossessed, with a wry acknowledgment that nothing can undo the destruction of the past. The Wright family's reuse of these forms in their textile block houses stands in dialogue with the ancient Maya ruins of Central America, refunctioning carved blocks into a strange and estranged domestic space. Tossin's work interrupts that dialogue, triangulates it, introducing living bodies into the spaces, throwing open the question of how to relate to these histories, when they are not legible, singular, or complete.[11] In her sculpture series, *The Mayan* (2017–18; pls. 37–40), cast body parts in terracotta-colored plaster—a dancing foot, gesturing hands—are placed in relation with silicone molds taken from the interior lobby

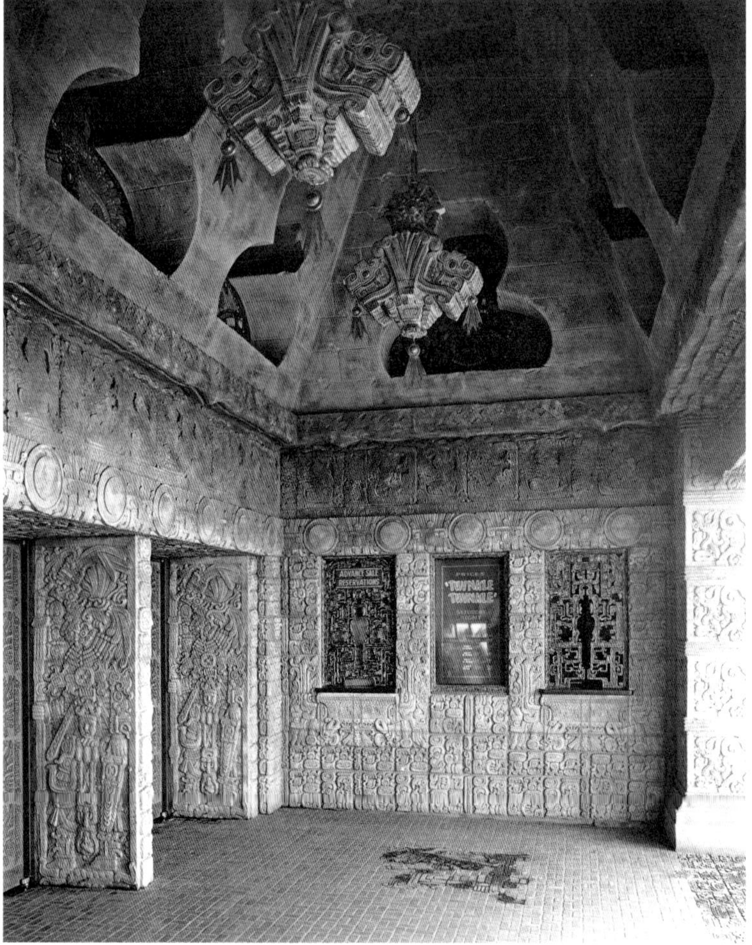

Fig. 5. Mayan Theater, Los Angeles, 1927. Designed by Morgan, Walls and Clements; sculpture by Francisco Cornejo. Courtesy of the California History Room, California State Library, Sacramento. Photo: Mott Studios

of the Mayan Theater, built in 1927 in Los Angeles (fig. 5). These are presented with black hair braided into extra-long ropes, with feathers at each end, and jaguar-patterned faux fur wrapped around carved walnut wood supports. Again, Tossin puts disparate elements together: the braided hair is synthetic, bought in a store; the translucent silicone skin, imprinted with architectural forms, drapes and sags like fabric, a scarf or a cloak for the implied dancer, who exists only as isolated gestures, broken-up movements that quote and repeat dances depicted on ancient Maya ceramics. This overlay and combination form a palimpsest, where writing is superimposed on writing, allowing an older text to come through, almost legible, but only in the context of more recent writings, like a woven fabric, back and forth, while the echo and reverberation of different elements, together with the evocation of dance, recall the way music works, building themes and variations and weaving them together.

The proliferation of cultural and historical references in Tossin's work is always anchored in deep formal structures that move the work beyond its specific engagement, for example with the Mayan Theater, toward an investigation of how meaning itself is made. *The Mayan* draws on specific architectural spaces and histories, opening up a formal dynamic between the two-dimensional and the three-dimensional, the façade in relation to the architectural plan, with the monumental presence of ancient carved stone and twentieth-century cast concrete remembered as tactile, patterned surfaces. Tossin consistently situates her work in a conversation among two-dimensional pieces, on the wall and in the middle of the room, and three-dimensional sculpture and installation, while her work in video explicitly brings time and performance into the formal equation. Sometimes the two-dimensional/three-dimensional articulation is the topic of the work: with her series *Unmapping the World* (2011; pl. 31), the artist creates a provisional globe by crushing tracing paper into a ball and drawing the continents on the crumpled surface in ink; she then flattens the paper out, showing how nonsensical this move from three dimensions to two can be. (Some of the crushed paper globes remain intact, providing a point of comparison.) In *Study for a Landscape (Mars)* (fig. 6), Tossin uses a color satellite photograph of the surface of Mars, folding it into an origami rocket, reenacting the paper planes of childhood. Unfolding it again, the folds leave white lines on the print, like the diagonal lines on old maps, or a diagram, or a model: two-dimensional representations with a purpose, a potential impact on our three-dimensional world.

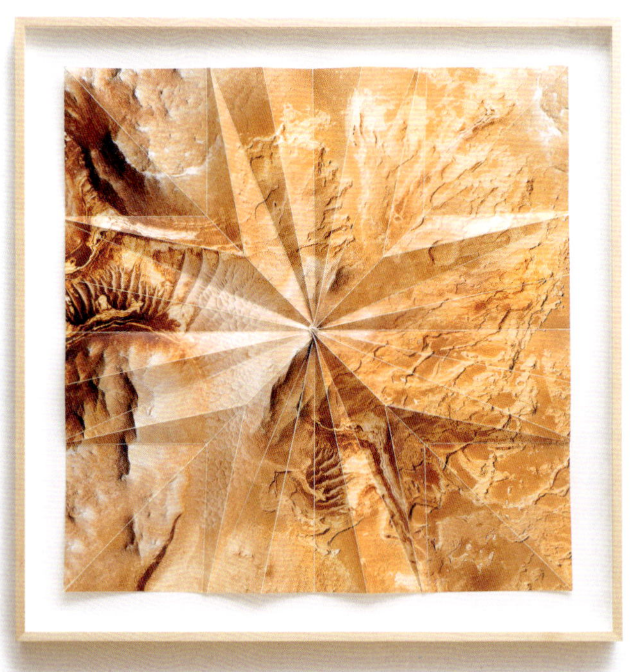

Fig. 6. *Study for a Landscape (Mars)*, 2012. Archival inkjet print. 30 × 30 in. Courtesy of the artist, Galeria Luisa Strina, São Paulo, and Commonwealth and Council, Los Angeles. Photo: Samuel Freeman

The predominance of two-dimensional forms in human culture, whether images, text, diagrams, or maps, exerts an implicit control over the turbulent flow of our being in the world. The three-dimensional is always beyond our capacity to take in at a glance; it has something to hide, something out of reach, an underneath and a behind, a part we can't see all at once. Maps lay it all out for us, distorting geographic forms in different projections, with Mercator's conceptualization of the continents perpetually haunting our sense of location and identity.[12] A two-dimensional photographic representation, whether on my phone, or a screen, or printed on paper, manages the ungainly excess of my biological being in the world, which is actually three-dimensional, taking up space and unfolding in time. Human consciousness perpetually anticipates the future: language itself (a time-based medium) requires me to guess what's coming, and I am always getting ahead of myself, discarding the moment for the next, and the next, and the next. Instagram now lets me pinch and swipe, moving into the image as it expands or contracts, discarding it without fear of loss. I sidestep the powerlessness of my biological existence through the fantasy of control afforded by the photographic image, which slices into space to make a two-dimensional rectangle and seems to perpetuate a moment indefinitely, especially in its digital form. Moving between two and three dimensions, Tossin opens up the space of representation itself for our consideration, linking our wish to control our world at the level of the individual with collective fantasies of distant conquest, as we put off the reality of our inevitable deaths.

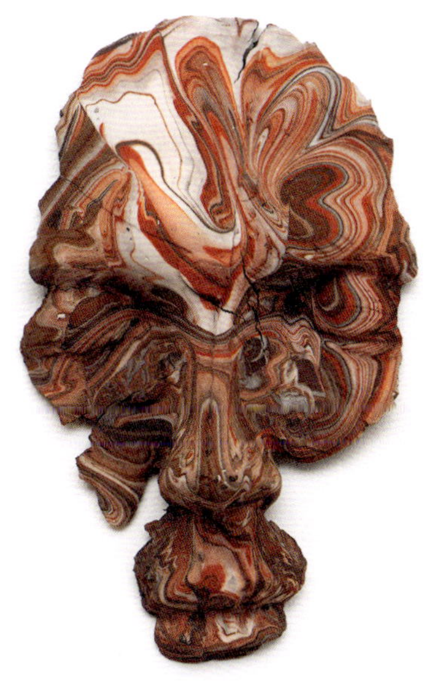

Fig. 7. *Becoming Mineral*, 2021. Fired clay. 7 × 4 × 1½ in. (approx.). Courtesy of the artist, Galeria Luisa Strina, São Paulo, and Commonwealth and Council, Los Angeles. Photo: Brica Wilcox

Three-dimensional casts of real objects and body parts reappear in Tossin's work, sometimes like fossils that replace living things, traces of a lost time and place, sometimes more like a death mask, capturing a moment before inevitable decay begins. Among other things, there are terracotta casts of CDs, printer cartridges, computer mouses, keyboards, and modems in *Nova gramática de formas #2 (New Grammar of Forms #2)* (2018; pl. 21); these translations of semi-obsolete technological items draw connections between the magical objects of our time and the pottery statues, whistles, and flutes of the Classic Maya period. The terracotta mouse won't work, although it is immediately recognizable as a mouse, designed for the ease and comfort of a human hand, because the cast is scaled to the real object.[13] In the cinema, the human face can take up the entire screen, as the edited film moves between long shots of the body and close-ups of an expression or a look. Digital images are fluid, moving easily, without impediment or interruption, bringing us closer, taking us farther away, in an extreme distortion of scale so familiar that we don't even notice it happening.[14] Here, these forms are replaced by a mode of representation that presents the object at one-to-one scale, insisting on the human body as the true measure of our shared world. Tossin takes us out of the digital, cinematic zone, into a material world where the cast is precisely mapping the real thing, where the pressure of the mold touches the surface of the actual object, where leftover clay in her studio can form a life mask of her own face, as with *Becoming Mineral* (2021; pls. 3–4 and fig. 7). In this way the work moves through the field of representation to return us to a shared reality, a tactile, dimensional space where we are alive and where someday we will die.

Tossin's early work, *Ladrão de Tênis (Sneaker Thief)* (fig. 8), shows a series of casts of the insides of discarded sneakers, a set of memorials to the various individuals whose repetitive wearing of the sneakers as time passed shaped them into these precise forms. The secret, dark, and utterly idiosyncratic interior of this consumer object is recorded in three dimensions; its inner surface, where the socked or naked human foot rubbed along with the manufactured shoe, is documented in the record of the empty space within. It is, perhaps, a play on the ideal of an indexical sign, that mark or trace of an actual event that remains to tell the tale, like a footprint, a material residue of a physical gesture that tells me *someone was here*. These ghostly casts are arranged in rows on clear acrylic shelves, a recollection of brand-new shoes in the Nike store. Like fossils, they recall mineral formations that fill the shaped space where an ammonite once lay. (How much time does it take to turn a corpse into stone? How much time does it take to wear away the inner contours of a trainer, so that the specific shape and movements of that particular foot are retained by its form?) Marks of wear and tear on clothing are an index of an individual's time and labor; like all memorials, these are inadequate to the task, falling short in their storytelling. Nevertheless, the work invokes the repetitions of identity, where what I wear tells both you and me who I am, and indicates the ways that such repetitions are subtly intertwined with death itself, providing an imaginary stability that affords me a sense of control, denying death even as I mimic it in these frozen forms.

Fig. 8. *Ladrão de Tênis (Sneaker Thief)* (detail), 2009. Hydrocal and acrylic shelves. Dimensions variable. Courtesy of the artist, Galeria Luisa Strina, São Paulo, and Commonwealth and Council, Los Angeles. Photo: Clarissa Tossin

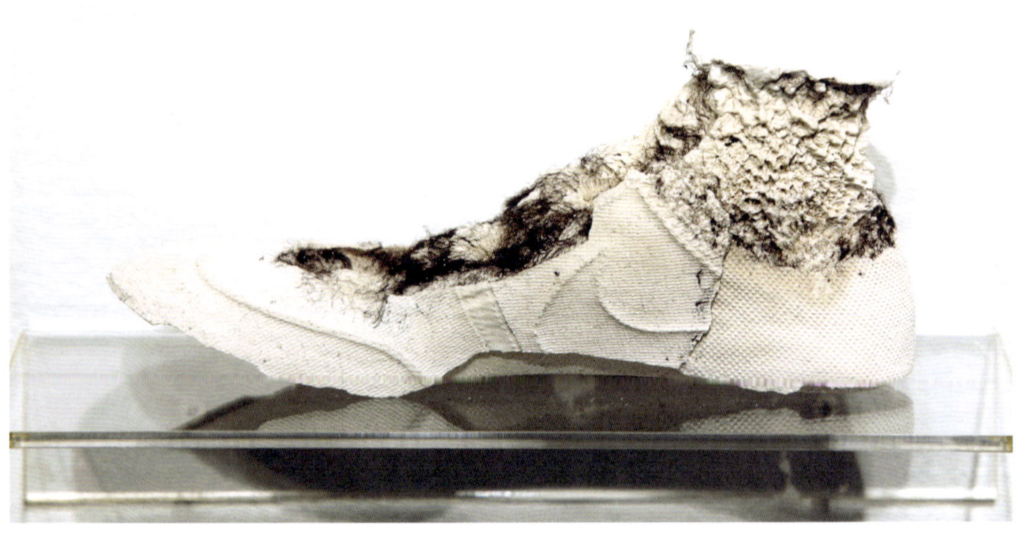

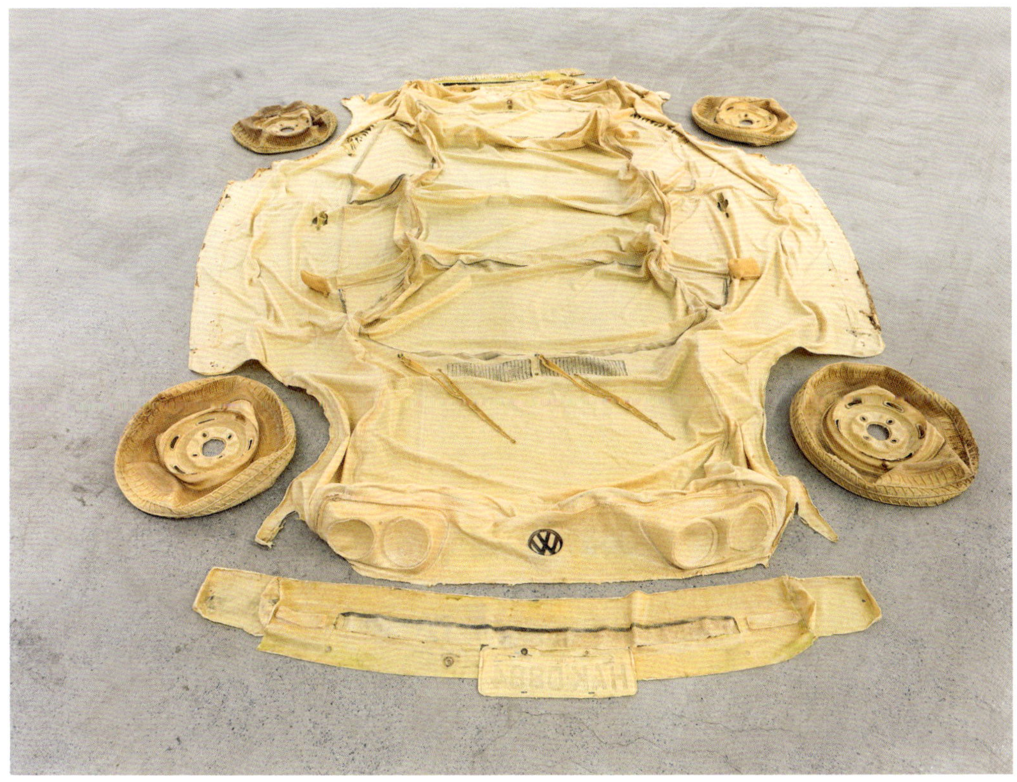

Fig. 9. *Transplanted (VW Brasília)*, 2012. Amazonian natural latex. 149 × 106 × 7 in. Private collection. Installation view, *Transplantado (VW Brasília)*, Galeria Luisa Strina, São Paulo, July 3–August 2, 2014. Courtesy of the artist and Galeria Luisa Strina. Photo: Edouard Fraipont

In *Transplanted (VW Brasília)* (fig. 9), Tossin deployed latex from Amazônia to form a skin, making a three-dimensional cast of the Volkswagen automobile named after the city of Brasília.[15] Her cast of the small station wagon preserves its complicated, illegible surface, as its dimensions in space collapse like an empty bag on the floor. Again, in this work, the surfaces are emphasized and recorded, as if the places where we touch the world is where history happens. If the car in this way becomes like a skin, translucent, soft to the touch, it's also a shoe, an object that creates a site for a human body to occupy, a place that holds me, with an inside and an outside, like a building or a dress.[16]

In *Vogais Portuguesas (Portuguese Vowels)* (fig. 10), sugar syrup was cast in a mold formed by alginate held in the mouth while a Portuguese vowel was voiced repeatedly, shaping the palate, the teeth, the tongue, so that time and sound are archived in the form of a translucent sweet object, just recognizable as the interior of a mouth.[17] The work preserves a specific sound in a lump of candy, as if one could suck on the vowels of one's native language, taking comfort in their forms while living in a strange environment, a place

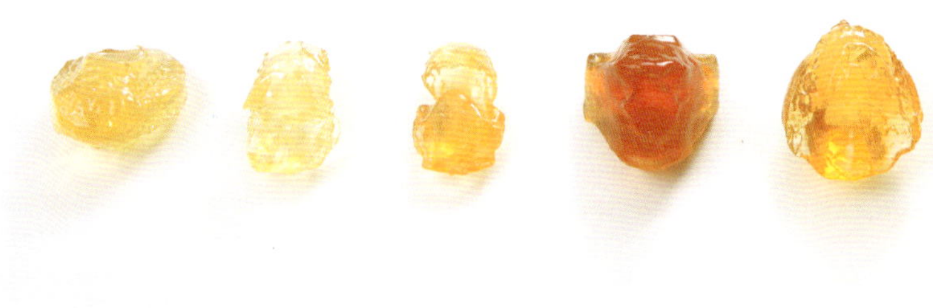

Fig. 10. *Vogais Portuguesas (Portuguese Vowels)*, 2008. Sugar. 3 × 4 × 3 in. each (approx.). Courtesy of the artist, Galeria Luisa Strina, São Paulo, and Commonwealth and Council, Los Angeles. Photo: Clarissa Tossin

where such subtle distinctions may not register. Except these candies are too big: the hard, gleaming, golden sweetness would choke and silence.

Tossin's *Spent / Gasto* (fig. 11) is a scatter of trash on the floor, the artist's own domestic trash, cast in porcelain. The crumpled tissues, used tampons (with strings!), Q-tips, and coffee cups have become fossilized, burnt to ash in the heat of the kiln as the porcelain slip was fired. What remains is a delicate shell, easily broken, one step away from dust and enigmatic fragments. Like the sneakers and the vowels, the passing of time is here reconstituted as objects taking up space, once again moving between different modes of representation to get at something that's overlooked. Each small piece of trash has a history: it was used, discarded, and then transformed and retained for another purpose: to map time passing, to remember traces of the body, to memorialize in miniature the infinite waste of resources belonging to our time. And the work remembers the ordinary maintenance work done, relentlessly, every single day.[18]

Tossin's video, *White Marble Everyday* (fig. 12), shows the daily washing of the vast marble floors of the Federal Supreme Court in Brasília, work done by a team of men and women whose expertise with quantities of water and suds preserves an architectural purity, repeating the utopian promise of Niemeyer's architecture. Wearing rubber boots, they scatter soap with watering cans and flood these surfaces with hoses, over and over again, slowly pushing giant squeegees across the floor. Paradoxically, their touch

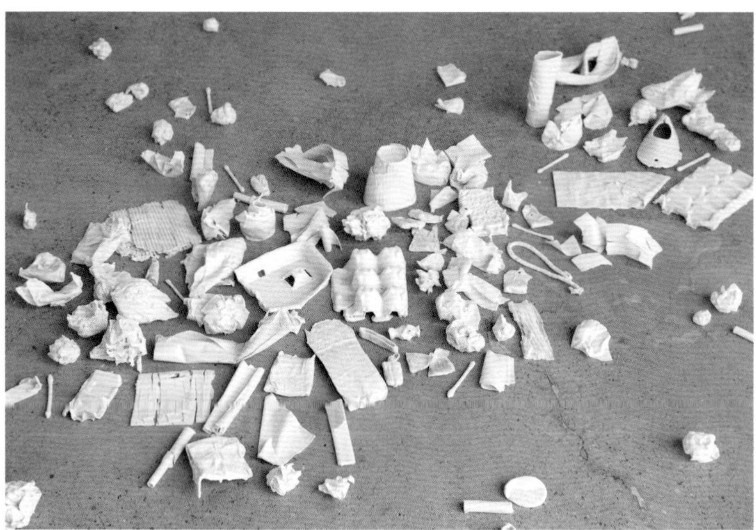

Fig. 11. *Spent / Gasto* (detail), 2009–11. Porcelain and trash. Dimensions variable. Private collection. Installation view, *Gasto*, Galeria Luisa Strina, São Paulo, June 29–July 30, 2011. Courtesy of the artist and Galeria Luisa Strina. Photo: Edouard Fraipont

erases history—removing footprints, dirt, dust—so that every day the building's ideological promise, an evocation of modernity and dynamic power, can once again be renewed in the expanse of bright stone.

With *Rising Temperature Casualty (Prunus persica, home garden, Los Angeles)* (2022; pl. 10), the silicone cast of a young dead tree is more like a corpse, a drowned body pulled out of the canal.[19] It resists sentiment: the traces of this particular, individual tree (unlike more human traces, unlike the intimacies of the interior of someone's sneaker, or someone's mouth) refuse my concern, resist signification. Then I discover, from the title, that the tree grew in the artist's back garden; it was a peach tree, with bright blooms in the spring, and I recognize it as a kind of companion, a friend. The silicone cast is another memorial: Tossin encountered this tree over and over again, through different seasons; possibly she herself planted this tree in the yard, and the young tree didn't make it. It is too hot in Los Angeles now.

The sedimentary form, where the passing of time is marked through the implied slow accretion of different layers of material, also appears as a deep structure in Tossin's recent works. In the sedimentary, what remains takes the form of strips, or stripes, layer upon layer producing an archaeology of knowledge that invokes a radically different timescale: geological time, hundreds of millions of years. There's a deep connection between the time zone this work invokes, and the space zone of unthinkable distance, hundreds of thousands of miles or even light-years away. Both are almost beyond

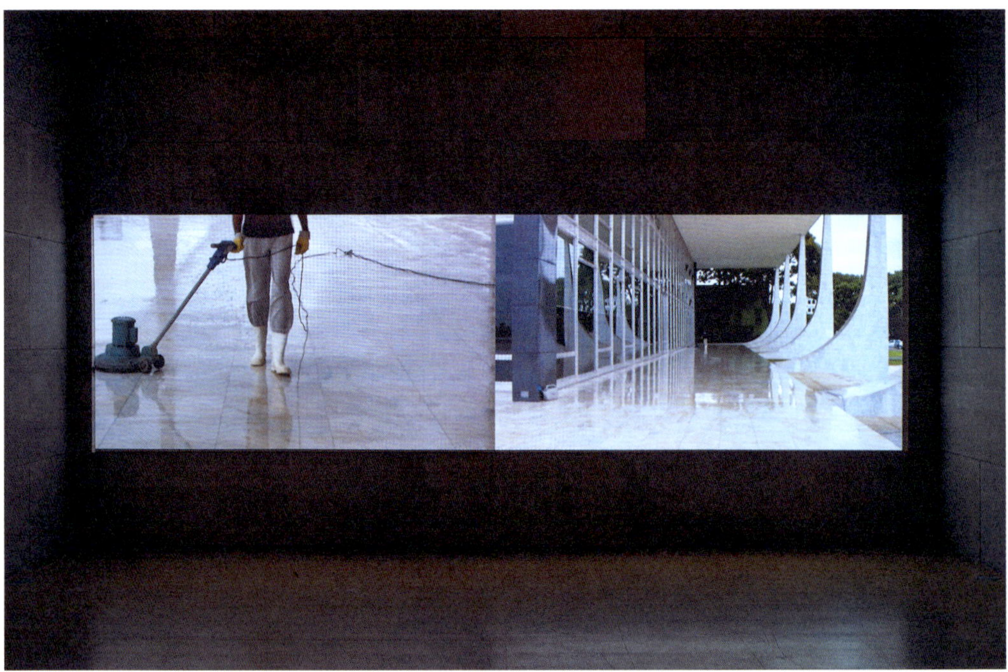

Fig. 12. *White Marble Everyday*, 2009. Two-channel digital video (color, sound); 5:42 min. Courtesy of the artist, Galeria Luisa Strina, São Paulo, and Commonwealth and Council, Los Angeles. Installation view, *Stereoscopic Vision*, Ezra and Cecile Zilkha Gallery, Center for the Arts, Wesleyan University, Middletown, CT, January 31–March 5, 2017. Courtesy of Center for the Arts, Wesleyan University. Photo: John Groo

our capacity to imagine: the sedimentary layers of Earth a kind of weighty corollary to the almost infinite expanses of outer space. We require certain formal structures to map or conceptualize what lies beyond the human scale: the planet hundreds of millions of years before "life" began, the universe outside our infinitesimally small time frames.

At the same time, the archaeological metaphor is fundamental to psychoanalysis: the unconscious imagined as multiple layers, overlaid one upon the other. You have to dig deep to uncover buried treasure; like an archaeologist, you have to put the broken pieces together, in an act of imagination and interpretation, and there's always something missing, something you can't access. It's incomplete, whatever's inside us, and it doesn't tell its story in a straightforward way. Tossin's work uses structuralist metaphors—the x/y axis of weaving, the palimpsest overlay, the dynamic between the two-dimensional and the three-dimensional, the sedimentary structure tracing the passage of time—as formal constructs, making palpable the different ways that human beings grasp reality, taking possession of it through representations of time and space.

Tossin's monumental work, *Future Fossil* (2018; pls. 25–26), projects a future where our compacted trash has become fossilized; the piece warps human time, dipping us into geological time, a core sample from a place and time where we are not. Imagining a future where interplanetary travel is commonplace, and the wide-open spaces of the Moon or Mars provide us with another site for extraction, opens up an expanse that is similarly mind-bending. In *The Only Lasting Truth Is Change* (2019; pl. 27), titled after verses in Octavia E. Butler's Earthseed trilogy, Tossin made a striped sphere out of compacted plastic refuse, combining the sedimentary logic of geology with the atmospheric effects of outer space, in striations of color and material. Because of science fiction movies and TV, we can't help but recognize this ball of plastic and rubbish as a planet, floating magically in the void even as it lies stranded on the gallery floor. It's made out of stuff that was lying around the studio: trash, aluminum foil, plaster, silicone, rocks. Yet its gooey materiality, melted, toxic, is suffused with potential: it may be open for business or abandoned by its inhabitants. Like the fossils and the maps, it's both a residue and the future, all at once.

Notes

1. The mythological woman warrior is an archer, also; the Amazon queen, Penthesilea, and her warrior sisters, each cut off one breast to be able to pull back the bow, letting the arrows fly.
2. Jeff Bezos's parents funded his business; they put almost $250,000 into it, which in 2022 dollars is equivalent to twice that amount. It didn't make a profit for seven years. Origin stories are always mythological: *A* to *Z*, beginning to end.
3. Jeff Bezos is one of a group of billionaires currently developing space exploration and travel as viable options.
4. Baskets are also containers, but each one, handmade, is unique.
5. For the problem too big to name, see Timothy Morton, *Hyperobjects: Philosophy and Ecology after the End of the World* (Minneapolis: University of Minnesota Press, 2013).
6. The paper punch cards used in jacquard weaving are regarded as an early form of computer program; see *The 8th Continent* (2021), digital loom jacquard tapestries with metallic thread, each 9 feet by 5 feet, depicting image maps of the Shackleton crater on the Moon, the South and North Poles of the Moon, and a view of Earth Rising.
7. The juxtaposition generates an absurd question: Is there a deep connection between Amazon Prime and *Star Trek*'s "Prime Directive"? Or is the company more like a prime number: is Amazon somehow *irreducible*?
8. The first iPhone was available for purchase in June 2007, only sixteen years ago. Many people believe that technology will solve the multiple challenges of what's often called—a fatal euphemism—*climate change*. They point to all the ways the smartphone changed our world, our everyday lives, and they wave their iPhone, always at hand; they say, "See, it can happen so quickly, *transformative technology*." ("Some tech person somewhere, probably in Seattle, will invent *something we can't even imagine* that will totally take care of the problem.") This attitude is a by-product of the implicit idealization of science and technology that underpins our discourse, a specific form of magical thinking. Other people believe that our planet will be destroyed and then discarded, and some very special humans will get to leave, loading up the silver spaceships for a new home in the sun, as Neil Young sang in 1970. Tossin's work reminds us that, without the maps and other representations of distant nebulae, animated by brilliant colors and sparkle effects, without the almost infinite promise of the power of technology—that shiny new phone in my hand—we can't go there. In demonstrating multiple ways that these ideas can be undone, re-functioned, and re-presented, her work invites us into

another relationship with our desires and denials, moving beyond wishful thinking towards a recognition of possibilities for real change.

9. *Ch'u Mayaa* translates as "Maya blue," a reference to the resilient blue pigment found in ancient Maya ceramics and murals. See Clarissa Tossin, "Ch'u Mayaa," accessed February 26, 2023, https://www.clarissatossin.net/Ch-u-Mayaa.

10. See Clarissa Tossin, "The Mayan," accessed February 26, 2023, https://www.clarissatossin.net/The-Mayan.

11. Approximately seven million Maya live in Central America today, with a large community, many undocumented, living in Los Angeles.

12. Mercator's Projection, presented by cartographer, geographer, and cosmographer Gerardus Mercator (1512–1594) in 1569, maps our world, showing the spherical globe in two-dimensional form, with meridians represented as equally spaced parallel vertical lines and latitudinal relations depicted by parallel horizontal lines that become further apart as they are more distant from the equator. Within this grid, north is always up and south is always down, yet local directions and shapes are preserved, making it extremely useful for navigation. However, Mercator's Projection distorts the size of masses more distant from the equator, making (for example) Greenland, Russia, and Antarctica appear much larger than they really are. A variant of Mercator's Projection, known as Web Mercator, was adopted by Google Maps in 2005 and continues to be the basis for almost all web-based mapping. For mental maps and their distortions, see https://www.nationalgeographic.com/culture/article/all-over-the-map-mental-mapping-misconceptions (accessed February 26, 2023).

13. Ceramic objects shrink approximately 10 to 15 percent in the kiln, so the fired terracotta mouse is in fact a little bit smaller than I remember, as memories often are.

14. My favorite example of this was the seven-year-old who approached a map displayed outdoors in a state park and tried to make the map larger by moving his fingers on the glass, the open-sesame reverse pinch, also known as the "stretch."

15. This work from 2012 foreshadows Tossin's Amazon work, as it exploits the generative potential of a corporate brand name. In the 1980s and 1990s, second- and third-hand VW Brasílias were beloved by the pool guys of the capital city, being relatively inexpensive, reliable, and the right size for their equipment. Within her large installation, *Brasília, Cars, Pools, and Other Modernities* (2009–13), Tossin's single-channel video depicts the arrival of one of these vehicles at the Strick House, designed by Oscar Niemeyer, a private house (with pool) in Santa Monica. Shockingly, this was Niemeyer's only solo project in the US and Tossin's work centers on an absurdity: the architect could not travel to the US in 1963 to visit the site or oversee construction, having been denied a visa on the grounds of his political beliefs. The beat-up car, however, gets there, somehow, decades later, complete with pool-cleaning nets, buckets, and vacuum. See https://hammer.ucla.edu/made-in-la-2014/clarissa-tossin (accessed February 26, 2023).

16. Around the same time, in *When Two Places Look Alike* (2012–13), Tossin made double images to mirror the forms of Henry Ford's almost identical workers' housing in Michigan and in Amazônia, built environments that were designed to structure the workers' relationships to each other and to the company. The artist's mirroring puts these radically different places together, folding them into an imaginary space dominated by Ford's indelible concept of what a house should look like. (In this context, the work raises a question: In what sense is a house [or my skin, or a dress] like a container, a box to hold something?)

17. It reminds me of the scene in *My Fair Lady* (1964), where the street seller Eliza Doolittle is required to hold a handful of marbles in her mouth as she is taught to enunciate proper English.

18. For maintenance work, see Mierle Laderman Ukeles, *Manifesto for Maintenance Art* (1969), in Patricia C. Phillips, *Mierle Laderman Ukeles: Maintenance Art* (New York: Prestel, 2016). In her series preserving shared napkins from 2007, Tossin memorialized meals with friends through the traces of food remaining on paper napkins, with the various foods listed in the materials. See *Shared Napkin (Andrezza, Guilherme, Ludovic and I)* (2007) (paper napkin, lipstick, grease, red wine, chocolate, tomato sauce, and coffee).

19. I am thinking of a scene in *Don't Look Now*, the 1973 film directed by Nicolas Roeg.

Flanking Sounds: Listening to *Mojo'q che b'ixan ri ixkanulab'* [1]

Vic Brooks

Mojo'q che b'ixan ri ixkanulab' / Antes de que los volcanes canten / Before the Volcanoes Sing (2022; pls. 41–54) undertakes a richly sensory journey across moments, languages, and music, roaming through architectural spaces that are variously imagined and real, cosmological, and colonized. In order to grapple with the history of Western architects using Indigenous motifs without significant reference to or engagement with their source, the Los Angeles–based Brazilian artist Clarissa Tossin works to restore such absent sounds by recording the musical performance of 3D-printed replicas of Maya wind instruments held behind glass in pre-Columbian collections in museums.

Mojo'q che b'ixan ri ixkanulab' originated from Tossin's research into these Indigenous cultural belongings dislocated from their original sites and housed in colonial museums, and manifests as an installation of moving image and sound within her solo exhibition at the Frye Art Museum. In the four intervening years between inception and completion, the project departed from research in the collection of the Denver Art Museum to traverse vernacular Los Angeles architectural pastiche, a Ukrainian 3D-printing studio, a performing arts and media production facility, contemporary Maya community centers, and ancient Guatemalan Maya landscapes. While the activities of Tossin and her artistic and technical collaborators within each of these sites of production are clearly inscribed onto the images we see on-screen, it is the articulation of what we *hear* that far exceeds the film's physical frame when we encounter the work in exhibition.

Told through the personal histories of its Maya protagonists, the film begins with K'iche'-Kaqchikel poet Rosa Chávez as she leads us through her Guatemalan community's vernacular architectures. Through poetry and commentary, Chávez traces a densely interwoven set of practices that have long articulated and preserved systematic understandings of time, language, and cosmology across cultural forms. These range from ancient temples to systems of healing, and from weaving techniques whose patterns encode complex information to the physical structure of the traditional temescal (steam room). As if in echo, these scenes filmed on location in Guatemala with Chávez are interwoven with its diaspora. Riverside-based Ixil Maya artist Tohil Fidel Brito Bernal works on his rigorously researched drafts of ancient Maya glyphs and calendars inside the Mayan Revival Sowden House in Los Angeles, surrounded by sculptural copies of the same motifs appropriated by the architect Lloyd Wright (Jr.). The poetry and artwork of Chávez and Brito Bernal are interwoven with spirited performances on replica Maya instruments by Mexican flautist Alethia Lozano Birrueta, with music composed by Michelle Agnes Magalhães and filmed variously in a concert hall, a theater, and a studio.[2]

The acoustic properties of architectural spaces are key to how we perceive our environment. Sound is crucial to our perception of space insofar as we hear the shape, quality, and location of a sound source because of how the waveform engages every single surface around us.[3] In Tossin's film, this happens on multiple levels. First, there are the acoustic qualities of the rooms in which the film was produced. For example, the long reverberation ("liveness") of sound reflecting off large surfaces of a concert hall is distinct from the "dry" character of a contemporary soundstage or recording studio designed to absorb specific frequencies. The consequences are significant: the intimate scale of a domestic interior filled with furniture and objects that reflect, absorb, and diffuse sound waves will contribute to an acoustic environment that might assist the listener to localize sounds, while the domed interior of the Maya temescal will tend to focus sound reflections in the center of the room. Second, these spaces are acoustically excited by voices and wind instruments, each of which contributes its own specific acoustic properties. For example, the resonance chamber of a globular flute (whose frequencies are determined by its volume and not, like a regular cylindrical flute, by its length) results in a mellow sound color; the sonic effect is additionally shaped by the pressure of the player's breath or the specific balance of the high-frequency bands of the speaking and singing human voice. Third, these two levels of acoustic characteristics are in turn shaped by the film's sound design, which manipulates, heightens, and spatializes the audio recordings in relation to what we see onscreen using digital tools.

Another interaction occurs as the loudspeakers amplify and project the soundtrack into the exhibition space to meet the architectural surfaces, the people, and the objects contained within the gallery. This web of sonic relations is the central concern of the field of psycho-acoustics (the study of sound perception and psychological response) and of what Barry Blesser and Linda-Ruth Salter term “aural architecture”[4] as “the aspect of [. . .] spaces that produce[s] an emotional, behavioral, and visceral response in inhabitants.”[5] However, while this theory expands on social dynamics and perceptual response to space, Nina Sun Eidsheim crucially articulates how we as listeners actively contribute to the production of a sound: “Listening is not a neutral assessment of degrees of fidelity but instead is always already a critical performance—that is, a political act.”[6] Attending to a site’s acoustics provides Tossin with not only a way to think about how its architectural design has the potential to communicate (and resonate) across timescales through amplifying perceptual response, but also a way to draw our attention to how architectural acoustics can articulate the inherent social dynamics of those who originally designed them and those who use them.[7]

What follows in this essay is structured by and through the act of critical listening to the traces and interactions of the acoustic fingerprints that inhabit Tossin’s film. Multiple layers of aural architecture surround and scaffold our encounter with the film’s premise, which centers on the capacity (and continuity) of ancient and contemporary Maya cultural production to give voice to Indigenous systems of knowledge and resist the ongoing process of colonial erasure by reclaiming space for Indigenous traditions in the present. Attending to the question of whether “spaces speak,”[8] this essay attempts to listen to the film’s sites of research, production, and exhibition, and to those who activate them, in order to mediate the complex web of dislocations of Maya cultural lineage at the heart of Tossin’s film. I will trace this through four distinct spaces and operations. First, through the acoustical properties of the colonial museum; second, the resonances between ancient and contemporary Maya architecture and its appropriation through the Mayan Revival style; third, the protocols of production and post-production; and finally, framed within the spaces of contemporary performance and exhibition.

Listening and sound are hardly the only preoccupations or operations of the film. Although specifically manifesting as a work of moving image, *Mojo’q che b’ixan ri ixkanulab’* is ambitious in its approach to multidisciplinary practice, which also encompasses art, poetry, archaeology, linguistics, music, and architecture and reaches across *longue durée* timescales. However, here I will focus in on the common sonic thread that I believe connects each of these registers within the film to ask: How does Tossin listen actively and critically *in relation to* the dislocation of Indigenous Maya peoples and their cultural belongings across time and geography? And what material and sonic techniques does the artist use to resituate and reframe the temporal, spatial, and experiential gaps produced by such acts of dislocation?

I. Reverberations of the Colonial Museum

Architectural acoustics is the physical study of the relationship between time and space in sound. One key measurement concerns the gap between the time it takes for an initial sound wave to reach you from its source and the time required for subsequent indirect sounds of that same wave to engage your eardrum after the wave bounces off surrounding surfaces. The duration of the reflected sounds bouncing around a space until they are no longer perceivable is the so-called "reverberation time."[9] It is directly correlated to the dimensions and surface area of a space and whether those surfaces reflect or absorb the energy of a sound wave. Over several centuries, the vernacular interior architecture of the Western colonial museum developed to be variations on the rectangular gallery, comprised of sound-reflective surfaces: high, flat, parallel walls; a ceiling with minimal ornamentation; and a hardwood or stone floor. Together these elements produce a highly reverberant space in which sound waves bounce directly back and forth between the surfaces with a very slow diffusion of their energy. Alongside the long reverberation of the overall space, additional "flutter" echoes are created by the parallel walls as the onset of sounds bounces between them. These layers of reverberation make it difficult for our ears to locate sound spatially and to decipher speech with its highly differentiated patterns of explosive consonants and finely shaped vowels. With my curatorial collaborator, Nida Ghouse, I argue that this type of design and its inheritance and proliferation in contemporary museum architecture has profound ideological and structural consequences in the ongoing silencing of peoples and cultural belongings.[10] To quote xwélmexw (Stó:lō/Skwah) artist, curator, and writer Dylan Robinson: "Such display culture removes the other senses from engagement with the belongings—a removal so that the eye can consume uninterrupted. No touch is permitted by the vitrine and glass, as the being and ancestor [. . .] are kept supported by the display, removed from touch, removed from sound, removed from land, and positioned for settler gaze."[11]

Pre-Columbian Maya wind instruments are usually displayed in what I would call an "unsounded" manner within glass vitrines for the sake of preservation and thus presented solely as visual evidence of an ancient culture "lost" to time. By implication, this display structure gestures to a cultural erasure of Indigenous peoples in the present through canceling the sonic prospect of hearing them at all. Reproducing the colonial logic that dislocated these instruments from their original sites to place them in museum collections, this very act of display dislocates them a second time, separating image from sound, and their essential function from those who wish to use them. The glass itself provides the material ground of this dislocation when viewed through the lens of its acoustic properties. Both metaphorically and literally, a glass vitrine keeps a sound-making object silent and, concurrently, its smooth, highly sound-reflective surface adds to the illegibility of vocal frequencies within the gallery in which it is contained. If museums have traditionally cared more for objects than the communities from which they originate, then their architectural acoustics and exhibition design provide audible evidence of this through the silencing of both object *and* audience.

Among the contemporary efforts to question the colonial basis of museum collections, the archaeologist Jared Katz[12] 3D-modeled a selection of pre-Columbian wind instruments from the Maya regions. Katz subsequently made an archive of the scans publicly available for the production of playable 3D-printed replicas.[13] Tossin pointedly does not film the museums or the instruments held there. Instead, using Katz's scans, she relocates their physical properties, and thus their potential for use and sounding, through the material process of reproduction. In endeavoring to produce instruments close to the originals in resonance, tuning, and playability, Tossin extensively experimented with 3D-printing techniques and materials, from standard resin and plastic compounds to ceramics, which are acoustic surfaces themselves that require friction from the pressure of breath to produce sound. Printing multiple versions from the same instrument scan, a specialist studio based in Ukraine generated them in terracotta using a multistage ceramic process. As a result of contraction and expansion during firing, each instrument's overall exterior and interior shape and size is unique and organically differentiated (fig. 1). Each provides a temporal and material connection to its original, but, crucially, each is also a product of the contemporary technique of its making.

Flautist Alethia Lozano Birrueta has played and recorded original Maya instruments from the collection of the Los Angeles County

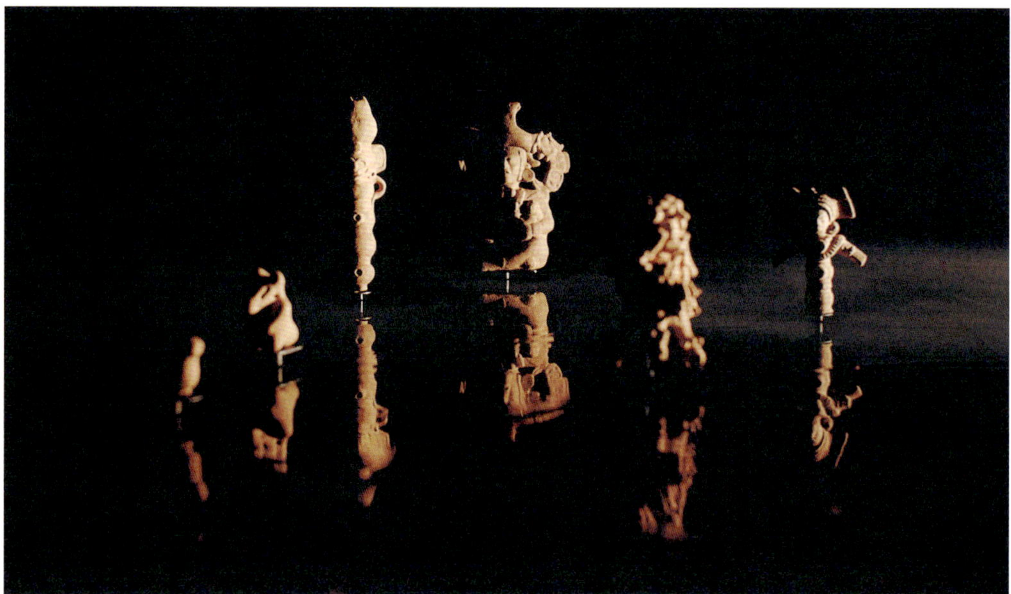

Fig. 1. *Mojo'q che b'ixan ri ixkanulab' / Antes de que los volcanes canten / Before the Volcanoes Sing* (still), 2022. Digital video (color, sound); 64:17 min. Courtesy of the artist, Galeria Luisa Strina, São Paulo, and Commonwealth and Council, Los Angeles

Museum of Art, and in experimenting with Tossin's versions, she initially attempted to recreate what she heard when playing the originals to "compensate for differences in tuning" that resulted from the (re)production process. Through practice, however, she realized "each flute had its own voice and tuning system, providing excellent resonance chambers for all the different playing techniques used for contemporary music."[14] Along with Tossin and composer Michelle Agnes Magalhães, Lozano Birrueta tuned into the potential to bridge ancient Maya musical technologies with contemporary techniques to create a hybrid musical language that does not attempt to recreate the music of the past, but instead aims to listen *in relation* and to forge new spatiotemporal connections. In having the instruments played in a traditional concert hall, in a recording studio, and within Los Angeles Mayan Revival–style buildings, Tossin plots an alternate historical, architectural, and geographical lineage that makes audible the influence of Maya culture on US cultural production, which has been erased by the multiple acts of dislocation and appropriation of Maya people, objects, architecture, and motifs caused by centuries of colonization.

If the temporal event of sound is an experience necessarily grounded in the present, these unique instrument copies produced through synthetic means could be described as historically acousmatic (that is to say, there is an unknowable dislocation between the sounding of the ancient instruments and our sonic experience of the replicas).[15] We have no record of what music was played on the ancient instruments—playing the originals is an act of interpretation in itself. Each version of Tossin's flutes and ocarinas must also be experimented with in order to play, and they do not necessarily conform to either Maya or Western musical traditions. The instrument-replicas often disturbed the assumptions Magalhães had presupposed of the instruments (for example, they did not always adhere to the principles of a pentatonic scale), and she described the flutes as "speaking a different language [that] we're trying to learn."[16] This gap between culturally standardized technical knowledge and the unique instruments' ability to play against these standards necessitated a working method by composer and flautist that explored the instruments on a "microscopic" and microtonal level. It was therefore necessary for Lozano Birrueta and Magalhães to interpret their own musical training in order to find "the way to release the music"[17] from the flutes.

Robinson quotes Métis artist and writer David Garneau's description of Indigenous Northwest Nations' "screen objects"[18] as versions of cultural belongings that "resemble the sacred things they imitate but do not include their animation . . . [They] have the patina of the originals but none of the meaning, ritual, or context. They are cultural *artifakes*—reasonable facsimiles designed for others and to give nothing essential away. The hope is that colonizers might settle for the appearance and leave the essential undisturbed."[19] In some ways, Tossin's instrument-reproductions take a parallel approach: they remain "reasonable facsimiles" that give "nothing essential away" in terms of empirical knowledge of their original musical performance, context, and style. Simultaneously, they produce a new hybrid form of musical experience that connects ancient and modern traditions in the present.

II. Sounding Maya Architecture and its Appropriation

Beyond the flutes themselves, Tossin narratively grounds the film's structure in architectural history, specifically the dislocation of forms and motifs of Maya cultural production through appropriation as ornamentation by the American Mayan Revival architectural style of the 1920s and 1930s. The artist's previous moving-image work, *Ch'u Mayaa* (2017; pls. 33–36), is located at Frank Lloyd Wright's Hollyhock House (1919–21), one of the most prominent examples of this tendency. Here, the choreographer and performer, Crystal Sepúlveda, bases her movements on the figuration from Maya pottery and murals; she moves in and out of the shadows cast by the pastiche of Indigenous motifs in an act of "re-signification" that seeks to reconnect the building with its Mesoamerican lineage. *Mojo'q che b'ixan ri ixkanulab'* goes a step further, directly connecting the vernacular design of Guatemalan Maya community centers, ancient ceremonial sites and landscapes, and glyph-adorned objects with the Los Angeles Mayan Revival architecture of Sowden House (1926), designed by Lloyd Wright, and the Mayan Theater (1927), designed by Stiles O. Clements with pre-Columbian-inspired ornamentation (fig. 2) by artist Francisco Cornejo.[20] The film does this by mediating the sites through the presence and voices of poet Chávez and artist Brito Bernal, and filling the volumes of the architectonic spaces with sound through Lozano Birrueta's performances of the flutes.

This question of language and re-signification is present from the film's first moments. *Mojo'q che b'ixan ri ixkanulab'* opens with a high-pitched whistle as the camera glides above a forest, toward a clearing of grassy mounds and geometric-stone walls that demarcate the boundary of an ancient Maya site at Q'umarkaj. The acousmatic voice of Chávez situates the image on-screen in K'iche' territory and marks the day as Kablajuj Tijax, a day of healing signified by sacred fires lit by Maya community members. As an individual instrument played by Lozano Birrueta becomes an ensemble of soaring pitches and rhythms, we are surrounded by trees and brought back to the earth to Chávez. We follow the poet

Fig. 2. *Mojo'q che b'ixan ri ixkanulab' / Antes de que los volcanes canten / Before the Volcanoes Sing* (still), 2022. Digital video (color, sound); 64:17 min. Courtesy of the artist, Galeria Luisa Strina, São Paulo, and Commonwealth and Council, Los Angeles

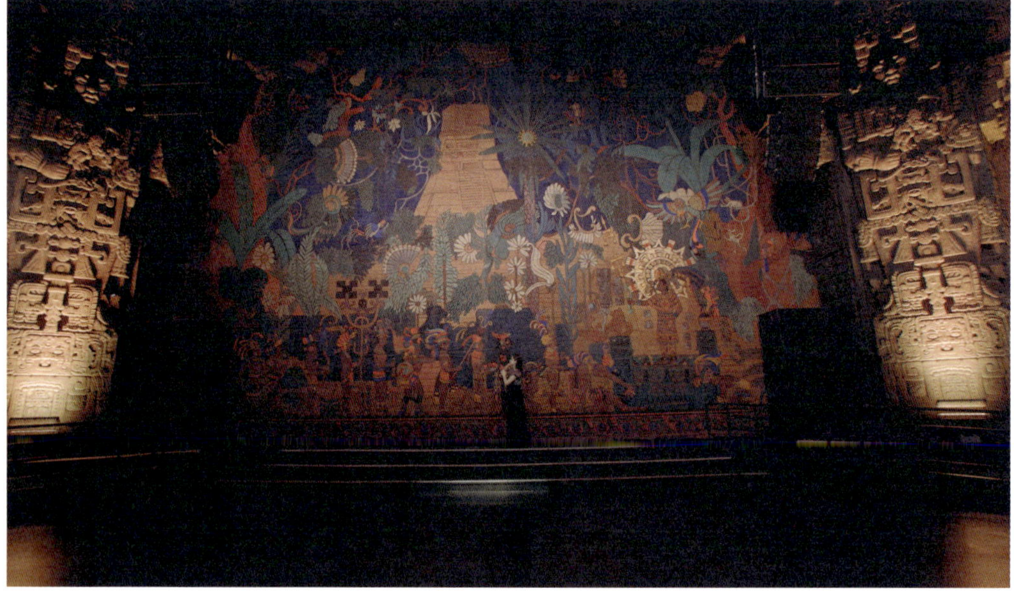

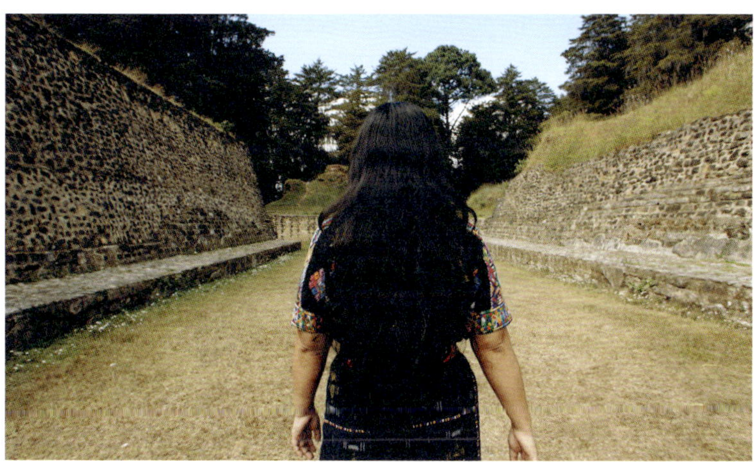

Fig. 3. *Mojo'q che b'ixan ri ixkanulab' / Antes de que los volcanes canten / Before the Volcanoes Sing* (still), 2022. Digital video (color, sound); 64:17 min. Courtesy of the artist, Galeria Luisa Strina, São Paulo, and Commonwealth and Council, Los Angeles

through the large clearing cut into forest, demarcated by high stone walls, as her voice performs "Dame permiso espíritu del camino," the poem from which Tossin's film takes its name (fig. 3 and pp. 114–16). The acoustic qualities surrounding Chávez's vocal delivery project the sense of an expansive interior environment at odds with our auditory perception of the open-air context in which we see her on-screen. As the camera moves past monumental rough-stone walls and grassy mounds, we hear the ceremonial chants emanating from Q'umarkaj's temple of Tohil entwine with Chávez's voice as she walks through the cavelike mouth of the temple. Originally pyramidal in shape with decorated stucco facing, it is now a tall, uneven stone structure topped with thick vegetation. With Chávez, we hear two different acoustic registers: her voice is grounded as she guides the camera through sites old and new to tell the story of community, yet it is reverberant when she is performing her poems, an effect that at times floats beyond the image on-screen to reach across time and space to inhabit the acoustic thumbprint of Q'umarkaj as it once stood.[21]

The words of the poem describe the active exchange of sound-source, listener, and language. She asks permission from and in relation to the sounds of stones, plants, and animals. Chávez's vocal performance moves between Spanish, her first language as a colonial subject, and K'iche',[22] and in doing so unites the past and present in a continuous act of listening *in relation* to her environment, an inherited ritual practice that encodes systems of meaning across geographies and time. Eidsheim describes the voice as "a complex event that, in addition to its myriad acoustic signals, constitutes of action, material, and social dynamics."[23]

Chávez herself points to this web of vocal relations in a conversation recorded during the film's production with Tossin and Brito Bernal, in which she describes (re)learning K'iche' as an act of relocating the continuity of the temporal-spatial specificity of Maya culture that was ruptured by colonization.[24] The recovery of her Indigenous language and the act of translation of her poems into K'iche' are active responses to a geographic displacement for her and her community. The sonic nature of language encodes within it a relation to physical space.[25] *Mojo'q che b'ixan ri ixkanulab'* connects the historical, cultural, and social contexts of Maya architectures so that it might allow us to listen in the present to the audible trace of the cultural lineage silenced by colonization. John Durham Peters notes: "Writing converts time and sound into space and vision; reading vocally, as most people seem to have done in history, converts space and vision into time and sound. Writing is a technical means of . . . transforming space into time and time into space, and for giving us access to a realm beyond time's irreversible flow."[26] This operation is also present in a different register when Chávez and weaver Delfina Par discuss the geometric patterns handwoven into the huipil. Explaining for the camera how the Maya calendar and language are camouflaged through pattern and color into the very fabric of their clothing, Chávez simply states: "The textiles are the books that colonization couldn't burn."

Classic Maya script is phonetic: it refers to the sound of speech. It is a complete writing system of logograms and syllabic glyphs that encodes vocal registration into the image and conjures sound through the transmission of syntax and vowels to those who know how to read it. While in the sixteenth century, Spanish priests used language against Indigenous peoples by writing in K'iche' and other Maya languages as an evangelizing tool, few Maya books written in the glyphic system survived colonization and the evangelical fires. What remains on paper is often limited to documentation by the colonizers themselves.[27] Beyond the page, however, the Maya also prolifically inscribed glyphs into buildings, monuments, and objects. This often took the form of bas-relief sculpture, which in itself serves an acoustic function, given how the high surface areas of the forms and intricately curved stone surfaces contribute to the diffusion of sound in space.[28] Guided by his teacher, Brito Bernal researches, decodes, and creates his own glyphs from these sources. By filming the artist's work on the translation and drafting of "before the volcanoes sing" into Maya glyphs as he inhabits Sowden House, Tossin visually, spatially, and vocally connects Brito

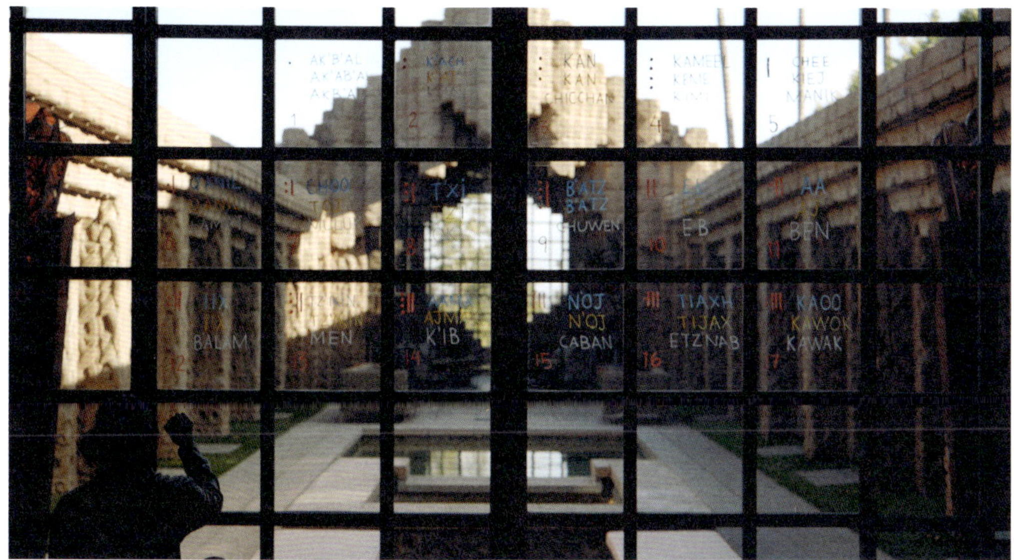

Fig. 4. *Mojo'q che b'ixan ri ixkanulab' / Antes de que los volcanes canten / Before the Volcanoes Sing* (still), 2022. Digital video (color, sound); 64:17 min. Courtesy of the artist, Galeria Luisa Strina, São Paulo, and Commonwealth and Council, Los Angeles

Bernal's study of his ancestral writing system to the appropriation and dislocation of Maya motifs by Lloyd Wright and his father. The figure of the Indigenous "screen-object" is pertinent again, but this time within the very act of appropriation. As the motifs are already taken without permission, the Indigenous strategy to protect meaning from extraction is clearly not operative here. Rather, as the glyphs and figures are divorced from the voice—their linguistic function—their resemblance is disconnected from Maya knowledge production and necessarily remains only surface deep. Brito Bernal's own presence decoding, reassembling, and speaking the component parts of the title, however, acts to resignify the meaning in the architecture's dislocated motifs.

Near the film's end, Brito Bernal writes the terms that make up the sacred calendar—called Cholq'ij (K'iche') or Tzolkin (Yucatec)—onto the vast interior glass doors that frame the geometric crenellation produced by the "textile blocks"[29] of Sowden House's pyramid-inspired façade (fig. 4). In a subtle act of reclamation, Brito Bernal writes and speaks the words in the Maya languages of Ixil, K'iche', Yucatec, and Náhuatl; the transparency of the glass overlays the words onto the appropriated architectural features of the building beyond it. Through his analysis of writing as media, Durham Peters explains:

> "Writing [marries] the two sensory modes of seeing and hearing. It got space to masquerade as time and the flat surface

> to hold markers that stood for sounds . . . The potential for writing is at the nexus linking the visual and the auditory channels of perception. Writing teaches the eye to behave like an ear, as McLuhan liked to say . . . Writing gives auditory objects (words, speech) a visual habitation, and temporal events a spatial home."[30]

Through physically superimposing action onto image, the film's sequence in essence reverses the function of the museum glass that silences the ancient flutes. The sound of Brito Bernal speaking the words fills the architectonic spaces at Sowden House, producing a performance of speech *as* space that animates the architecture and makes it his own. Essentially creating what Durham Peters describes as a "voice resonator," this act of writing onto the building's glass doors transforms the architectural features, which (like writing on "turtle shells and metal bells") act as "both inscription surface[s] and sound amplifier[s]."[31]

III. The Space and Sound of Production

This practical effect of superimposition produced by Brito Bernal as he inscribes the calendar onto the surfaces of Sowden House is exemplary of Tossin's approach to the production of film. Durham Peters goes on to describe the spatiotemporal relationship of recording media as an operation that "chop[s] and freeze[s] temporal events and inscribe[s] them onto spatial coordinates."[32] *Mojo'q che b'ixan ri ixkanulab'* records its action "onto spatial coordinates" both through practical effects such as the glass writing, and through digital experiments with montage, compositing, speed ramping, and time-lapse. Each is a technique characteristic of the artist's approach to her earlier video work *Ch'u Mayaa* (2017; pls. 33–36), but they expand in scope here to produce a dramaturgy able to link together resonances between the film's locations. Through visual and auditory effects that collapse past and present, and time and space, the film sensorially exceeds its linear timeline. For example, as Chávez guides us into the incense-filled, cavelike temple of Tohil, Tossin cuts to the scale-shifting passageways and expansive, hyperreal landscapes bound to the undulating interior and exterior form of the monkey flute (figs. 5, 6). The scale shift is produced using a macro lens[33] that is long and narrow enough to enter the resonance chambers of a larger, unplayable version of the flute, which Tossin had 3D-printed. Like the Indigenous screen-object, this enlarged flute's essential use is subverted. Divorced from its practical use

Figs. 5–7. *Mojo'q che b'ixan ri ixkanulab' / Antes de que los volcanes canten / Before the Volcanoes Sing* (stills), 2022. Digital video (color, sound); 64:17 min. Courtesy of the artist, Galeria Luisa Strina, São Paulo, and Commonwealth and Council, Los Angeles

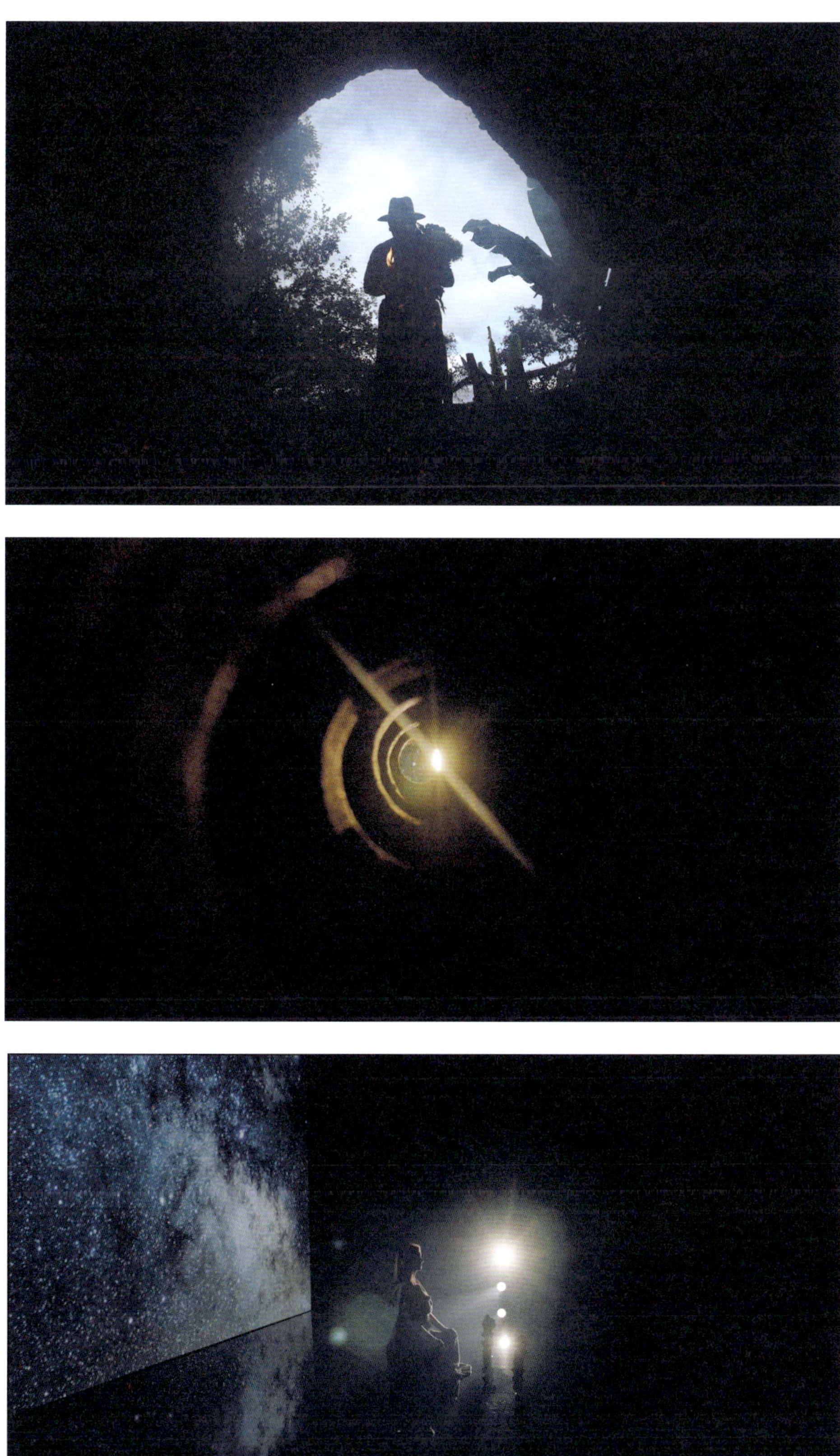

as a musical instrument, it nevertheless resonates in acoustic form with the temescal, temple, and concert hall. It visually enacts an "aural architecture" by collapsing the space between the instrument and the rooms in which it can be heard.

This exchange between digital and physical space was produced at EMPAC—the Curtis R. Priem Experimental Media and Performing Arts Center, a building in which acoustically tunable studios and theatrical infrastructures are networked with digital-production tools. Tossin was able to activate and deploy each of these venues' acoustical properties differently to sculpt that conjunction between temporality and architecture so central to how the film communicates through cinematic means.[34] However, in the same way that architectural features of the colonial museum are inherited by the contemporary art exhibition space, biases inherited from auditory technologies (such as radio) still affect the standards upon which new technologies are built.[35] There is a long history of audio communications technologies favoring the vocal range of the male voice, for example. Likewise, the advent of radio and the development of dedicated recording studios had a ripple effect on how we listen, by training our ears to the idea that "good" sound had very little reverberation time.[36] This epic aural shift over the past century of how we hear the relationship between space and sound therefore gradually reformulated how we listen by tending to dislocate a space's material structure and scale from the propagation of sound within it (fig. 7). Such a shift is central to Tossin's project, particularly in how it experiments directly with the exchange between digital and physical locations and between vernacular architectures based around acoustic systems of communication that propagated sound and contemporary spaces conversely designed for their acoustic invisibility for sound reproduction. In the final moments of the film, Chávez stands in the shallows of the lake, facing the volcanoes. Raising two stones above her head, she connects them in a series of percussive beats that marks the ritual with sound. As the stones fall through the water and merge with studio-produced effects, the sonic register shifts, as the medium through which the sound travels transforms from air to water, from the aural liveness of the landscape to the dampened and regulated sound of the studio.

IV. Listening with the Exhibition

In the film, each breath played through tiny bird ocarinas and flutes, which sculpturally represent monkey, jaguar, and other deities of Maya mythology, activates layers of music that expand the slippery temporalities of the film's themes and are then heightened even further through the film's proliferating digital effects. Lozano Birrueta performs each instrument on the Concert Hall stage among multiple digital versions of herself, fully occupying the space with sound. Pauline Oliveros[37] famously termed her meditative acoustic practice "Deep Listening" after playing music in an underground cistern with a forty-five-second reverberation time. The elongated sonic effect turned the room into an instrument in and of itself, filling the space with waves of resonating sound in response to her accordion.

On completion of the film at EMPAC, *Mojo'q che b'ixan ri ixkanulab'* was presented for a single evening in the Concert Hall, where several of Lozano Birrueta's performances had been recorded (fig. 8). Performing one final spatiotemporal superimposition, the film was projected in front of the acoustically ornamented stage wall, its score and sound design dramatized spatially throughout the hall's volume by Magalhães and audio engineer Jeff Svatek on an immersive Ambisonic array of sixty-four loudspeakers surrounding the audience. The hall was "tuned" through the manipulation of inbuilt acoustic banners to reduce the reverberation time to balance between music and dialogue. Concert halls are usually designed

Fig. 8. *Mojo'q che b'ixan ri ixkanulab' / Antes de que los volcanes canten / Before the Volcanoes Sing*, 2022. Digital video (color, sound); 64:17 min. Courtesy of the artist, Galeria Luisa Strina, São Paulo, and Commonwealth and Council, Los Angeles. Installation view, EMPAC—the Curtis R. Priem Experimental Media and Performing Arts Center, Rensselaer Polytechnic Institute, Troy, NY, February 9, 2022. Courtesy of EMPAC. Photo: Kris Qua

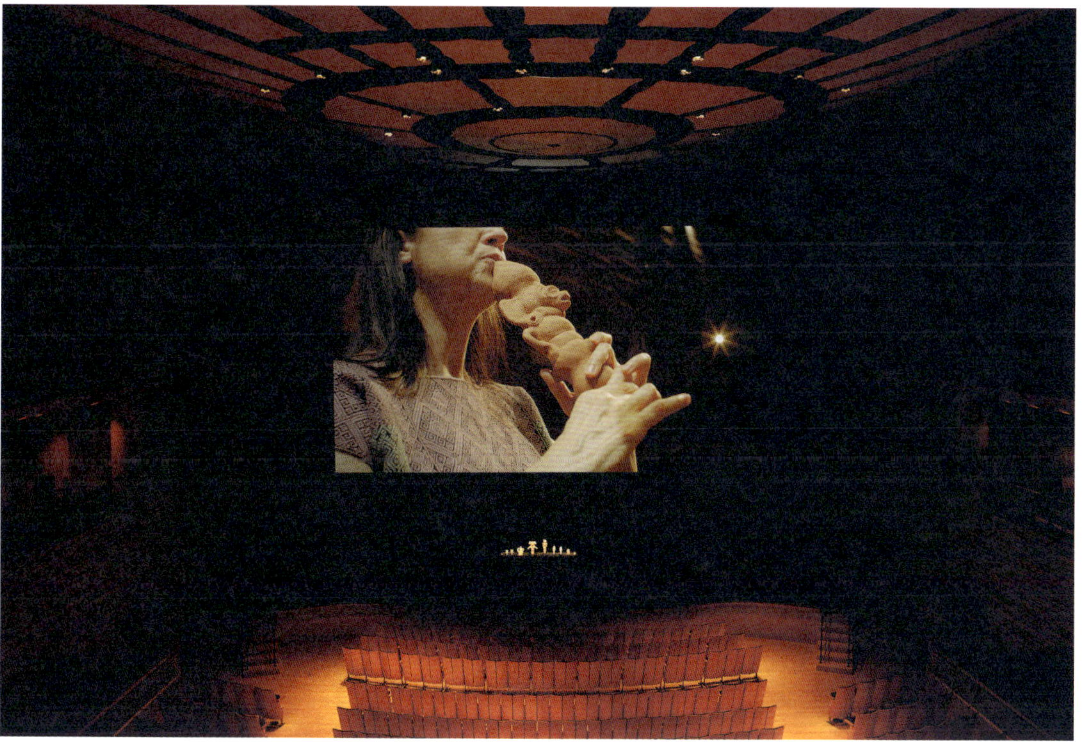

with an extended reverberation time to lengthen a given note or pitch across the large interior spaces. However, built for the sonic optimization of orchestral music (like many museum interiors), they compromise the intelligibility of "short sounds"—such as those of speech.

At the Frye, the film will be presented at one end of a long rectangular gallery with a thirteen-foot ceiling. An exhibition space with these dimensions and no acoustic treatment to absorb the sound would usually produce an environment at odds with the presentation of the film's dialogue to its audience. In this exhibition, however, clerestory walls that surround the room extend well beyond the ceiling, a design choice that dramatically increases the interior surface area of the exhibition space.[38] The sonic result of this layout is that the voids around the circumference of the ceiling can act to subtlety diffuse the sound, reducing the reverberation time and supporting our ability to localize sounds. This architectural feature conversely also contributes to "flanking sound," more commonly (and perhaps tellingly) termed "sound-bleed," which describes sound waves able to travel indirectly to the spaces that surround it. The film's soundtrack thus resonates beyond the gallery's walls. It becomes fugitive, subverting and escaping the architecture that contains it, and instead starts to permeate the building. Robinson reminds us that "[w]hether the white cube of the gallery, the proscenium stage-concert hall, the outdoor festival stage, or the black box, each site urges us to think and listen to music in particular ways that may not be conducive to the kinds of listening otherwise we might hope to advance."[39] To listen to this work within the exhibition, the film demands that we listen critically and in awareness of our communal positionality. Eidsheim writes: "Attending to the acousmatic question [*Who is this?*] tells you only who is listening: who you are. Indeed, who *we are*."[40]

Notes

1. Acknowledgments: This essay is indebted to my conversations with Clarissa Tossin, as well as to her collaborators both in front of and behind the camera: Alethia Lozano Birrueta, Rosa Chávez, Tohil Fidel Brito Bernal, Michelle Agnes Magalhães, Jeremy Glaholt, Jared Katz, Ryan Jenkins, Jeff Svatek, and the whole EMPAC team. To the continual tuning of language and ideas by Evan Calder Williams, Johannes Goebel, and Todd Vos, and to thinking museum acoustics with Nida Ghouse and Jonas Braasch.
2. Vic Brooks, "Introduction," in *Clarissa Tossin: Mojo'q che b'ixan ri ixkanulab' / Antes de que los volcanes canten / Before the Volcanoes Sing*, eds. Vic Brooks and Jo Stewart (Troy: Rensselaer Polytechnic Institute, 2022), 6. Description abridged from the program book for the work's premiere at the Concert Hall at EMPAC—the Curtis R. Priem Experimental Media and Performing Arts Center at Rensselaer Polytechnic Institute in Troy, New York, on September 16, 2023. *Mojo'q che b'ixan ri ixkanulab'* was originally commissioned by EMPAC and developed through a series of production residencies at the Center, as well as on-location film productions in Los Angeles and Guatemala.
3. For a comprehensive history of architectural acoustics and the changing "soundscapes" of early twentieth-century America, see Emily Thompson, *The Soundscape of Modernity: Architectural Acoustics and the Culture of Listening in America, 1900–1933* (Cambridge / London: MIT Press, 2002).
4. Barry Blesser and Linda-Ruth Salter, *Spaces Speak, Are You Listening? Experiencing Aural Architecture* (Cambridge/London: MIT Press, 2007), 1–9.
5. Barry Blesser and Linda-Ruth Salter, "Questions and Answers about: *Spaces Speak, Are You Listening? Experiencing Aural Architecture*," accessed December 5, 2022, http://www.blesser.net/downloads/Q-A%20Dialog%20Handout.pdf.
6. Nina Sun Eidsheim, *The Race of Sound: Listening, Timbre, and Vocality in African American Music* (Durham/London: Duke University Press, 2019), 25. See also Dylan Robinson, *Hungry Listening: Resonant Theory for Indigenous Sound Studies* (Minneapolis/London: University of Minnesota Press), 10.
7. For example, architecture can be modeled in digital space or as physical scale models to design a concert hall with the "perfect" acoustics of several seconds of reverberation time, standardized as optimal for the Western tradition of classical music. However, when that hall is built and physically encountered, there may be a difference between our perceptual response or "feeling" upon entering and a scientific understanding of how the sound waves are actually operating in the room when measured acoustically. For the first comprehensive study of concert hall acoustics see Leo L. Beranek, *Music, Acoustics & Architecture* (New Jersey: John Wiley & Sons, Inc., 1962).
8. Referring to the title of Blesser and Salter's *Spaces Speak, Are You Listening?*
9. Thompson, "Wallace Sabine and the Reverberation Formula," *The Soundscape of Modernity: Architectural Acoustics and the Culture of Listening in America, 1900–1933* (Cambridge / London: MIT Press, 2002), 33.
10. Vic Brooks and Nida Ghouse, "Shifting Center," Andy Warhol Foundation for the Visual Arts Curatorial Fellowship, accessed December 5, 2022, https://warholfoundation.org/grants/archive/vic-brooks-and-nida-ghouse.
11. Robinson, *Hungry Listening*, 69.
12. Jared Katz was a consulting curator at the Denver Art Museum at the time of Tossin's research there.
13. Jared Katz, "Gentle Flutes and Blaring Horns: An Analysis of Ancient Maya Music and Musical Instruments in Daily and Ceremonial Activities" (Riverside: UC Riverside, 2018), accessed December 5, 2022, https://escholarship.org/uc/item/60b4z9qm.
14. Alethia Lozano Birrueta, "In Collaboration," in *Clarissa Tossin: Mojo'q che b'ixan ri ixkanulab' / Antes de que los volcanes canten / Before the Volcanoes Sing* program book, interview by Mariana Fernández (Troy: Rensselaer Polytechnic Institute, 2022), 35.
15. The term "acousmatic" refers to the experience of hearing a sound with no perceptible source.
16. Michelle Agnes Magalhães, "In Collaboration," 35.

17. Michelle Agnes Magalhães, "In Progress: Clarissa Tossin, Before the Volcanoes Sing" (Work-in-progress presentation, EMPAC—the Curtis R. Priem Experimental Media and Performing Arts Center, Rensselaer Polytechnic Institute, Troy, NY, November 7, 2019).
18. David Garneau, "Imaginary Spaces of Conciliation and Reconciliation," *West Coast Line*, Summer 2012, 33. Accessed December 5, 2022, https://inhabitinginheritance.files.wordpress.com/2016/02/pages-from-west-coast-line-74-1.pdf.
19. Robinson, *Hungry Listening*, 22.
20. Jesse Lerner points to the architectural landmark and "monument" status of preservation accorded to both Frank Lloyd Wright's Hollyhock House and lthe Maya ruins of Chichén Itzá, Uxmal, Calakmul, Palenque, Quiriguá, and Tikal in Jesse Lerner, "Ch'u Mayaa and the Re-Appropriated Past," unpublished manuscript, 2021.
21. Even in partial ruin, the material structure of the forest surrounding the site—thick stands of tall trees at multiple distances from the clearing, whose texture and surface area refract and absorb the energy of the sound waves—and the acoustic qualities of the materials (rough stone, mud, lime, and sand) with which the site was built points to a lively and acoustically diffusive environment in which the voice would be legible and localized, while resonant enough that acoustic music from a flute would carry some distance through the air into the surroundings. The audio effect of Chávez's sound-poems at Q'umarkaj frames the way in which the formal properties of a site (including architectural design, natural landscape features, and foliage) can encode a sonic support structure, which extends acoustic communication across generations and scales of time. New technologies for mapping archaeological sites, including the use of aerial lidar to reveal how sites such as Teotihuacán, Mexico, were laid out, are leading to new ways of studying the acoustics of these sites. See also Nida Ghouse's work with Indian acoustic-archaeologist Umashankar Manthravadi on his acoustic measurement of premodern performance spaces in India. Ghouse's exhibition is documented by a series of publications: see "An Archaeology of Listening," ed. Nida Ghouse (Berlin: Archive Books, 2021).
22. K'iche' translations of her poems are by Vianna González Ajiataz, produced in collaboration with Chávez.
23. Eidsheim, *The Race of Sound*, 4.
24. Chávez is specifically referring to the importance of language and its continuity to the transmission of ancestral knowledge and cultural techniques. Practices of assimilation by colonial conquests and subsequent settler societies, like Indigenous language suppression, engender a secondary dislocation from cultural, educational, and spiritual practices embedded in systems of writing and communication that follows the community's removal from their lands and ways of living.
25. Chávez discusses the relationship between language recovery and migration in "Mojo'q che b'ixan ri ixkanulab': Rosa Chávez and Tohil Fidel Brito in conversation with Clarissa Tossin and Mariana Fernández," EMPAC at Rensselaer Polytechnic Institute, March 17, 2021, https://empac.rpi.edu/events/2021/mojoq-che-bixan-ri-ixkanulab.
26. John Durham Peters, *The Marvelous Clouds: Toward a Philosophy of Elemental Media*, (Chicago: University of Chicago Press, 2015), 304.
27. Judith Maxwell, "Revitalization Programs and Impacts in Latin America and the Caribbean," *Indigenous Language Revitalization in the Americas*, eds. Serafín M. Coronel-Molina and Teresa L. McCarty (London / New York: Routledge, 2016), 251. The Maya mythos-historic narratives in *Popol Vuh*, written by Fray Francisco Ximénez, are still used extensively today as "a mystic charter for all Maya." See also Gloria Elizabeth Chacón, *Indigenous Cosmolectics: Kab'awil and the Making of Maya and Zapotec Literatures* (Chapel Hill: The University of North Carolina Press, 2018) for in-depth reading on the complexity of translation and contemporary poetry, literature, and theater by Indigenous Mesoamerican artists.
28. For a related thesis on the interaction of architectural acoustics and ornament, see Zackery Belanger, *Acoustic Ornament* (Detroit: Arcgeometer LC, 2021).
29. For the architectural context of textile block houses, see Jesse Lerner, "Frank Lloyd Wright's Textile Block Houses and the Maya Revival" (KCET, March 7, 2018), accessed on December 5, 2022, https://www.kcet.org/shows/artbound/frank-lloyd-wrights-textile-block-houses-and-the-maya-revival. See also Clarissa Tossin's exhibition, *21st Century Wisdom: Healing Frank Lloyd Wright's Textile Block Houses*, 18th Street Arts Center, Santa Monica, January 22–March 29, 2019.
30. Durham Peters, *The Marvelous Clouds*, 303.

31. Durham Peters, *The Marvelous Clouds*, 304.
32. Durham Peters, *The Marvelous Clouds*, 308.
33. A macro lens is a wide-angle lens that allows for greater depth of field at close focusing distances. To film inside the flutes, a Laowa 24mm "probe" lens was used, which has LEDs on its end to capture footage inside the vessels.
34. In collaboration with the technical expertise of the EMPAC engineering team and Tossin's cinematographer, Jeremy Glaholt.
35. Digital tools, from audio software to communications technologies, also have architectural properties and protocols, which have a profound effect on the film's effects. When the film's production schedule was interrupted by the pandemic, Tossin continued to rehearse the score with Magalhães and Lozano Birrueta from a distance on Zoom. The platform's inbuilt "optimizations" were immediately recognizable and reflected back into Tossin's reparative method and approach. The algorithm driving the preset filters that optimize vocal legibility by reducing background "noise" in fact silenced the complex sounds produced by Lozano Birrueta's exhalation each time she played a flute. The emphasis on amplifying Lozano Birrueta's breath as she plays the instruments, particularly as she gets to and from a note to release it, was crucial. Rather than conforming to the hierarchy of occidental musical traditions, which tend to privilege pitch and rhythm, the film instead centers on the material and sonic properties of the performing body as a tool of communication. By listening closely to the production, Tossin was able to hear how certain implicit protocols of technical calibration are hardwired into the tools.
36. See Emily Thompson's account of the architectural acoustic development of recording studios and sound stages, which developed in concert with the rise of audio recording and amplification tools. She refers to such spaces as "subtly defined by the absence, not presence of sound," 198.
37. Electronic music pioneer Pauline Oliveros (1932–2016) was distinguished professor of music at Rensselaer Polytechnic Institute and worked regularly in EMPAC's Concert Hall. For her "Oliveros at 80," Jonas Braasch, professor of architectural acoustics and associate director of research at EMPAC, worked with Oliveros to recreate a simulation of the long reverberation time of the Fort Worden Cistern within the Concert Hall, where Tossin's work was filmed and premiered. See "Oliveros at 80" (Performance, EMPAC, Rensselaer Polytechnic Institute, Troy, NY, May 10, 2012), https://empac.rpi.edu/events/2012/oliveros-80 and *Mojo'q che b'ixan ri ixkanulab' / Antes de que los volcanes canten / Before the Volcanoes Sing* (Screening and Ambisonic installation at EMPAC, Rensselaer Polytechnic Institute, Troy, NY, September 9, 2022), https://empac.rpi.edu/events/2022/mojoq-che-bixan-ri-ixkanulab-antes-de-que-los-volcanes-canten-volcanoes-sing.
38. It is helpful to return to Blesser and Salter's definition of aural architecture here: "The composite of numerous surfaces, objects, and geometries in a complicated environment creates an aural architecture. As we hear how sounds from multiple sources interact with the various spatial elements, we assign an identifiable personality to the aural architecture, in much the same way we interpret an echo as the aural personality of a wall," 2.
39. Robinson, *Hungry Listening*, 61.
40. Eidsheim, *The Marvelous Clouds*, 24.

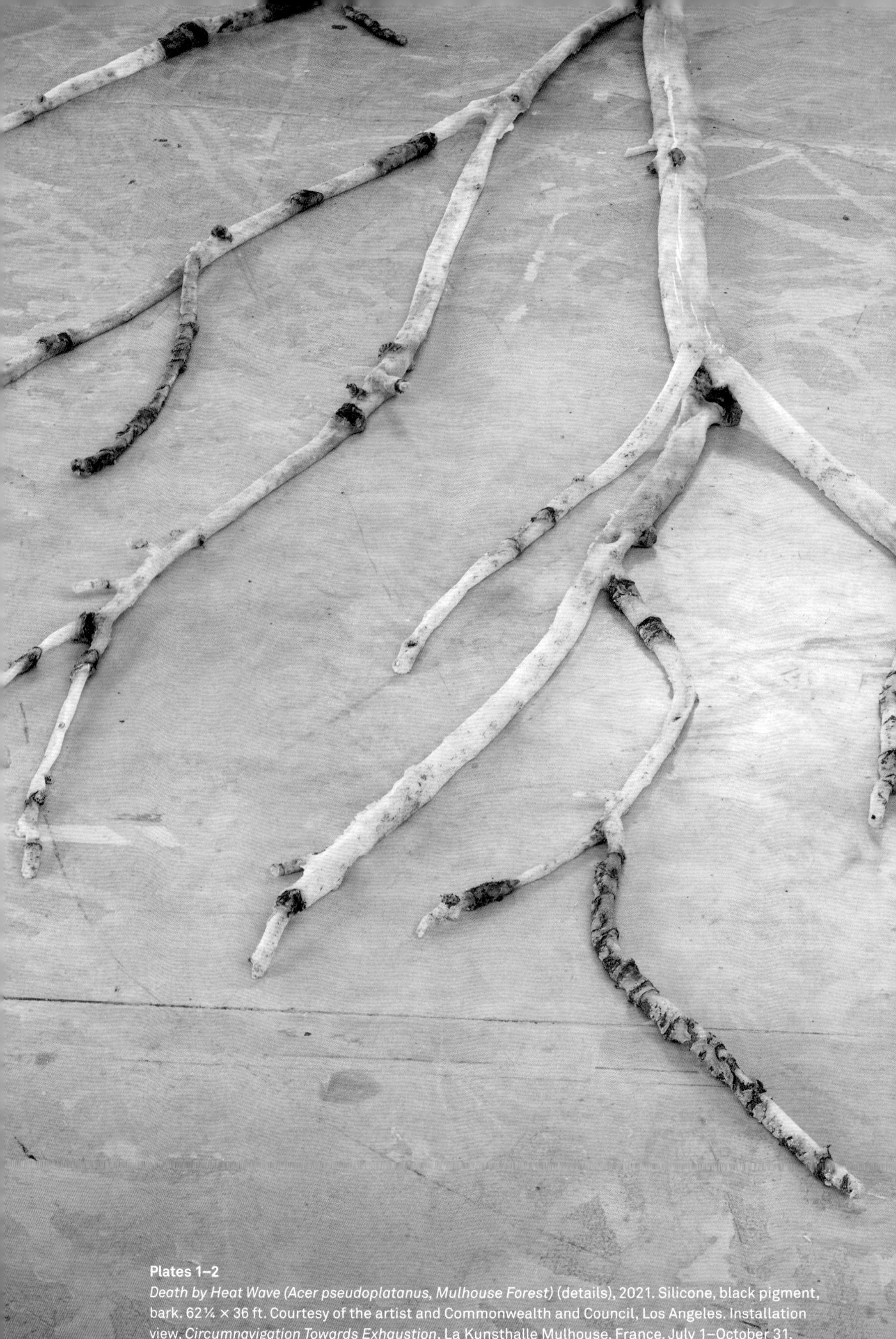

Plates 1–2
Death by Heat Wave (Acer pseudoplatanus, Mulhouse Forest) (details), 2021. Silicone, black pigment, bark. 62¼ × 36 ft. Courtesy of the artist and Commonwealth and Council, Los Angeles. Installation view, *Circumnavigation Towards Exhaustion*, La Kunsthalle Mulhouse, France, July 1–October 31, 2021. © La Kunsthalle Mulhouse. Photo: Michel Kurst

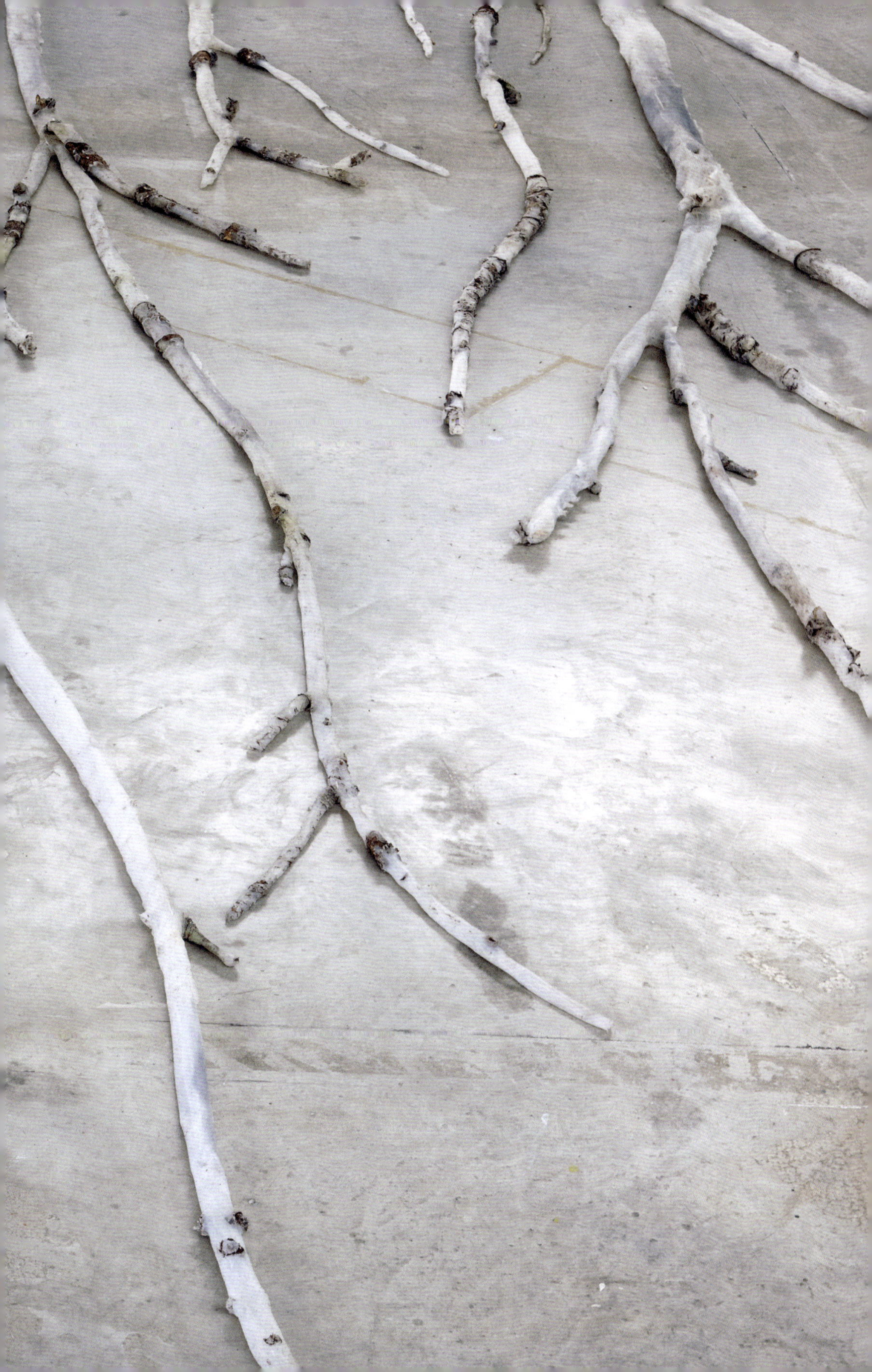

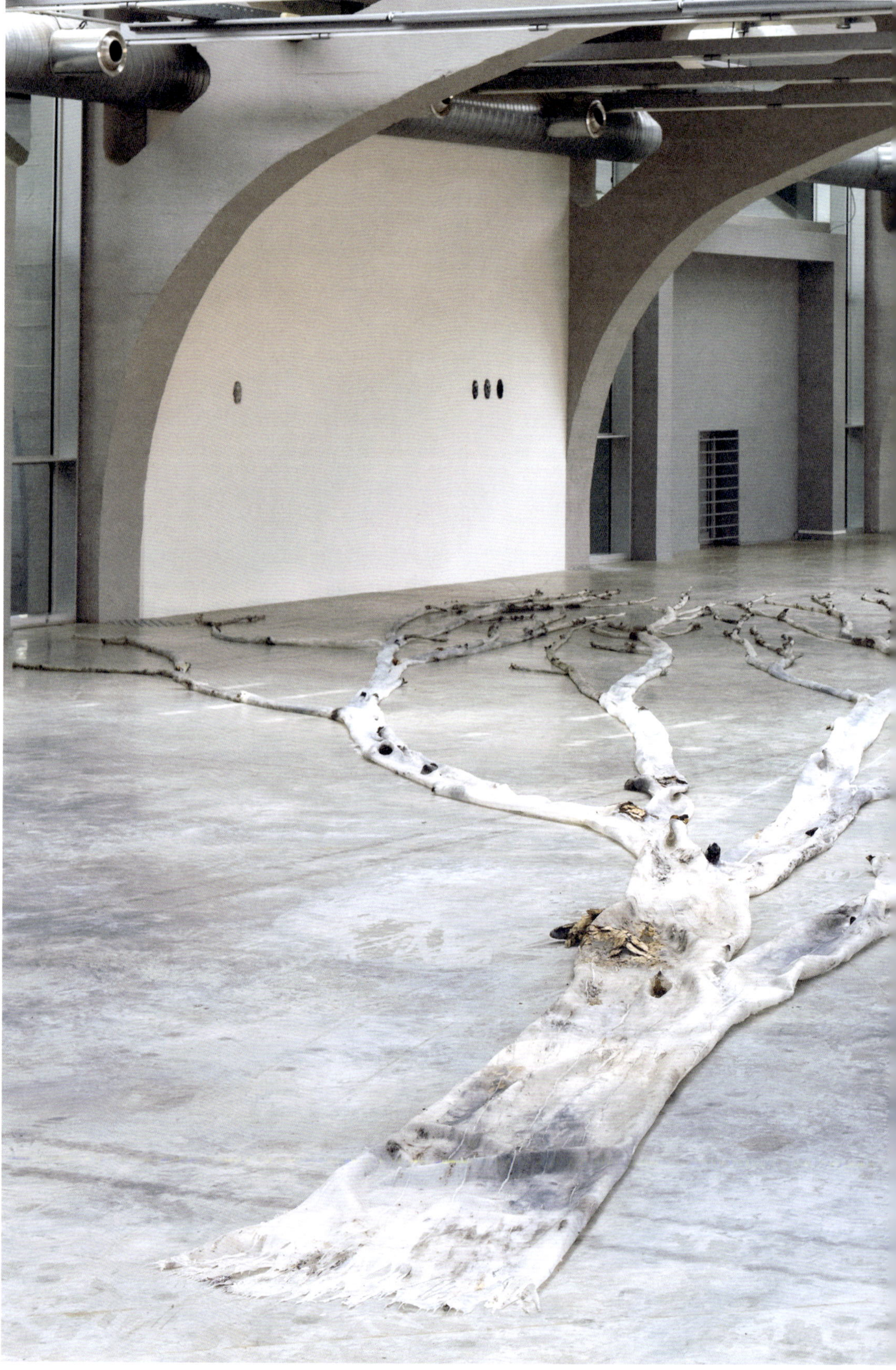

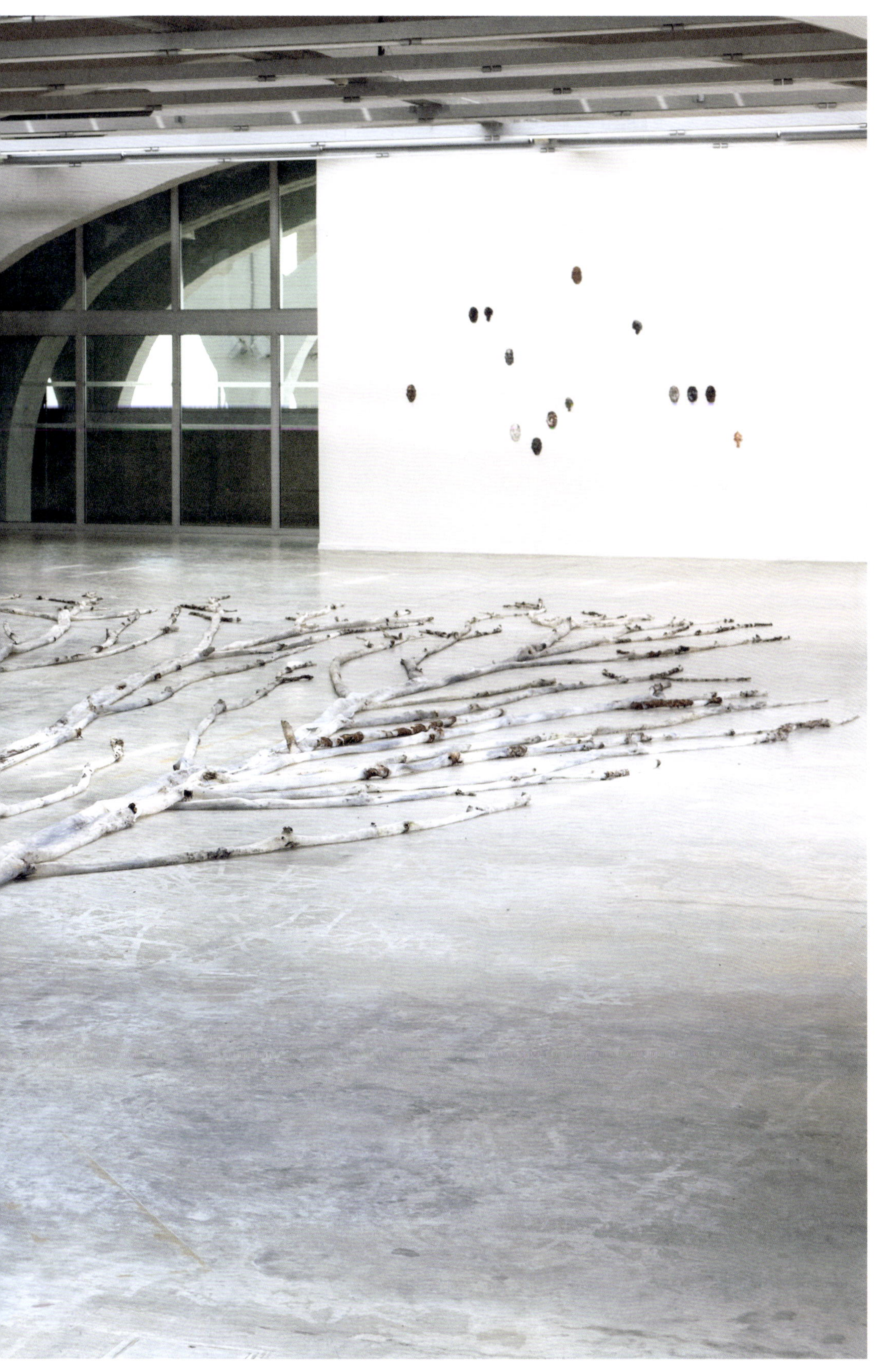

Plate 3
Becoming Mineral, 2021. Fired clay, terracotta, and porcelain. 7 × 4 × 1½ in. each (approx.). Courtesy of the artist, Galeria Luisa Strina, São Paulo, and Commonwealth and Council, Los Angeles. Installation view, *Clarissa Tossin: Falling From Earth*, Museum of Contemporary Art Denver, June 3–August 28, 2022. Courtesy of MCA Denver. Photo: Wes Magyar

Plate 4
Becoming Mineral, 2021. Porcelain. 8 × 6 × 1½ in. Frye Art Museum, Purchased with funds provided by the Contemporary Council, 2023.005.02. Photo: Brica Wilcox

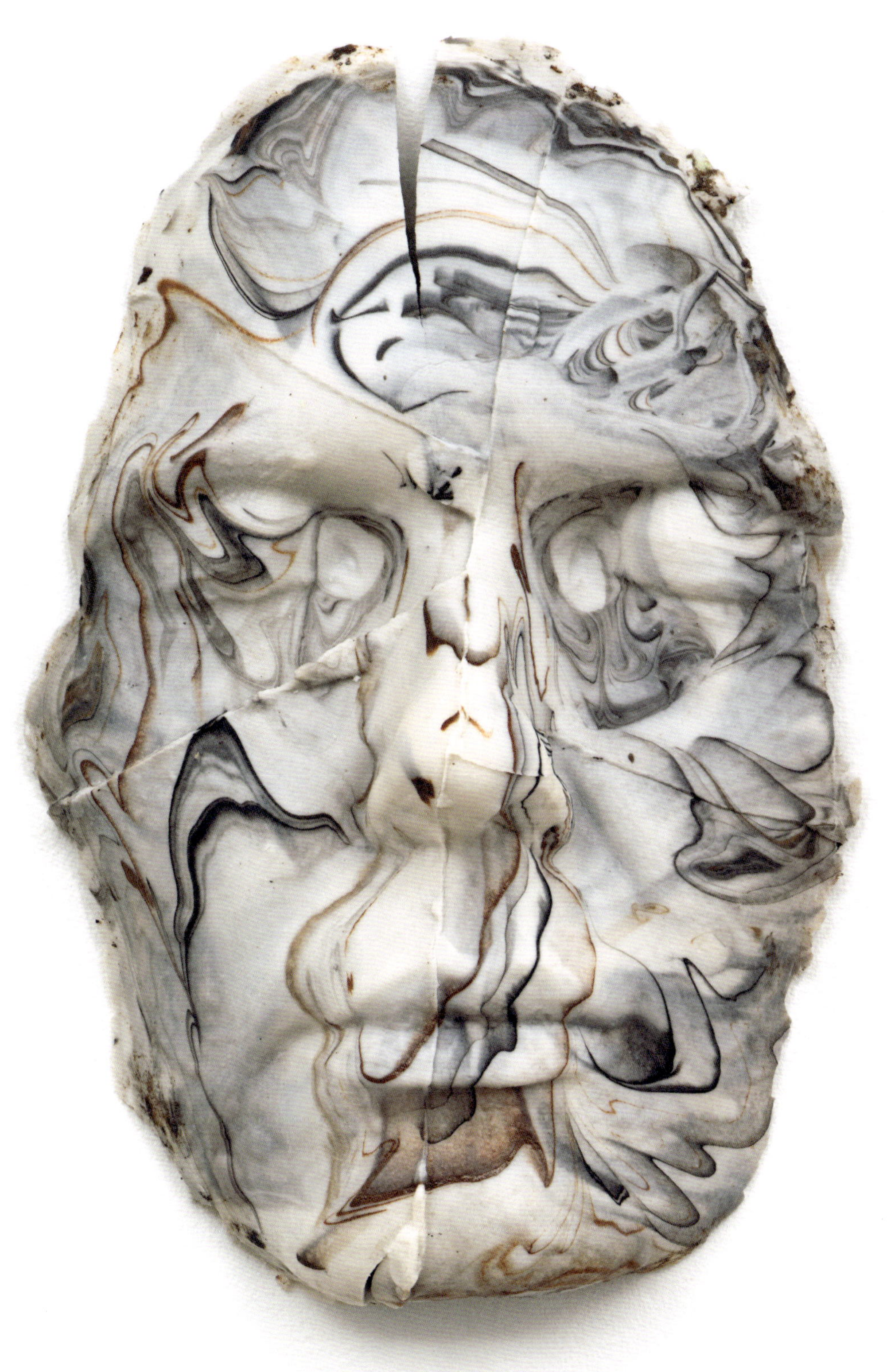

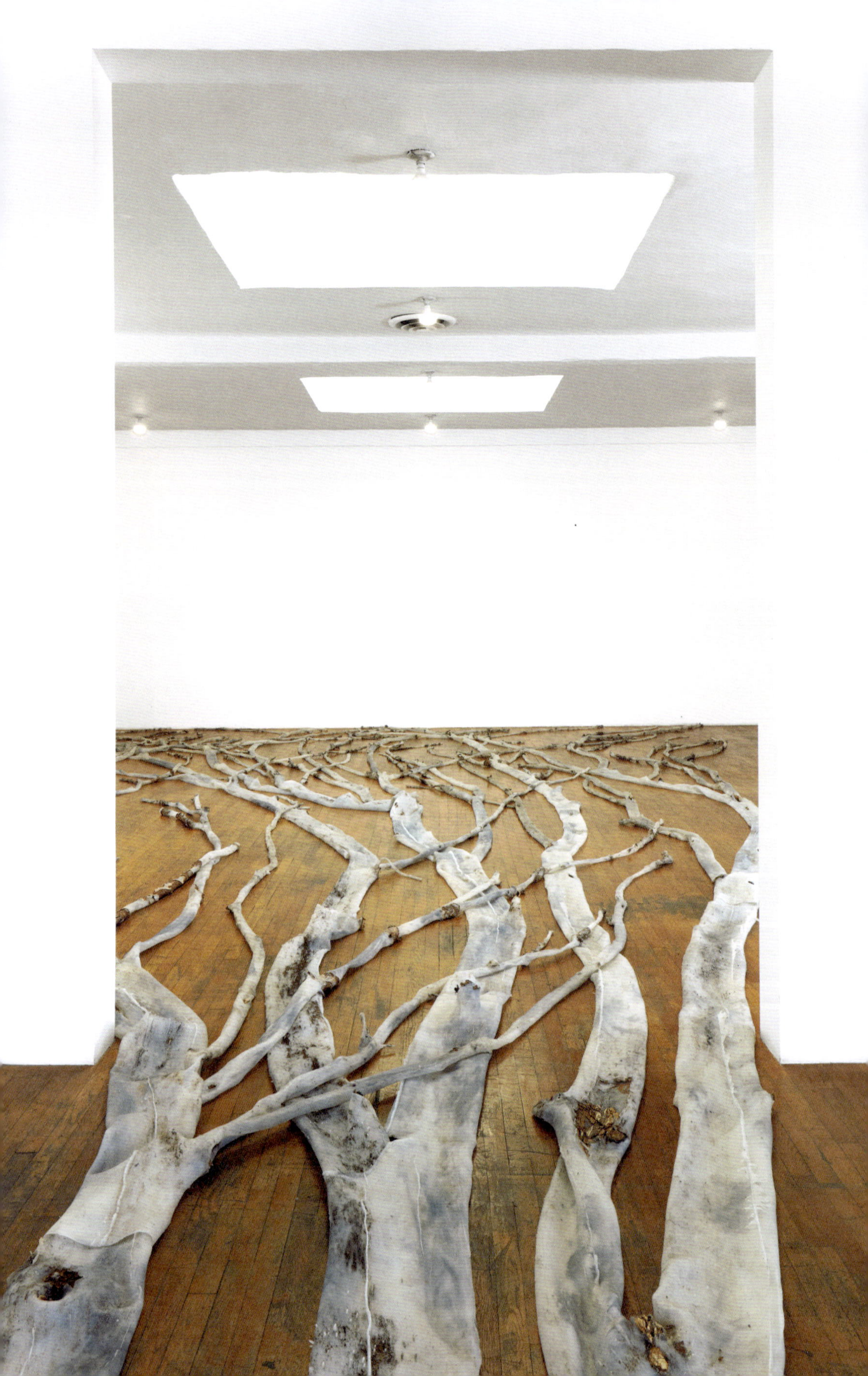

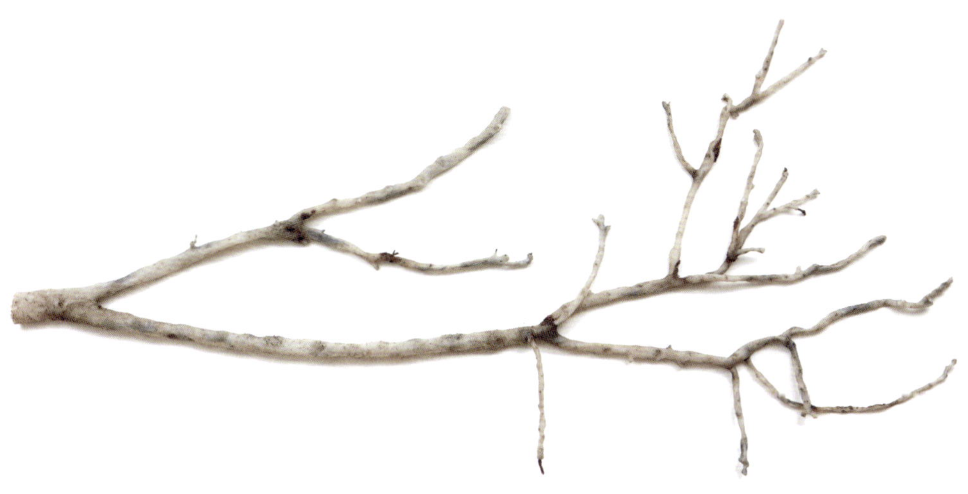

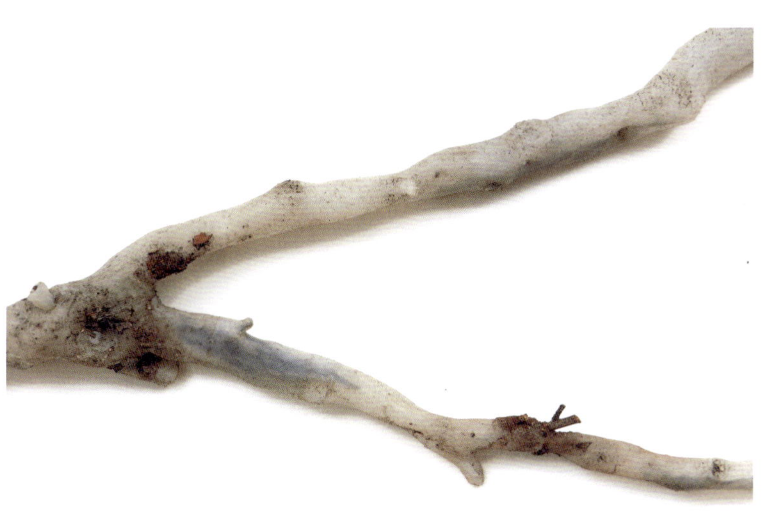

Plate 5
Death by Heat Wave (Acer pseudoplatanus, Mulhouse Forest) (detail), 2021. Silicone, black pigment, bark. 62¼ × 36 ft. Courtesy of the artist and Commonwealth and Council, Los Angeles. Installation view, *Disorientation Towards Collapse*, Commonwealth and Council, Los Angeles, January 15–February 19, 2022. Photo: Paul Salveson

Plates 6–7
Rising Temperature Casualty (Prunus persica var. nucipersica, home garden, Los Angeles), 2021. Silicone, black pigment, tree bark. 44 × 115 × 4 in. (approx.). Courtesy of the artist and Commonwealth and Council, Los Angeles. Photo: Paul Salveson

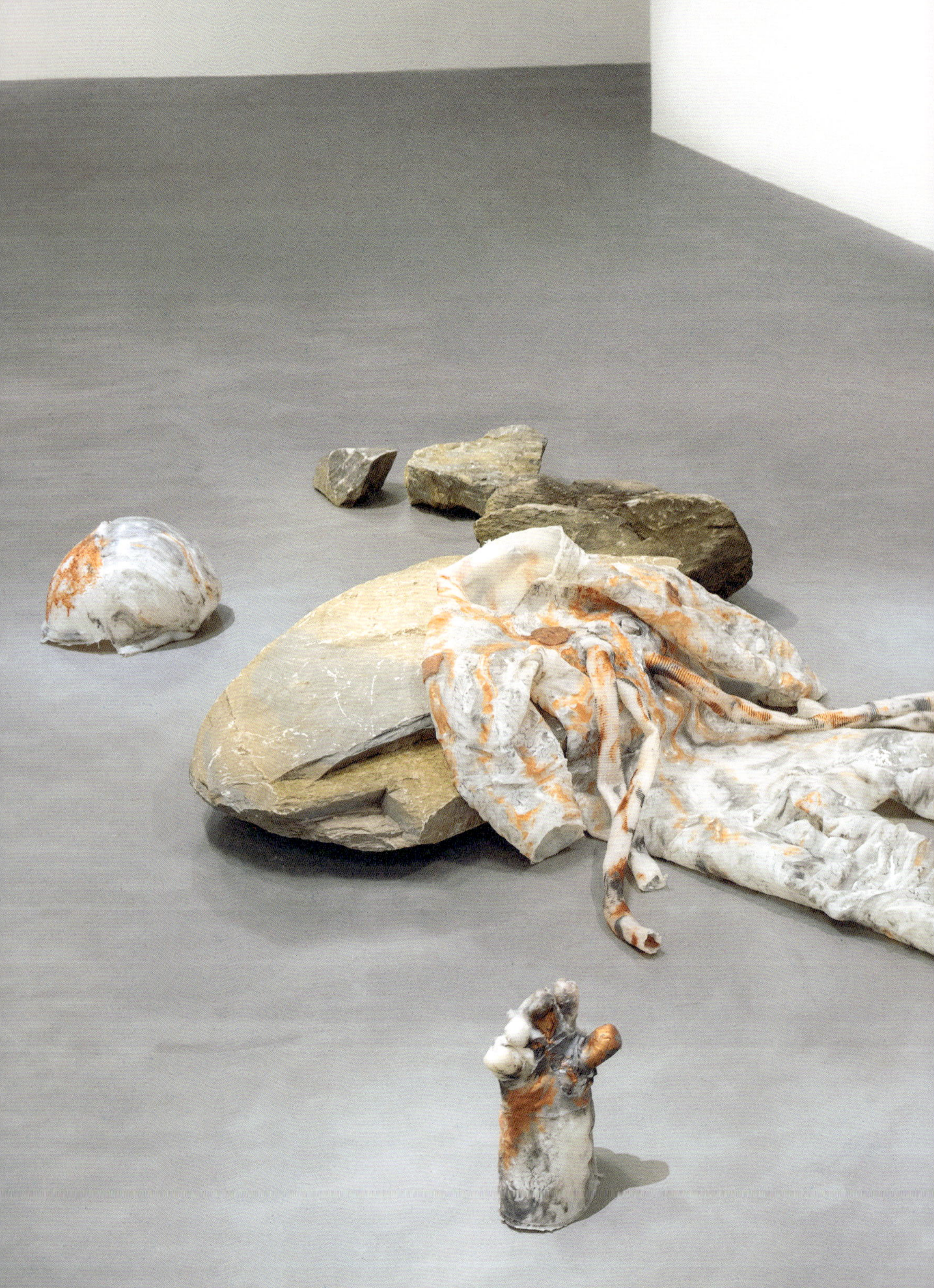

Plate 8
Vulnerably Human #2, 2022. Silicone, meteorite powder, pigment. Dimensions variable. Courtesy of the artist and Galeria Luisa Strina, São Paulo. Installation view, *Vulneravelmente Humano*, Galeria Luisa Strina, São Paulo, March 25–April 29, 2023. Courtesy of Galeria Luisa Strina. Photo: Edouard Fraipont

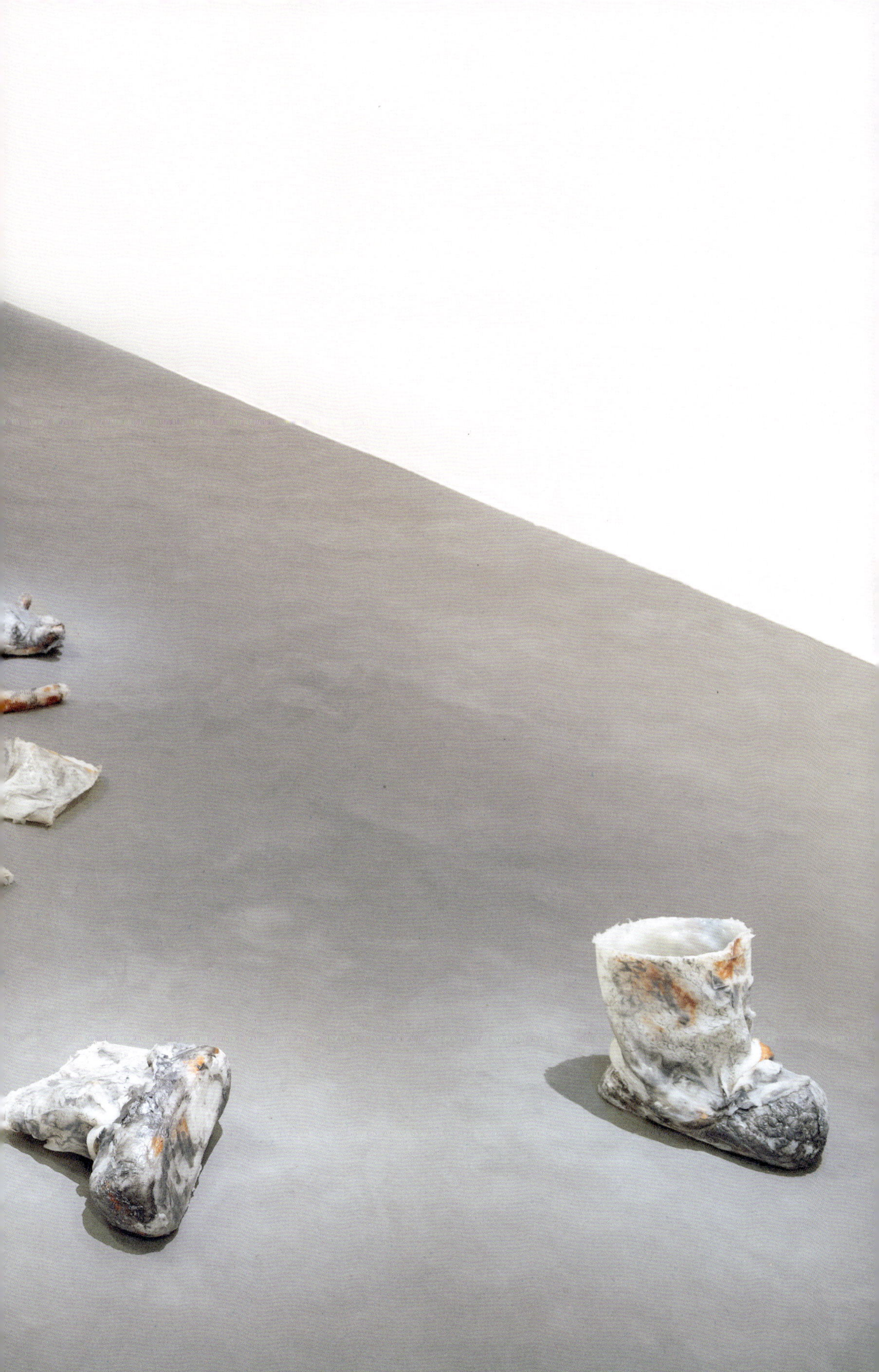

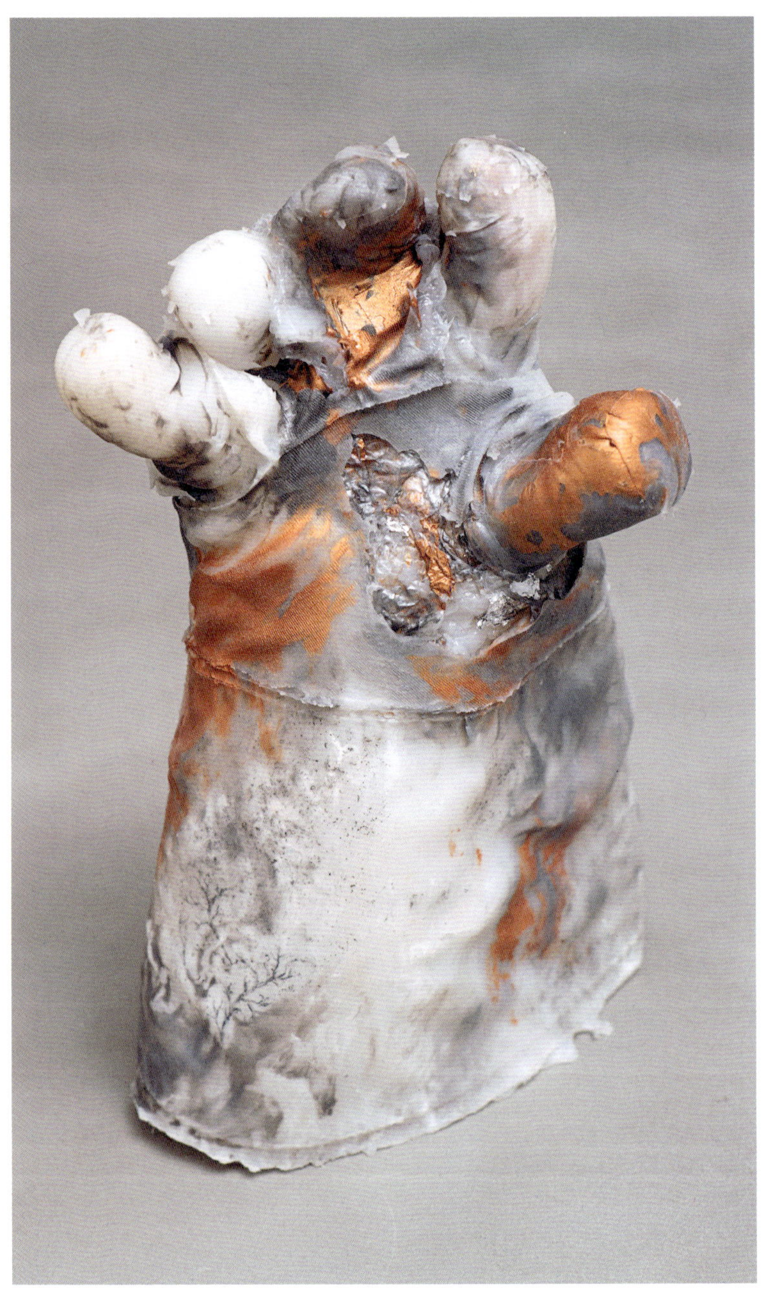

Plate 9
Vulnerably Human #2 (detail), 2022. Silicone, meteorite powder, pigment. Dimensions variable. Courtesy of the artist and Galeria Luisa Strina, São Paulo. Photo: Edouard Fraipont

Plate 10
Rising Temperature Casualty (Prunus persica, home garden, Los Angeles), 2022. Silicone, black pigment, tree roots. 126 × 48 × 58 in. (approx.). Frye Art Museum, Purchased with funds provided by the Contemporary Council, 2023.005.01. Installation view, *Clarissa Tossin: Falling From Earth*, Museum of Contemporary Art Denver, June 3–August 28, 2022. Courtesy of MCA Denver. Photo: Wes Magyar

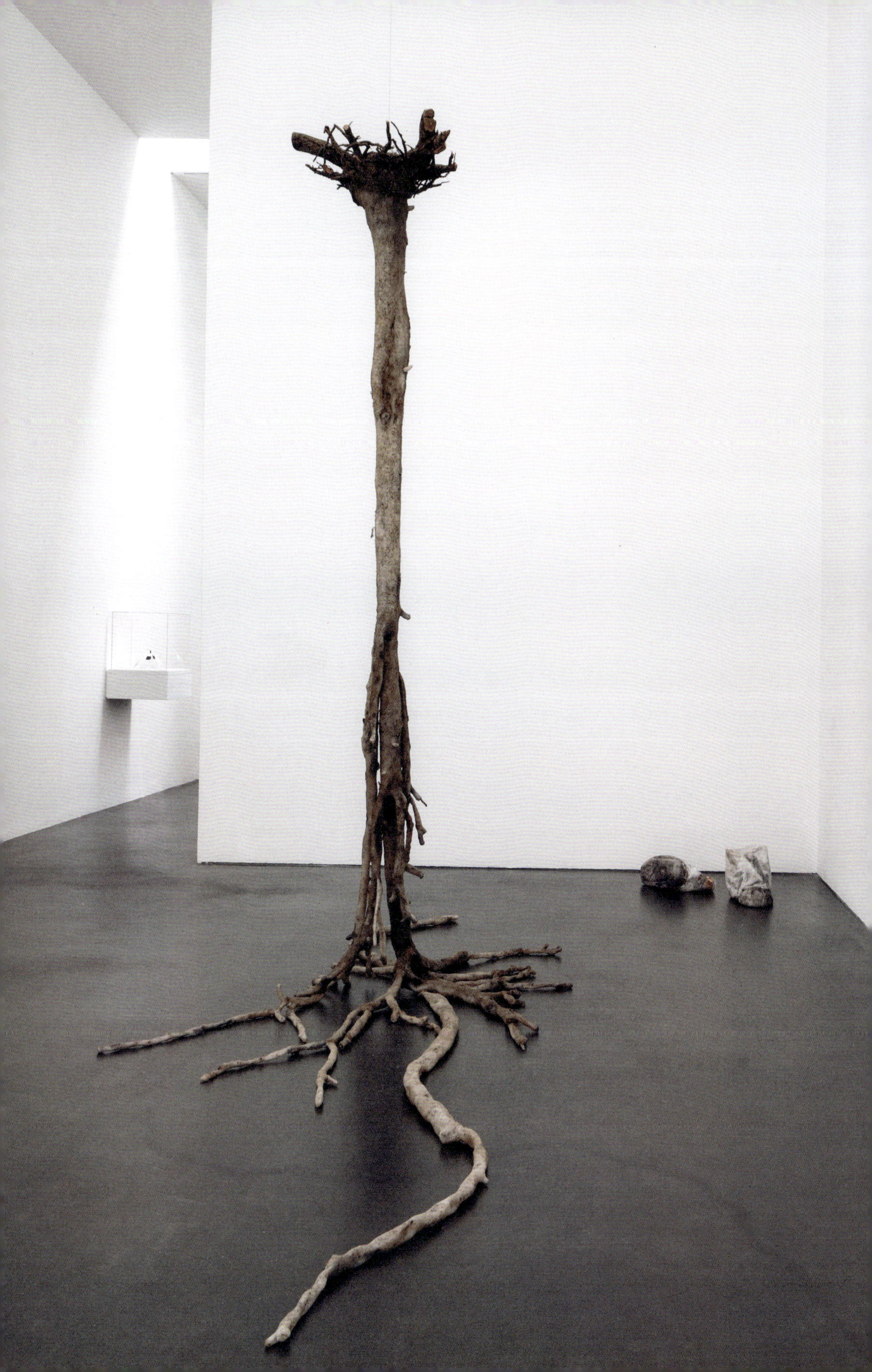

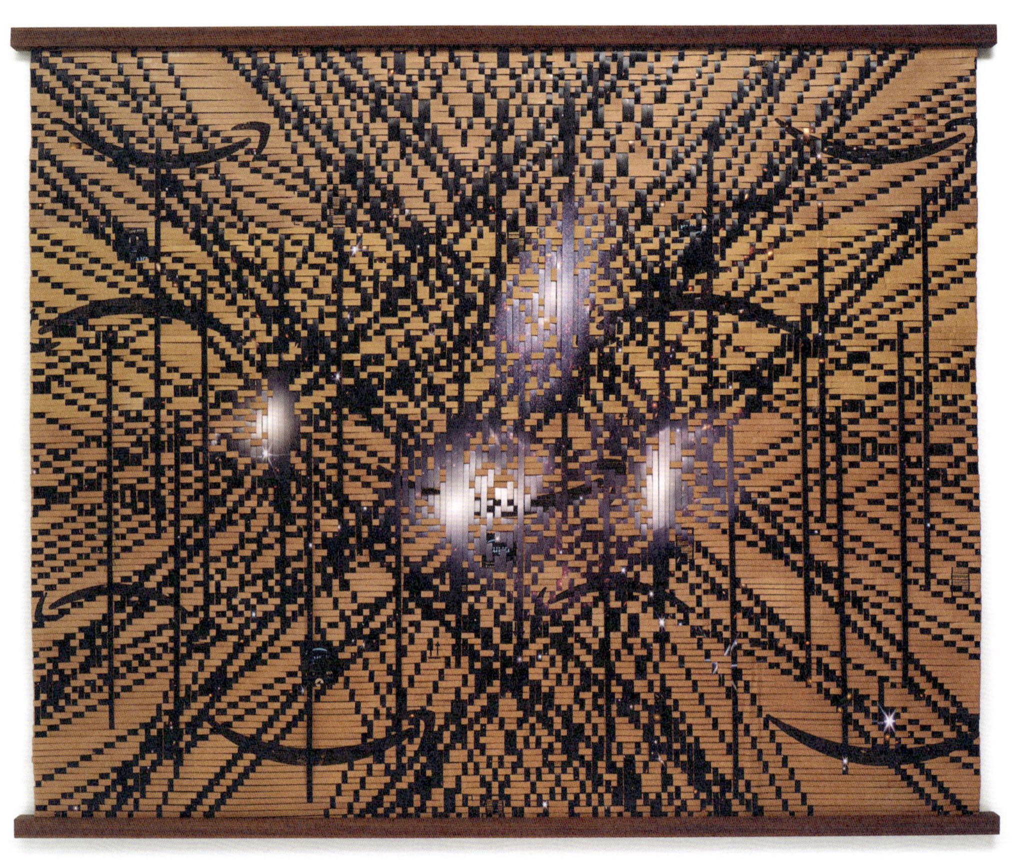

Plate 11
Future Geography: The Five Galaxies of Stephan's Quintet, 2022. Used Amazon.com delivery boxes, archival inkjet print on photo paper with lamination, wood. 66 × 79½ × 1½ in. Commissioned by the Frye Art Museum. Courtesy of the artist, Galeria Luisa Strina, São Paulo, and Commonwealth and Council, Los Angeles. Photo: Brica Wilcox

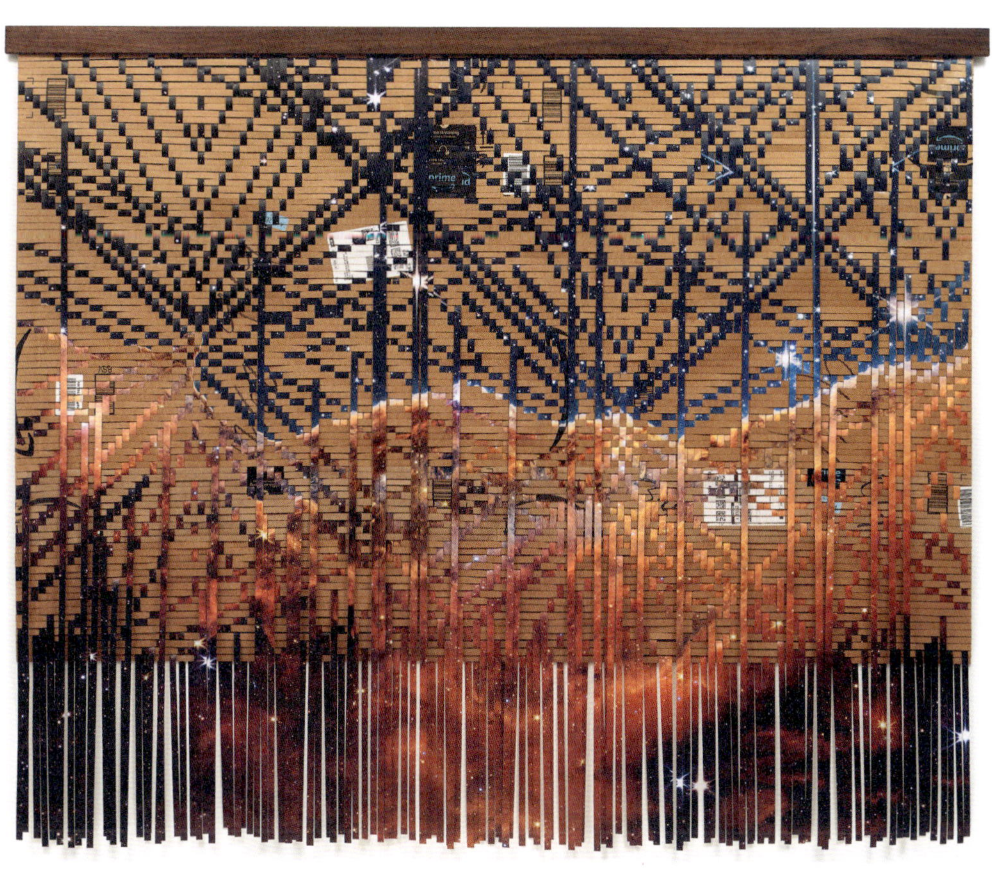

Plates 12–13

Future Geography: Cosmic Cliffs, 2023. Used Amazon.com delivery boxes, archival inkjet print on photo paper with lamination, walnut. 60 × 71½ × 1 in. Commissioned by the Frye Art Museum. Courtesy of the artist, Galeria Luisa Strina, São Paulo, and Commonwealth and Council, Los Angeles. Photo: Brica Wilcox

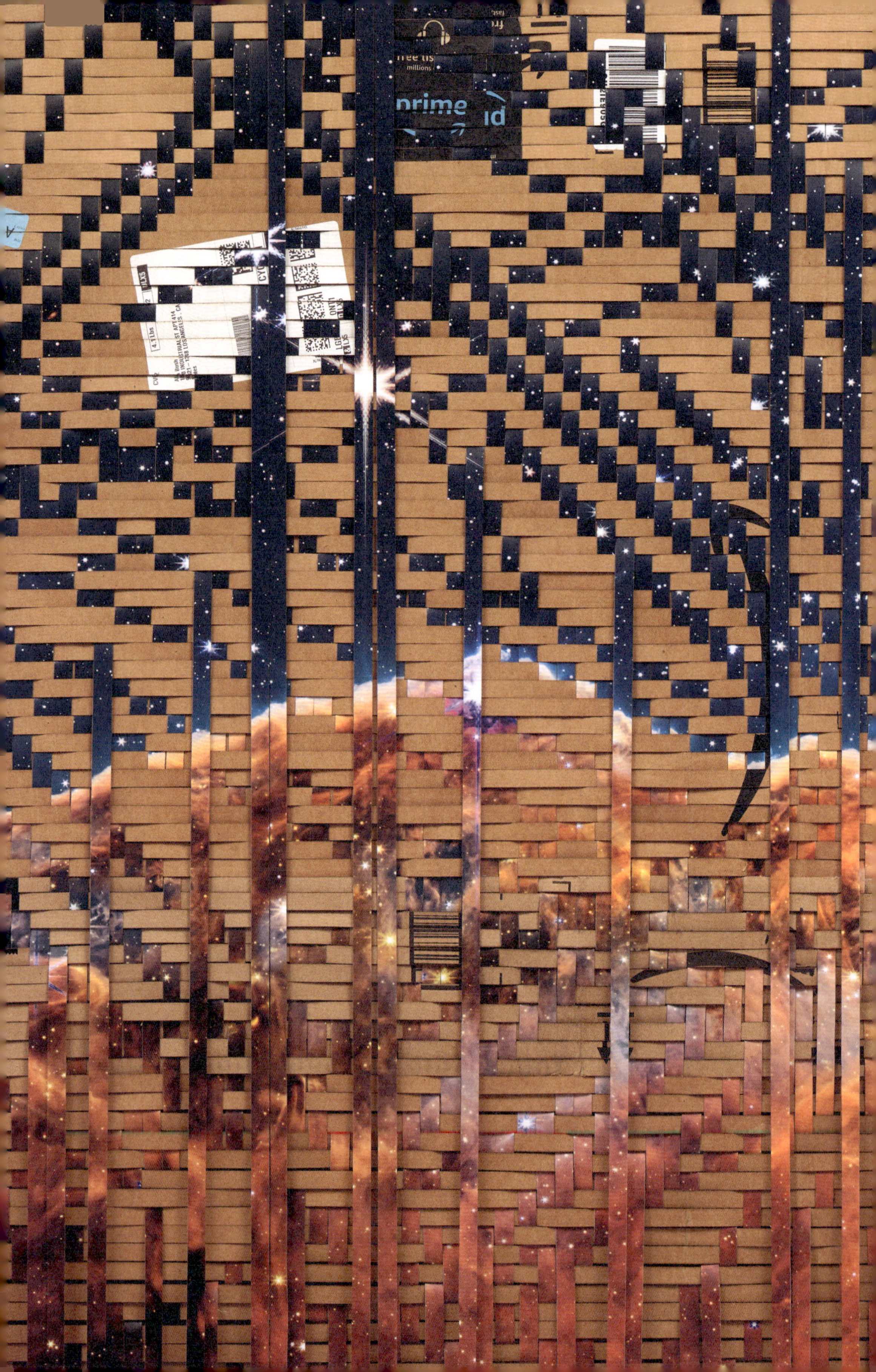

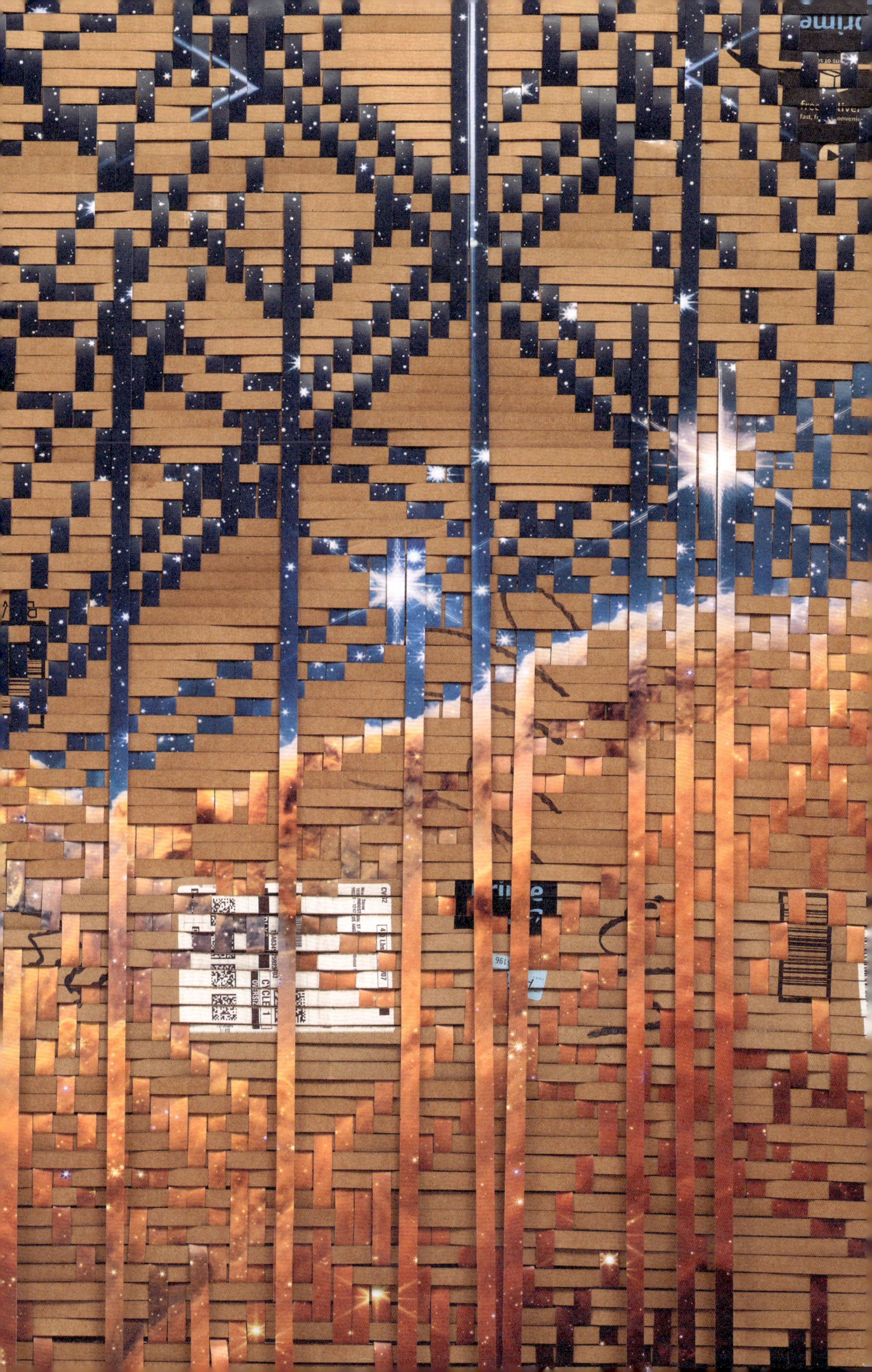

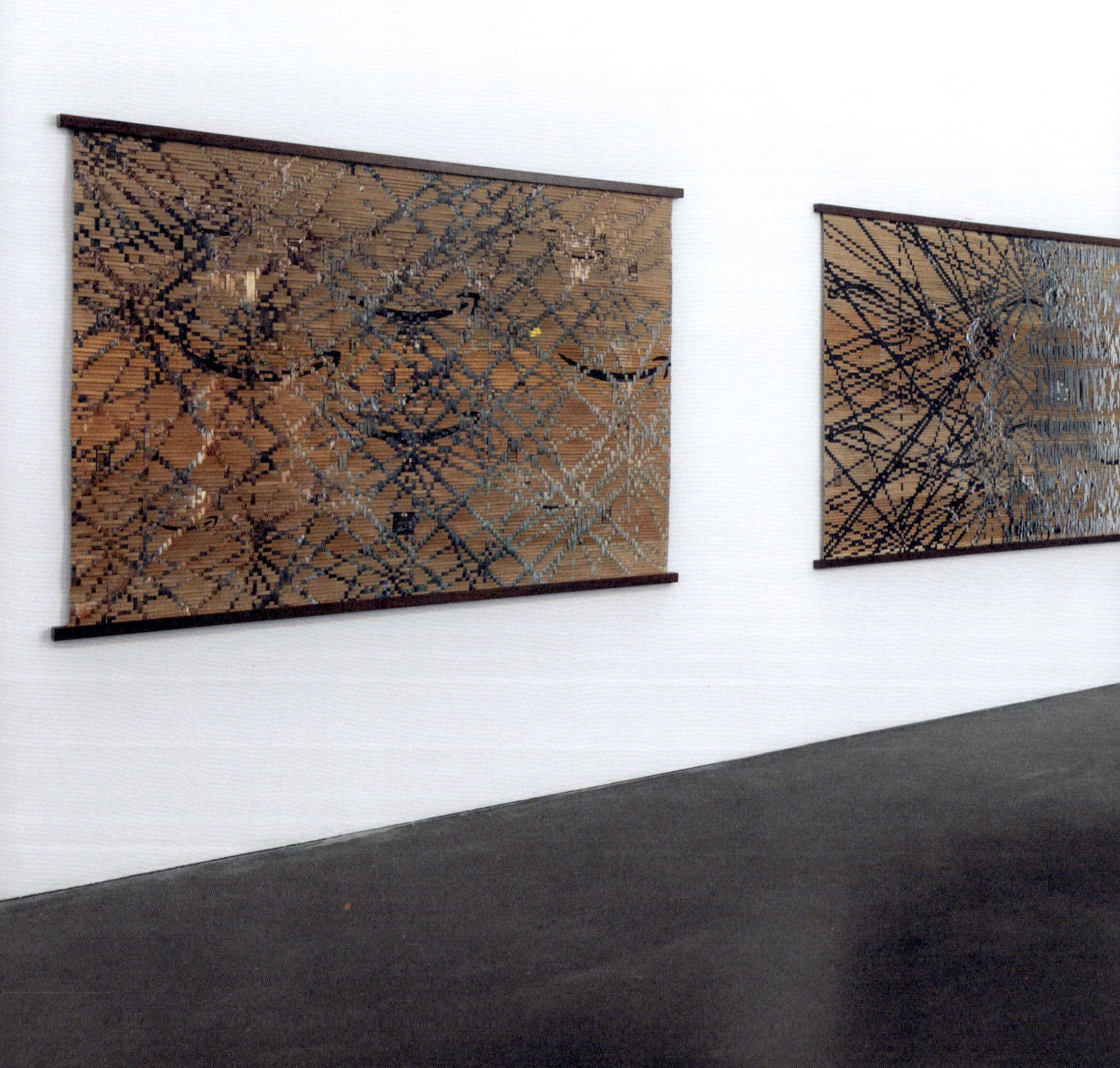

Plate 14
Future Geography series, 2021. Installation view, *Clarissa Tossin: Falling From Earth*, Museum of Contemporary Art Denver, June 3–August 28, 2022. Courtesy of MCA Denver. Photo: Wes Magyar

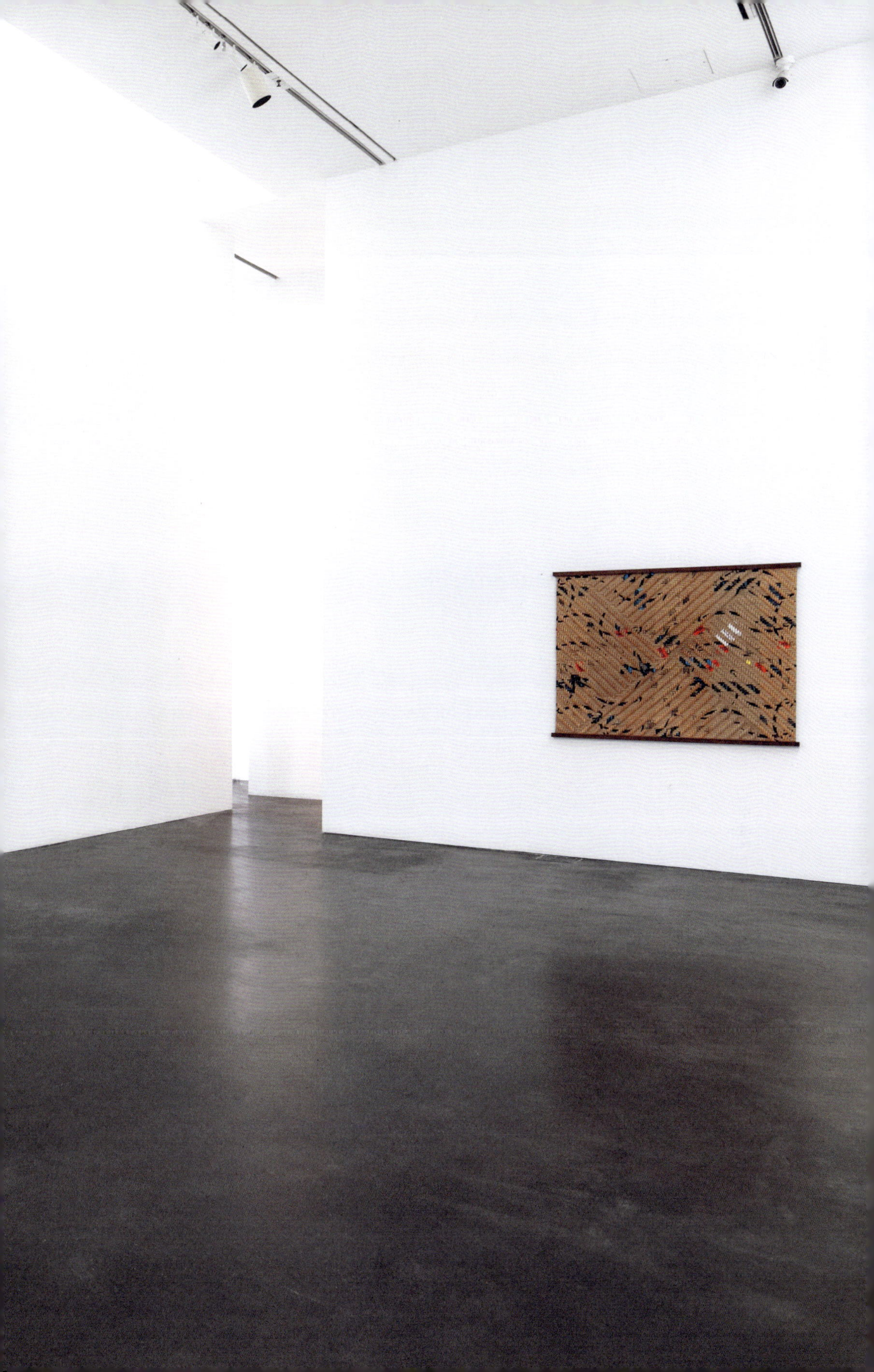

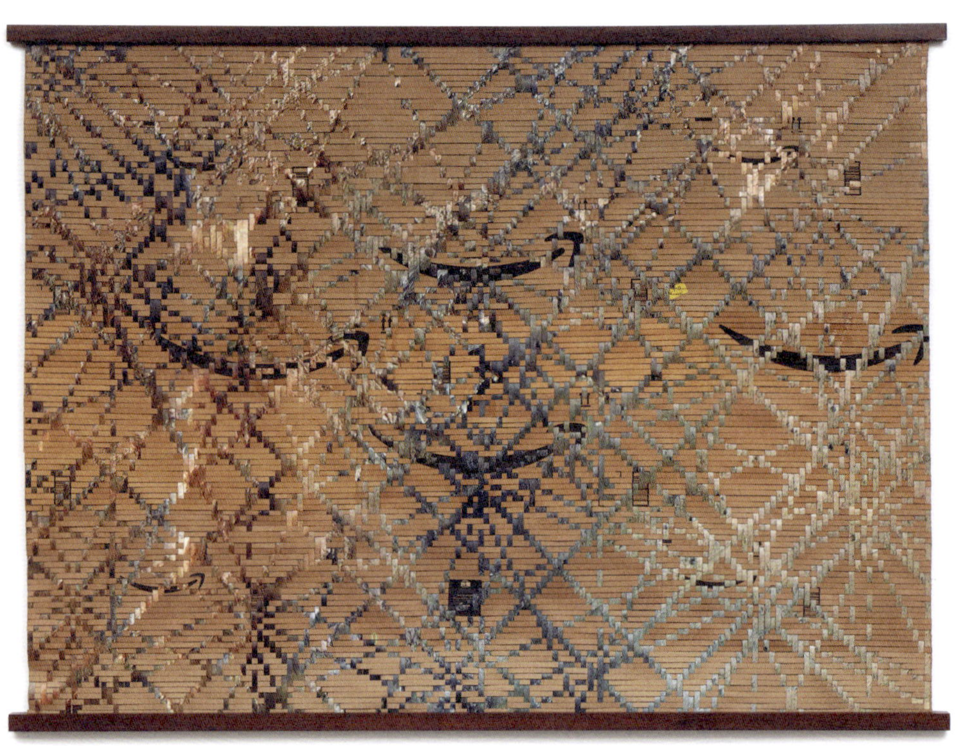

Plate 15

Future Geography: Jezero Crater, Mars, 2021. Used Amazon.com delivery boxes, archival inkjet print with matte lamination, wood. 60 × 84 × 1½ in. Private collection. Courtesy of the artist and Commonwealth and Council, Los Angeles. Photo: Paul Salveson

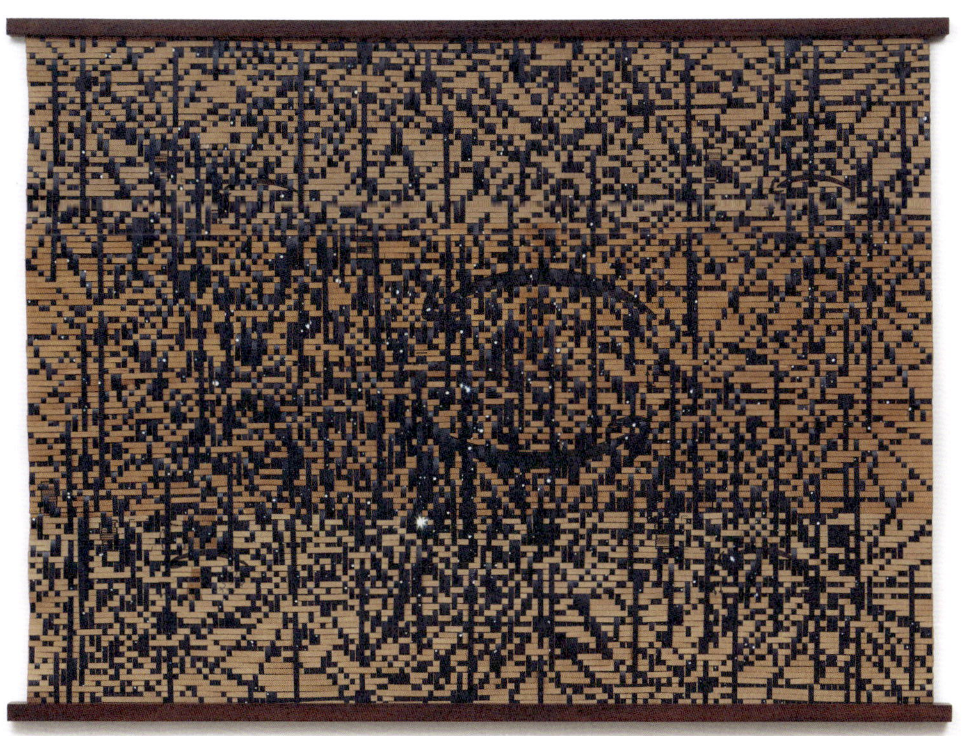

Plate 16
Future Geography: Hyades Star Cluster, 2021. Used Amazon.com delivery boxes, archival inkjet print with matte lamination, wood. Private collection. 60 × 84 × 1½ in. Courtesy of the artist and Commonwealth and Council, Los Angeles. Photo: Paul Salveson

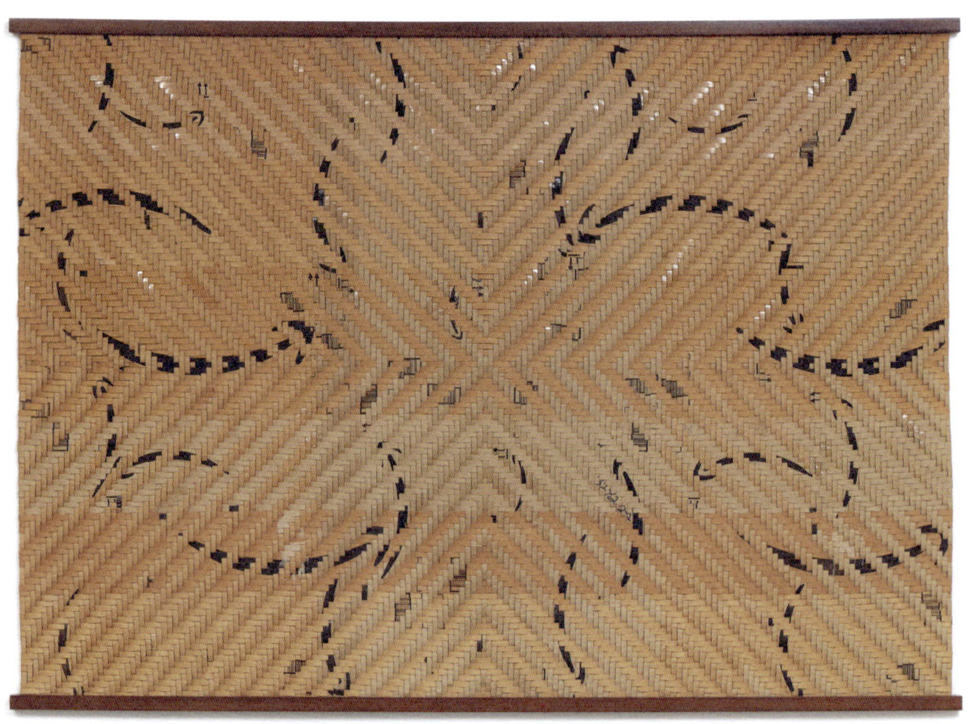

Plates 17–18
Disorientation Towards Collapse, 2020. Used Amazon.com delivery boxes, wood. 60 × 84 × 1½ in.
The Mohn Family Trust. Courtesy of the artist and Commonwealth and Council, Los Angeles.
Photo: Paul Salveson

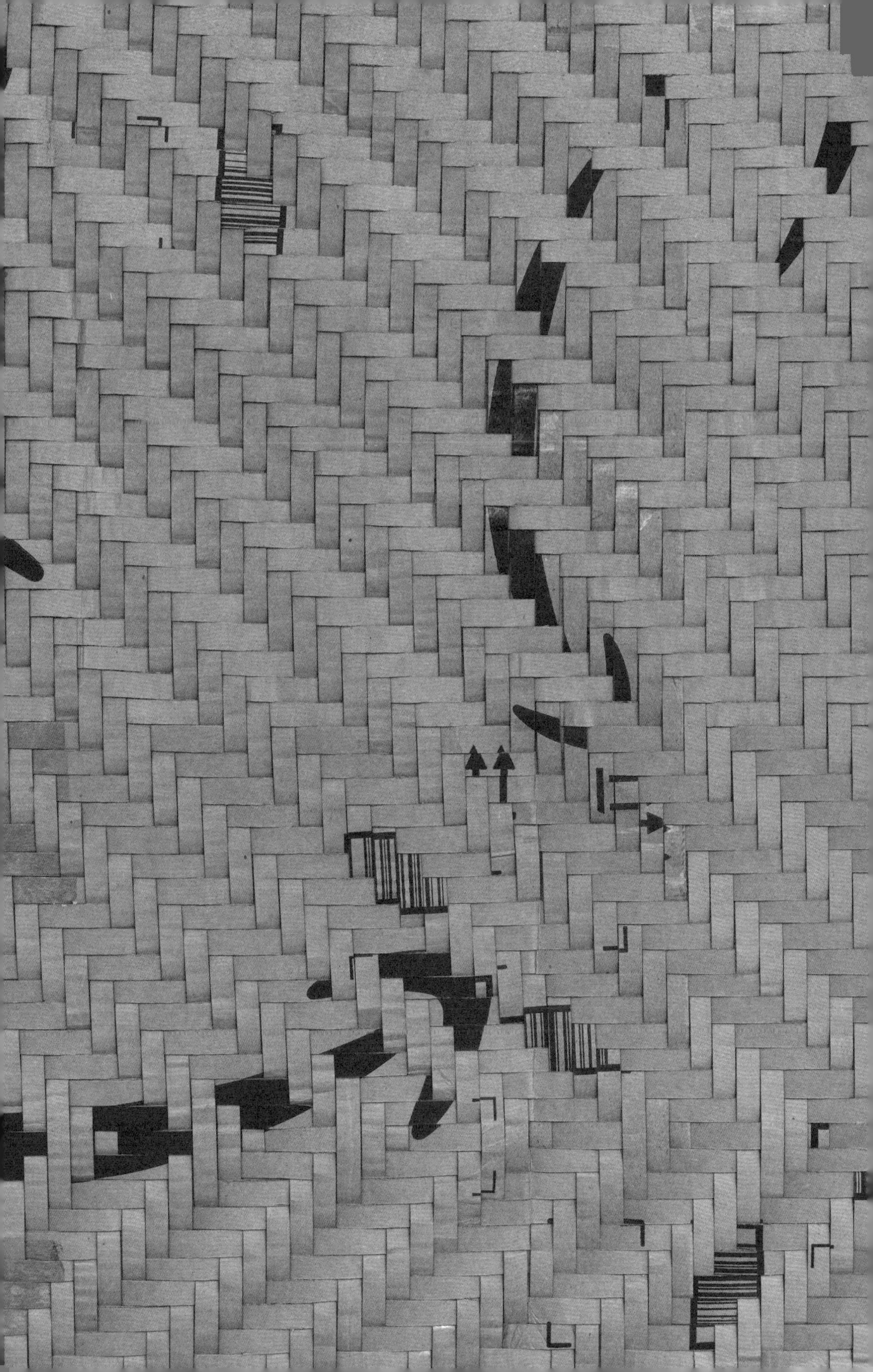

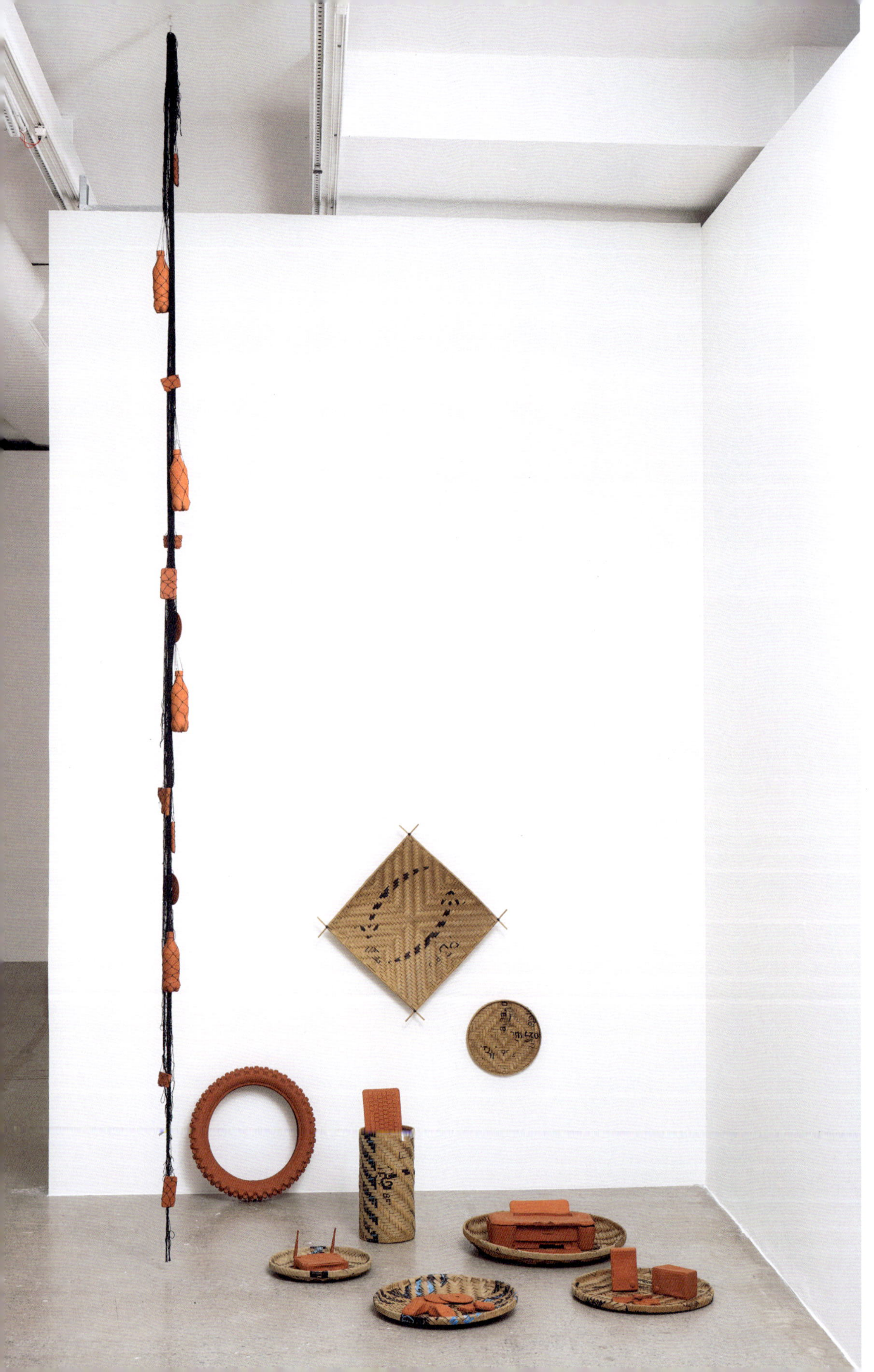

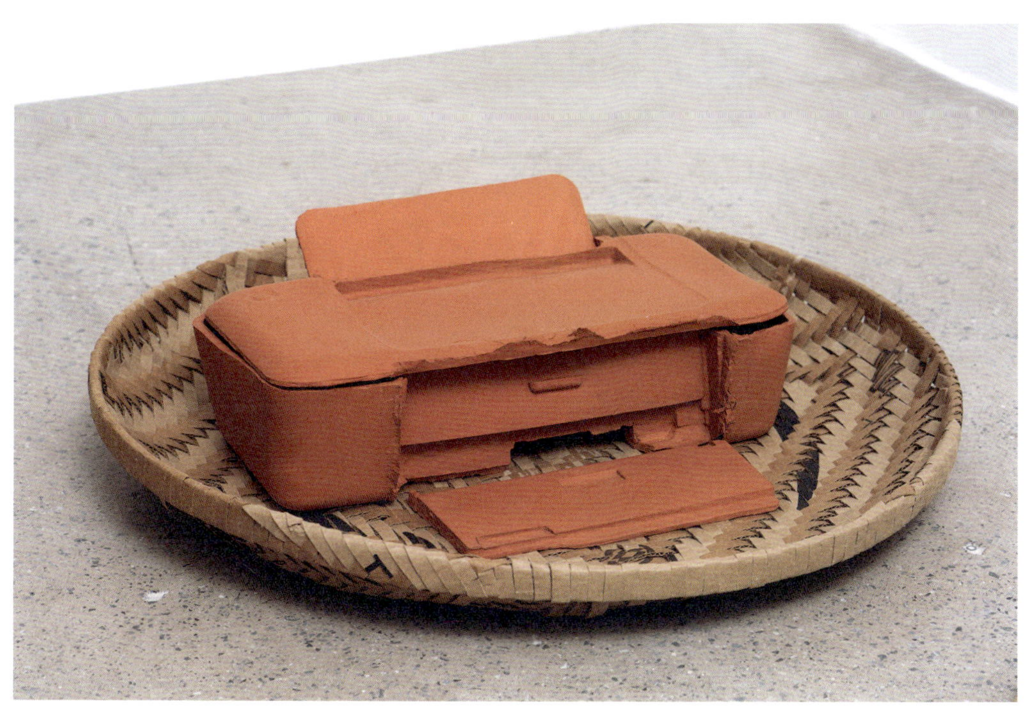

Plates 19–20
Nova gramática de formas #1 (New Grammar of Forms #1), 2018. Terracotta objects, baskets woven from used Amazon.com delivery boxes, thread, wood, fishing net. Dimensions variable. Private collection. Installation view, *Azul Maia*, Galeria Luisa Strina, São Paulo, 2018. Courtesy of the artist and Galeria Luisa Strina. Photo: Edouard Fraipont

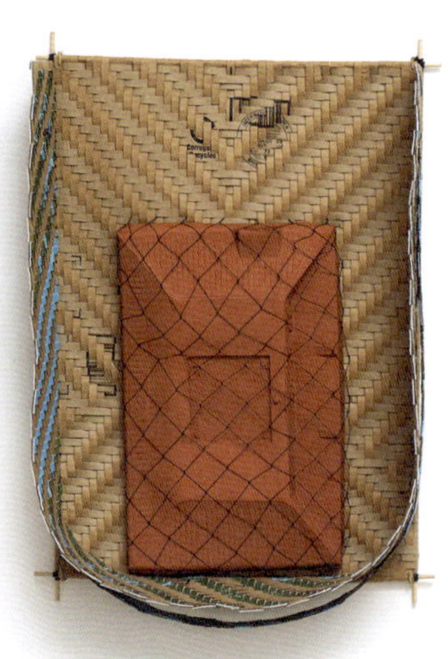

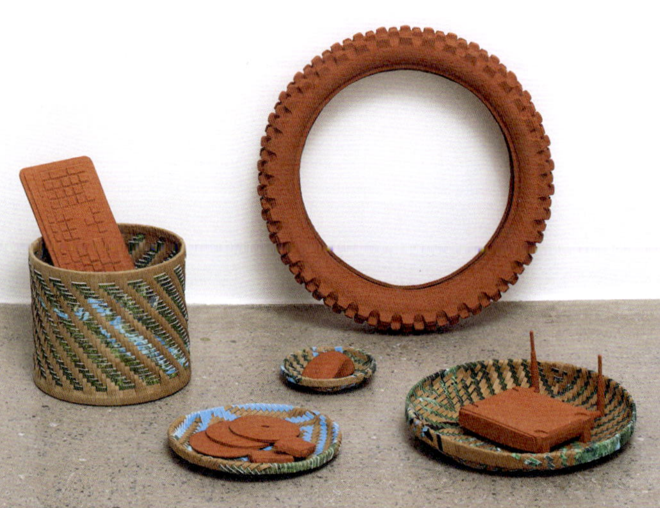

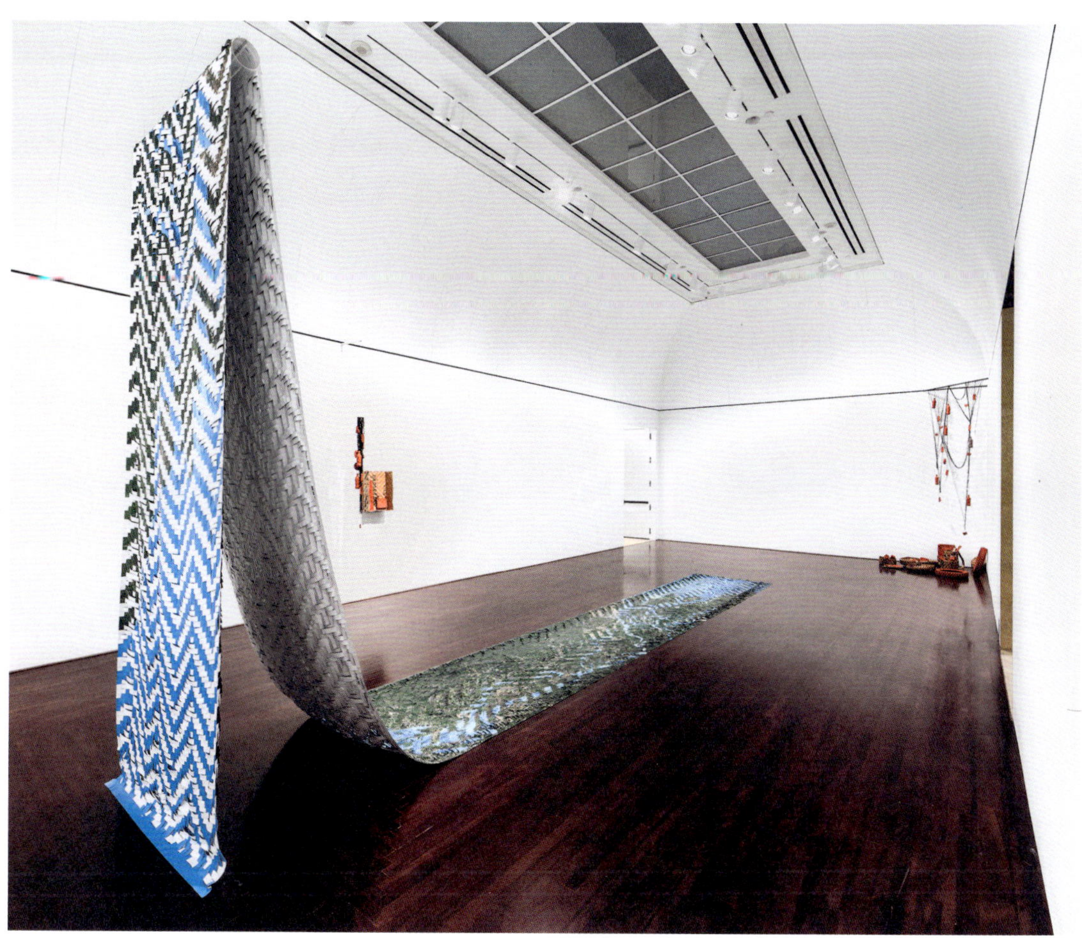

From left:

Plate 21
Nova gramática de formas #2 (New Grammar of Forms #2), 2018. Terracotta objects, baskets woven from used Amazon.com delivery boxes and archival inkjet prints, thread, wood. Dimensions variable. Collection of Janice Niemi and Dennis Braddock, Seattle; Promised gift to the Seattle Art Museum. Installation view, *Azul Maia*, Galeria Luisa Strina, São Paulo, 2018. Courtesy of the artist and Galeria Luisa Strina. Photo: Edouard Fraipont

Plates 22–24
Encontro das Águas (Meeting of Waters), 2016–18. Woven archival inkjet print on vinyl, terracotta objects, fishnet, thread, woven baskets, backpack made out of used Amazon.com delivery boxes. Instituto Inhotim Collection, Minas Gerais, Brazil. Installation view, *Clarissa Tossin: Encontro das Águas (Meeting of Waters)*, Blanton Museum of Art, University of Texas at Austin, January 13–July 1, 2018. Courtesy of the Blanton Museum of Art. Photo: Colin Doyle

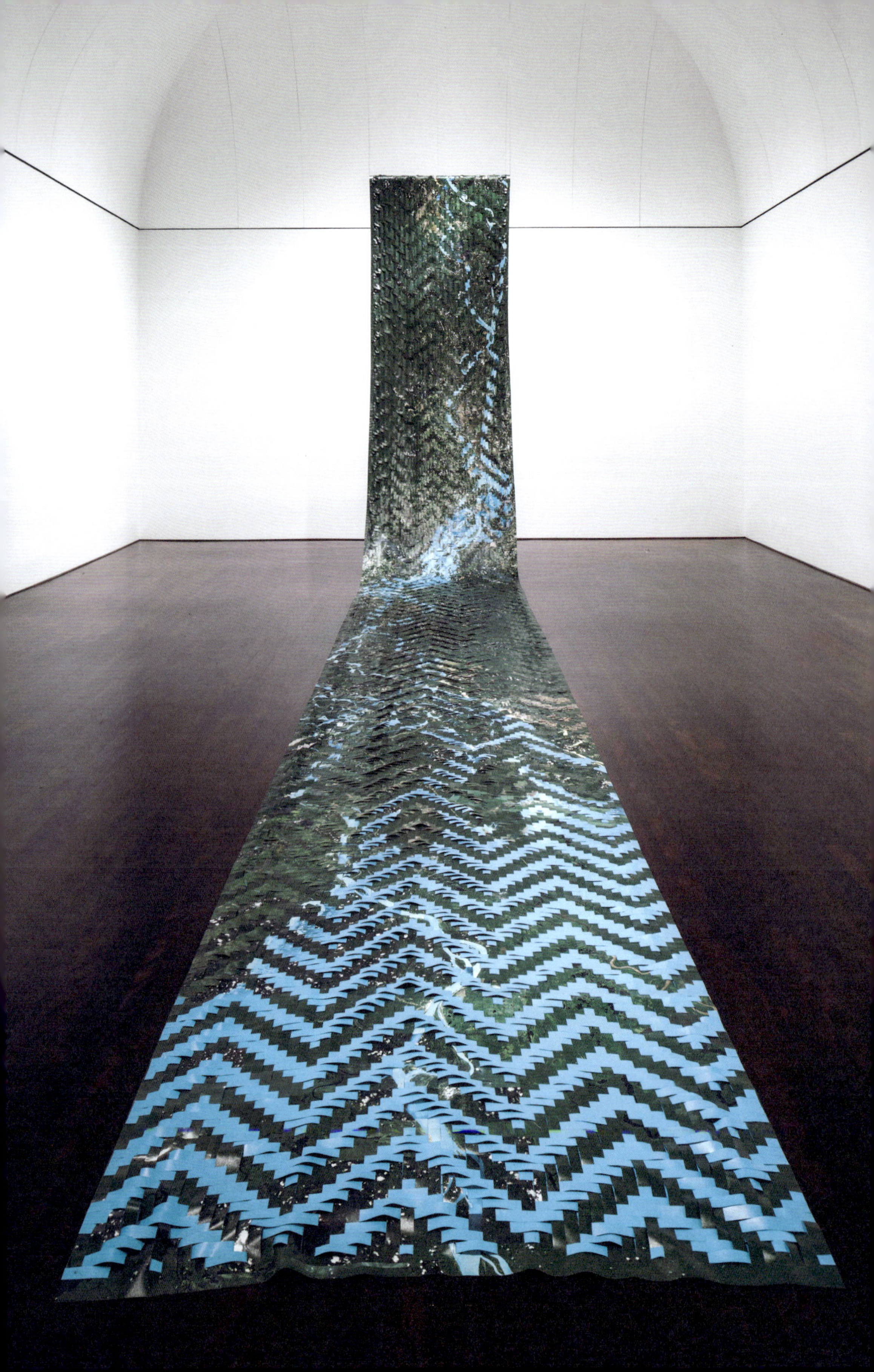

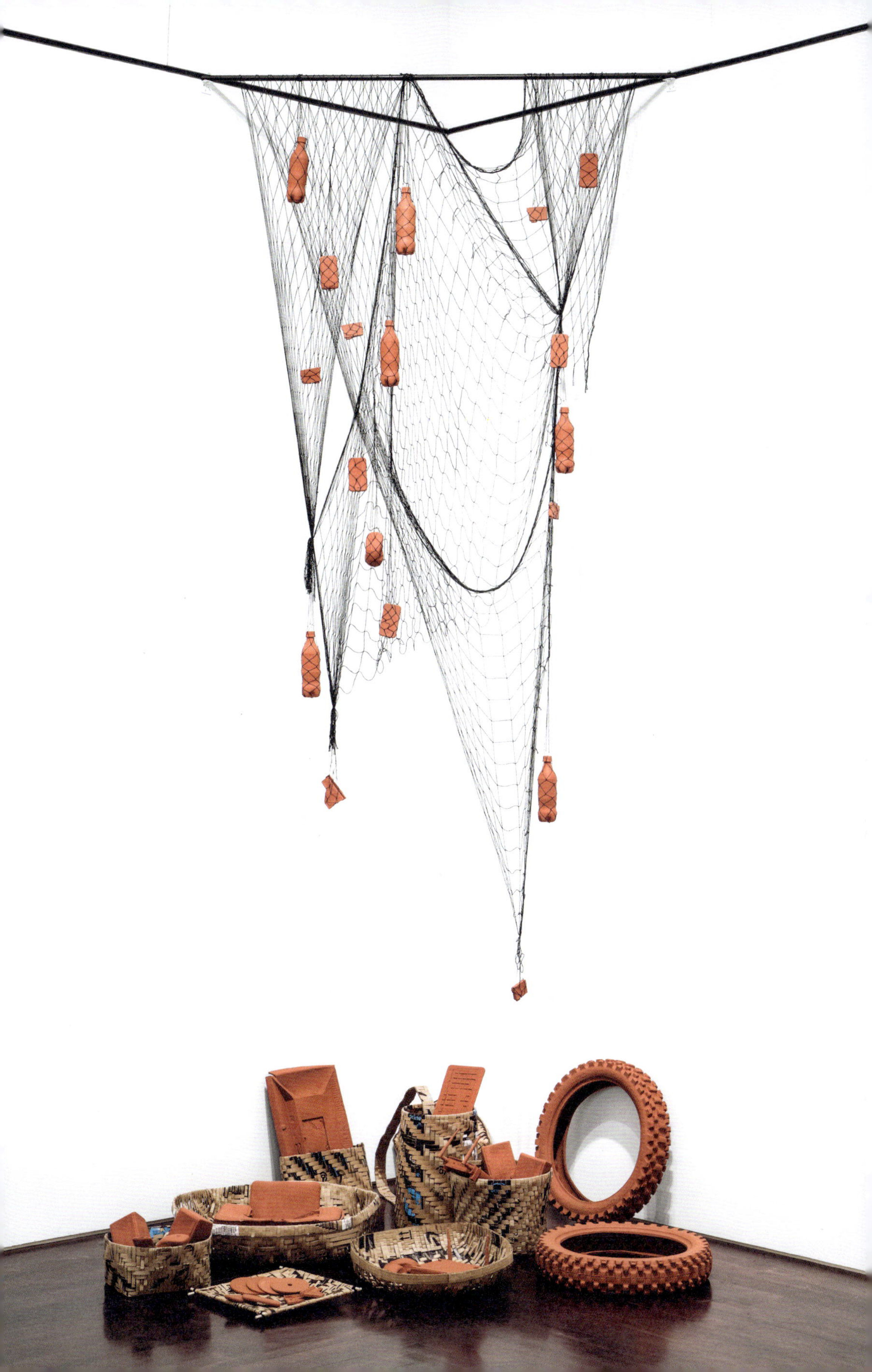

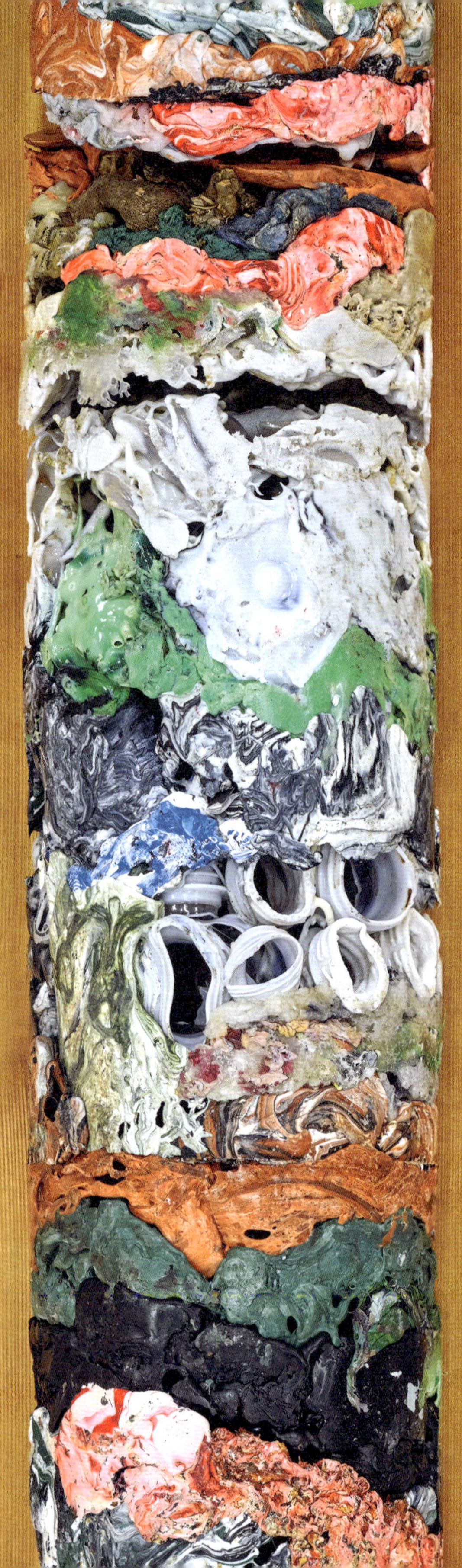

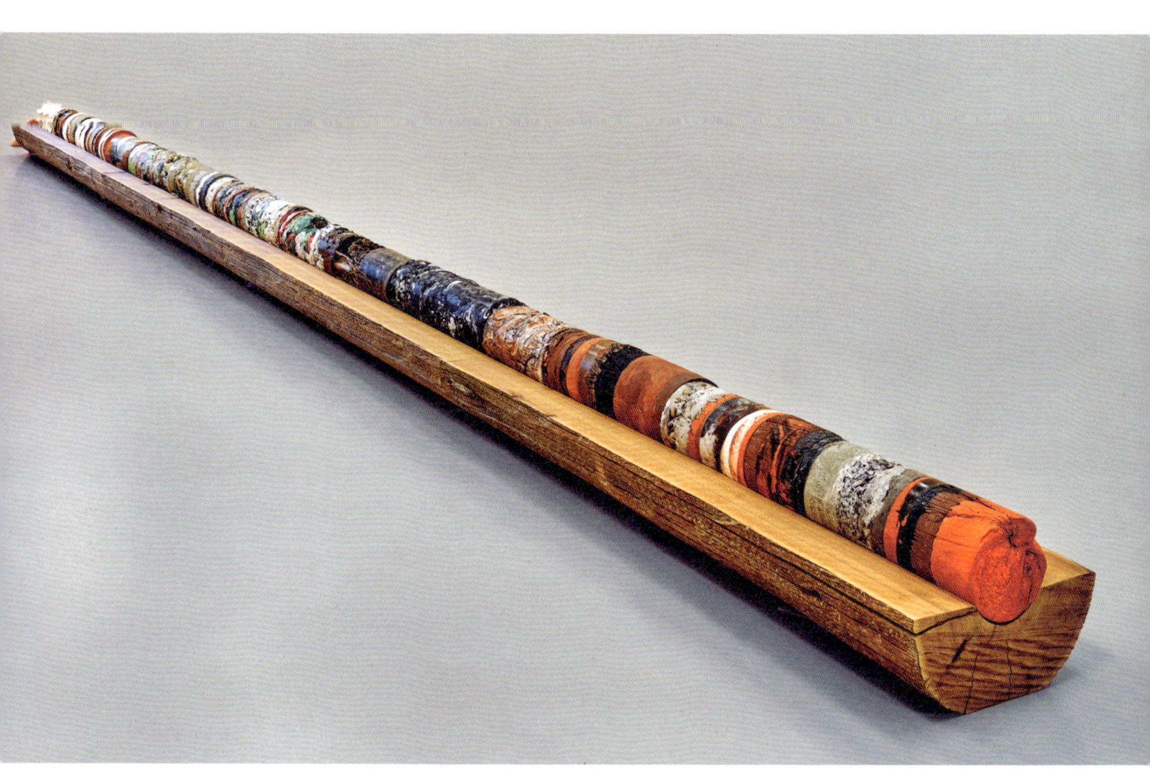

Plates 25–26
Future Fossil, 2018. Cedar tree trunk, rocks, roots, leaves, bark, soil, sand, plaster, cement, silicone, foam, resin, aluminum foil, electronic waste, recycled plastics (PET, HDPE, LDPE, PP, and PS). 14 × 240 × 17 in. Los Angeles County Museum of Art, Purchased with funds provided by AHAN: Studio Forum, 2019 Art Here and Now purchase. Installation view, *Future Fossil*, Harvard Radcliffe Institute for Advanced Study, Johnson-Kulukundis Family Gallery, January 31–March 16, 2019. Image courtesy Harvard Radcliffe Institute for Advanced Study. Photo: Stewart Clements

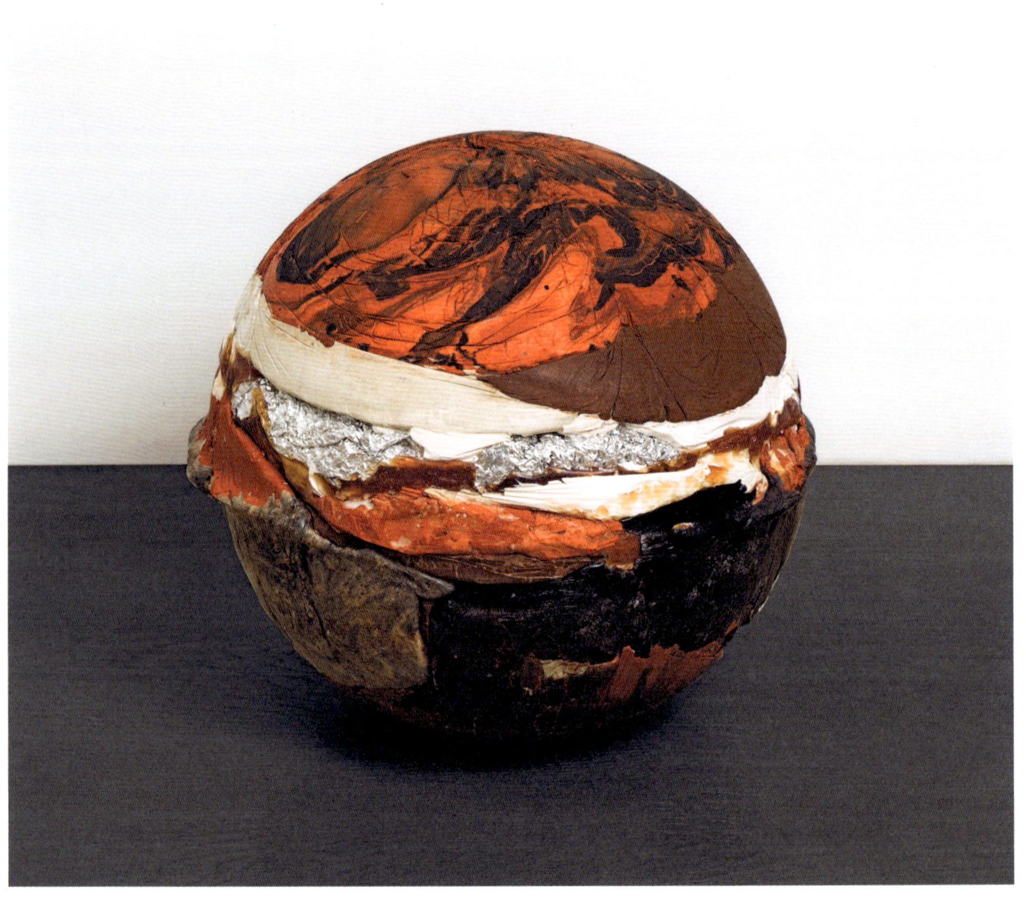

Plate 27
The Only Lasting Truth Is Change, 2019. Plaster, cement, foam, urethane, silicone, aluminum foil. 12 in. diam. Courtesy of the artist and Commonwealth and Council, Los Angeles. Photo: Ruben Diaz

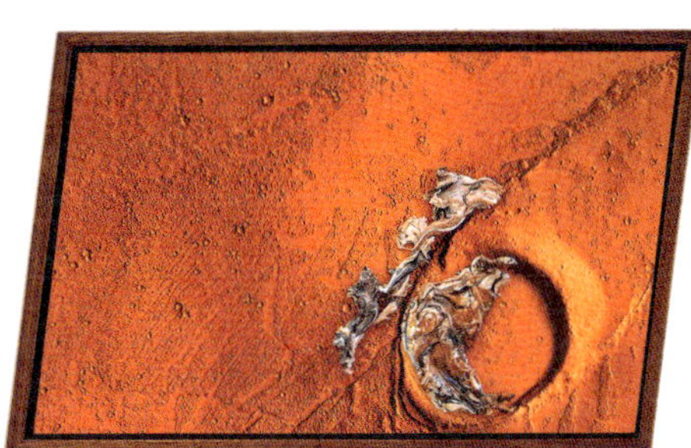

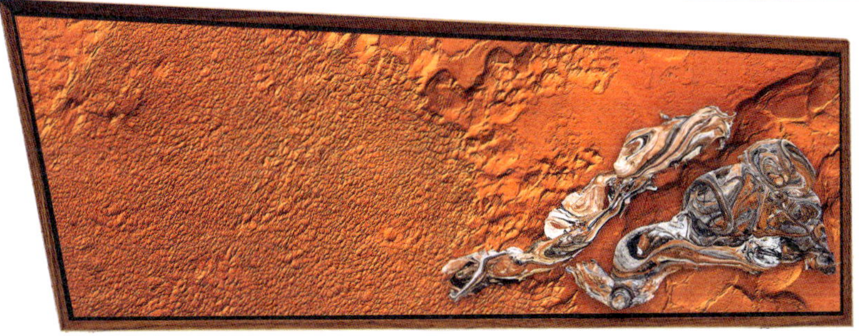

Plate 28
#AmazonisPlanitia2, 2018. Archival inkjet prints on glossy photo paper, recycled plastic from artist's own waste. 20¾ × 29⅞ in. and 11¼ × 19⅝ in. Courtesy of the artist and Commonwealth and Council, Los Angeles. Installation view, *Future Fossil*, Harvard Radcliffe Institute for Advanced Study, Johnson-Kulukundis Family Gallery, January 31–March 16, 2019. Image courtesy Harvard Radcliffe Institute for Advanced Study. Photo: Stewart Clements

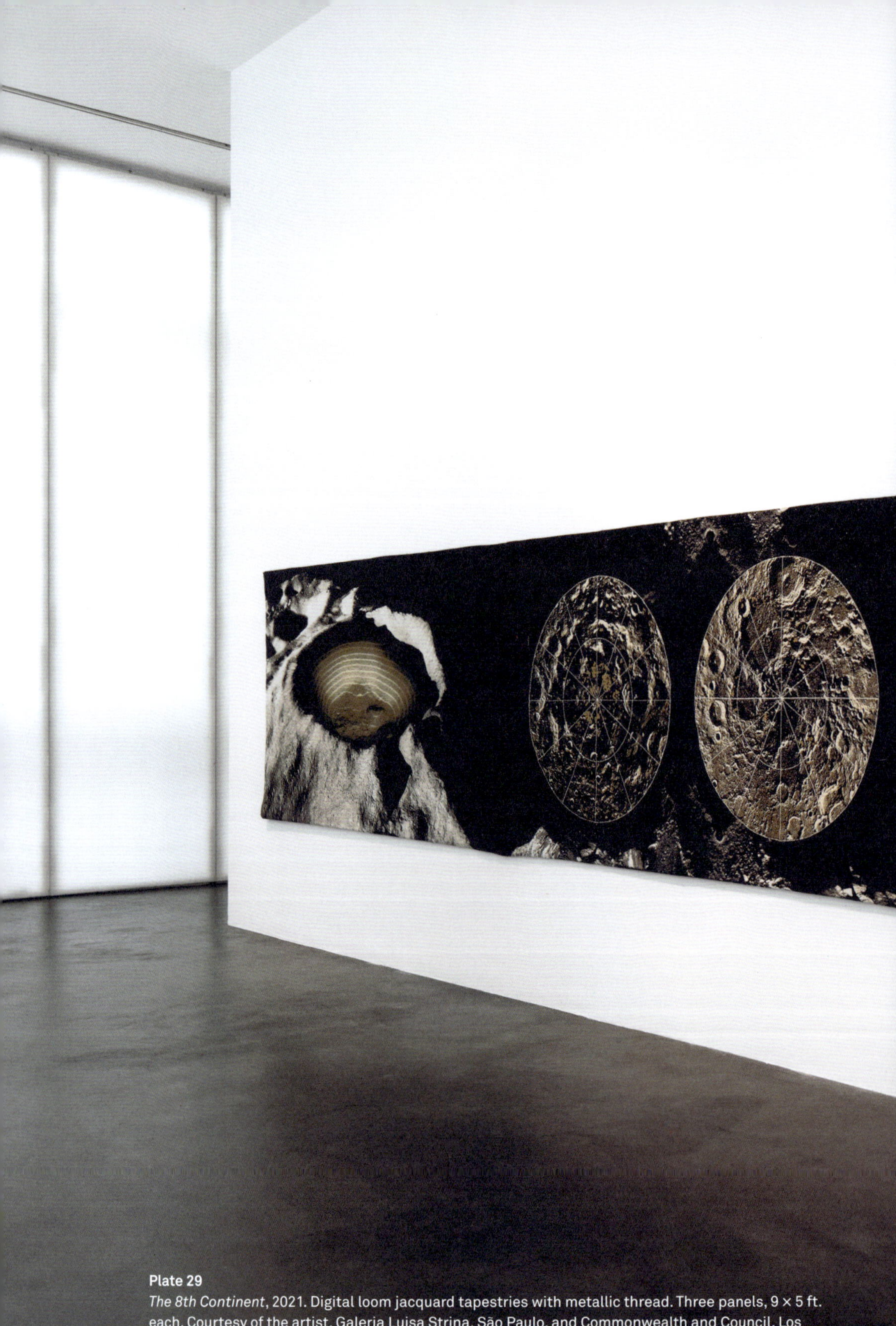

Plate 29
The 8th Continent, 2021. Digital loom jacquard tapestries with metallic thread. Three panels, 9 × 5 ft. each. Courtesy of the artist, Galeria Luisa Strina, São Paulo, and Commonwealth and Council, Los Angeles. Installation view, *Clarissa Tossin: Falling From Earth*, Museum of Contemporary Art Denver, June 3–August 28, 2022. Courtesy of MCA Denver. Photo: Wes Magyar

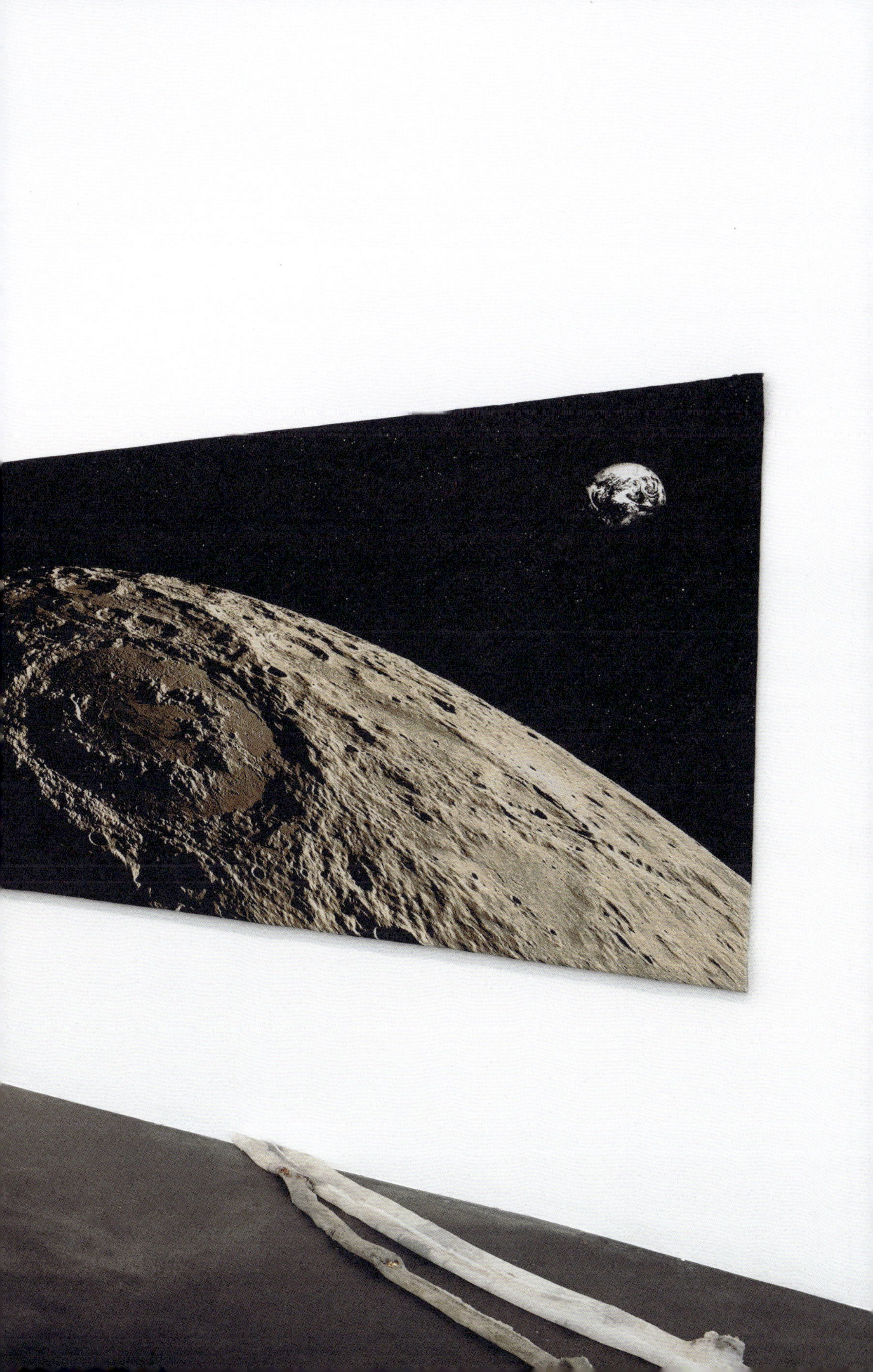

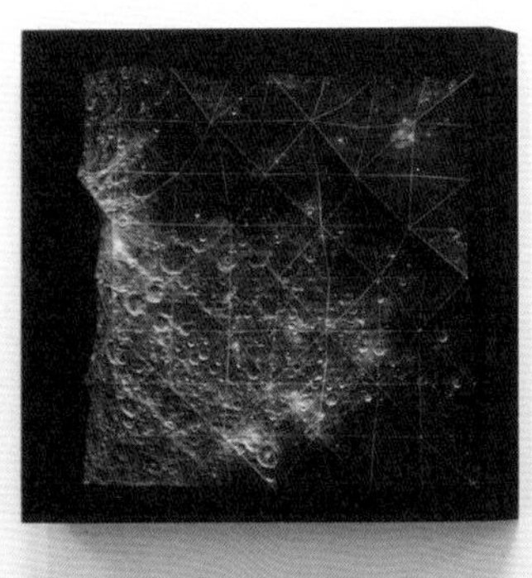

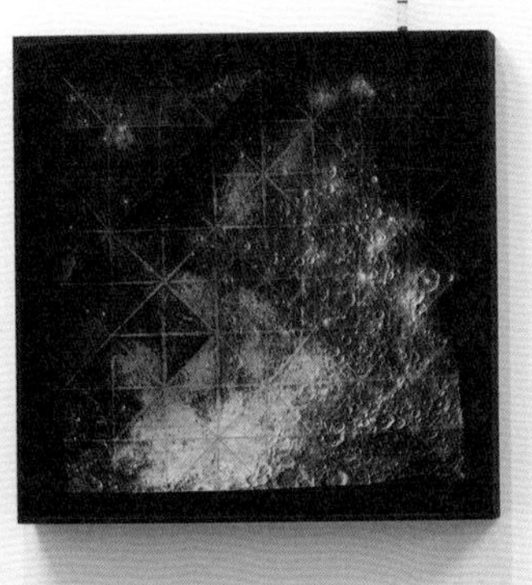

Plate 30
Valuable Element, 2022. Archival inkjet print, inkjet dust, glass vial. 34 × 34 × 1½ in. each. Courtesy of the artist, Galeria Luisa Strina, São Paulo, and Commonwealth and Council, Los Angeles. Installation view, *Vulneravelmente Humano*, Galeria Luisa Strina, São Paulo, March 25–April 29, 2023. Courtesy of Galeria Luisa Strina. Photo: Edouard Fraipont

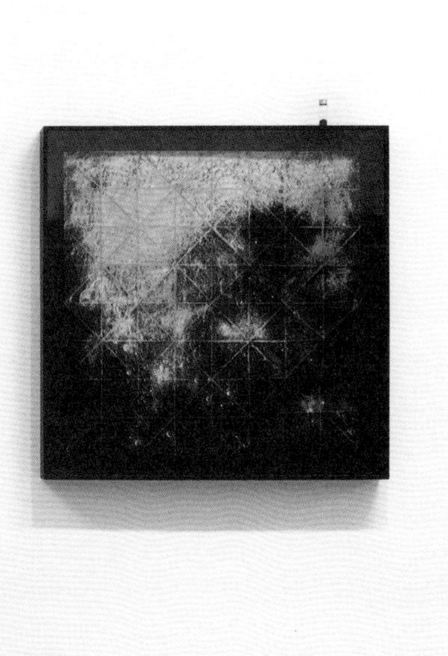
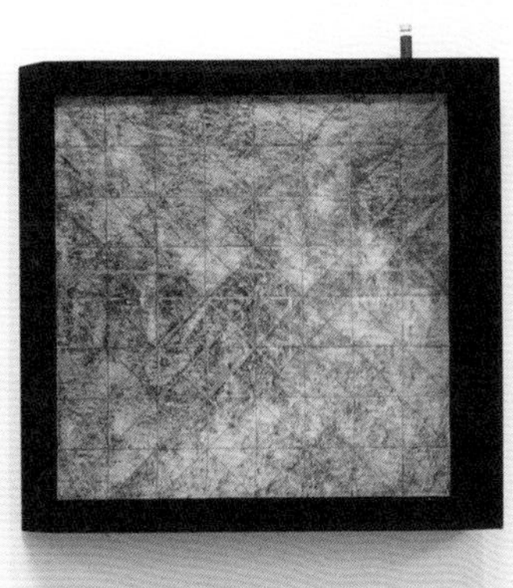

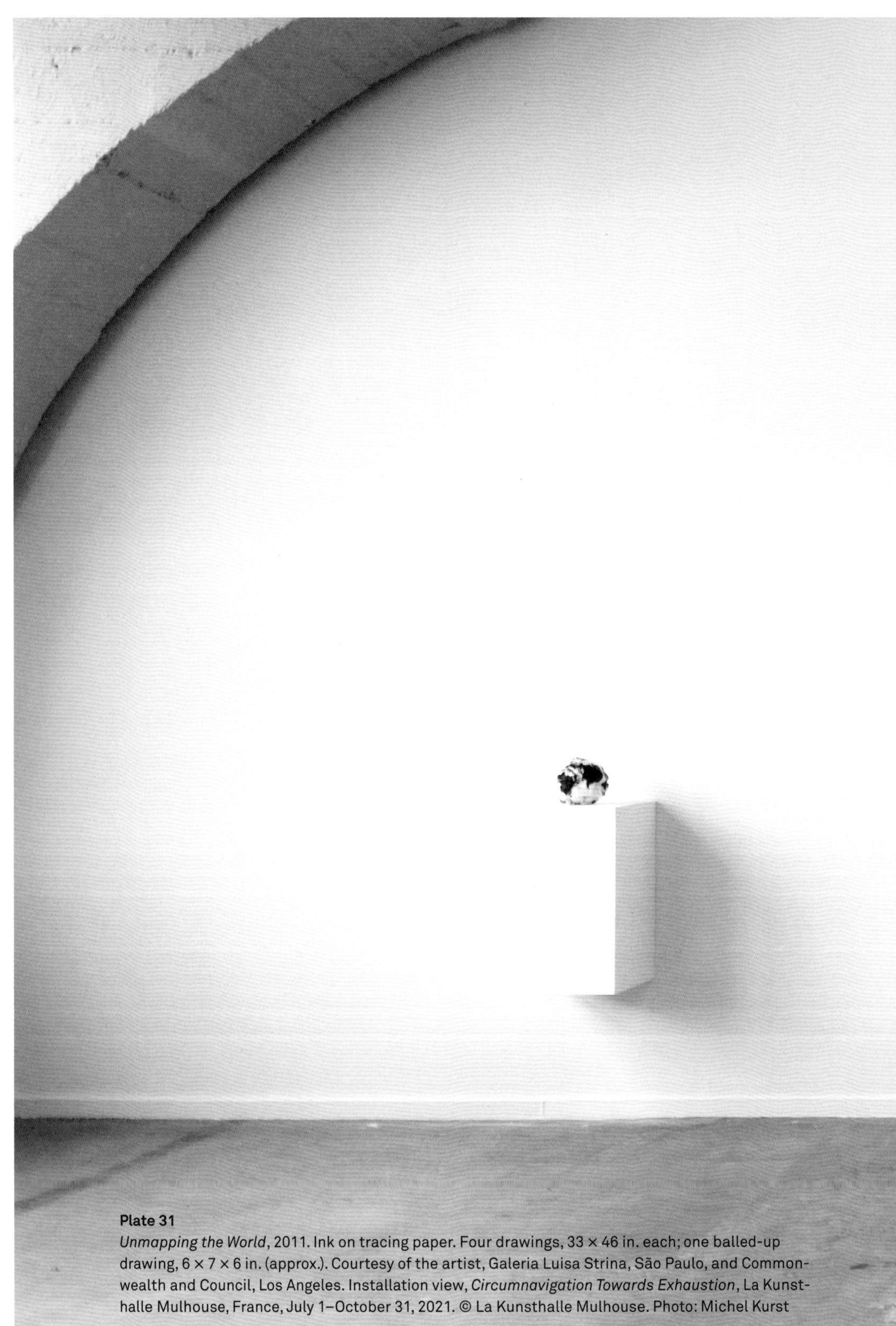

Plate 31
Unmapping the World, 2011. Ink on tracing paper. Four drawings, 33 × 46 in. each; one balled-up drawing, 6 × 7 × 6 in. (approx.). Courtesy of the artist, Galeria Luisa Strina, São Paulo, and Commonwealth and Council, Los Angeles. Installation view, *Circumnavigation Towards Exhaustion*, La Kunsthalle Mulhouse, France, July 1–October 31, 2021. © La Kunsthalle Mulhouse. Photo: Michel Kurst

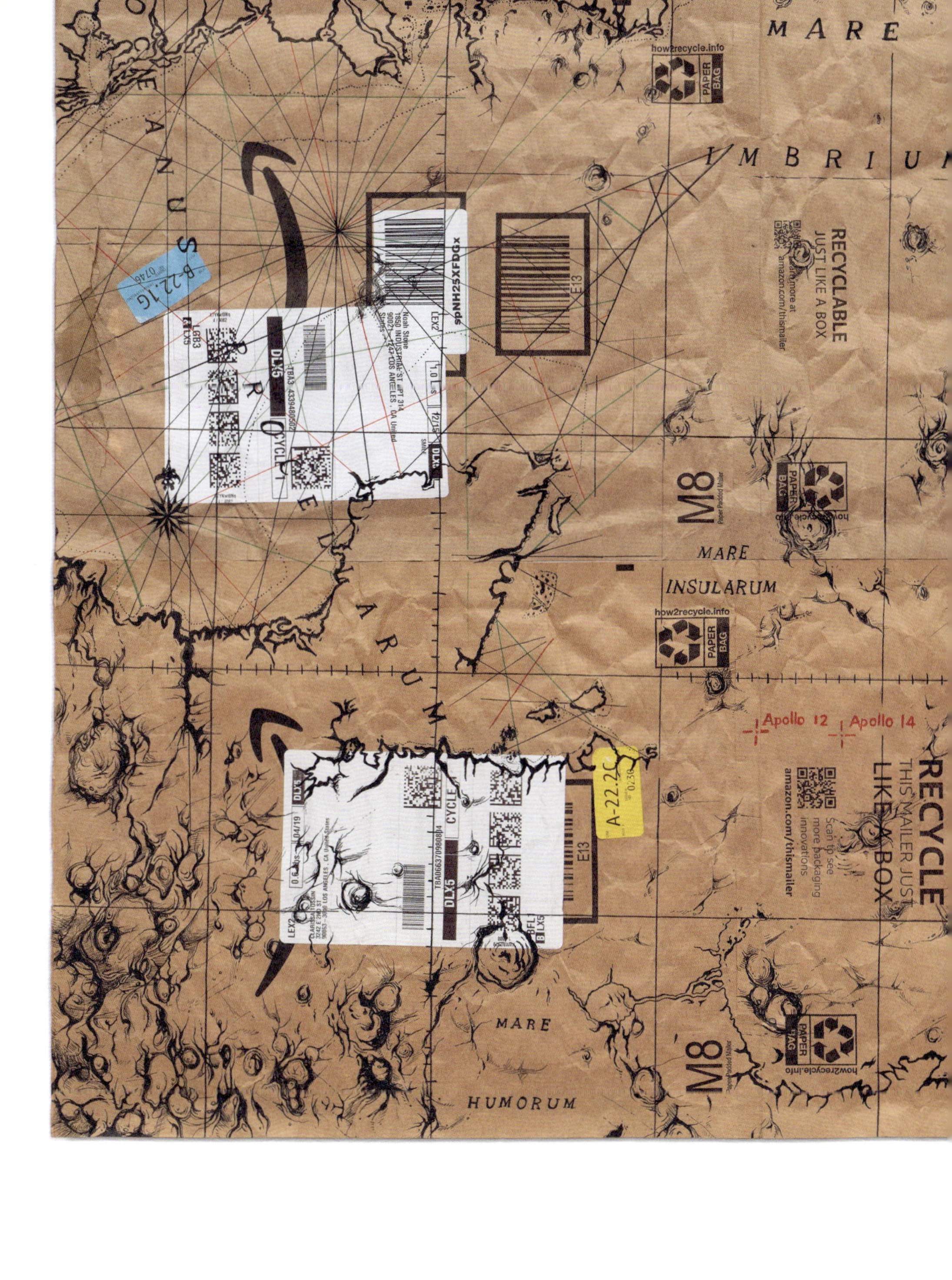
MARE
IMBRIUM
MARE
INSULARUM
Apollo 12
Apollo 14
MARE
HUMORUM
how2recycle.info
PAPER BAG
RECYCLABLE
JUST LIKE A BOX
amazon.com/thismailer
M8
RECYCLE
THIS MAILER JUST
LIKE A BOX

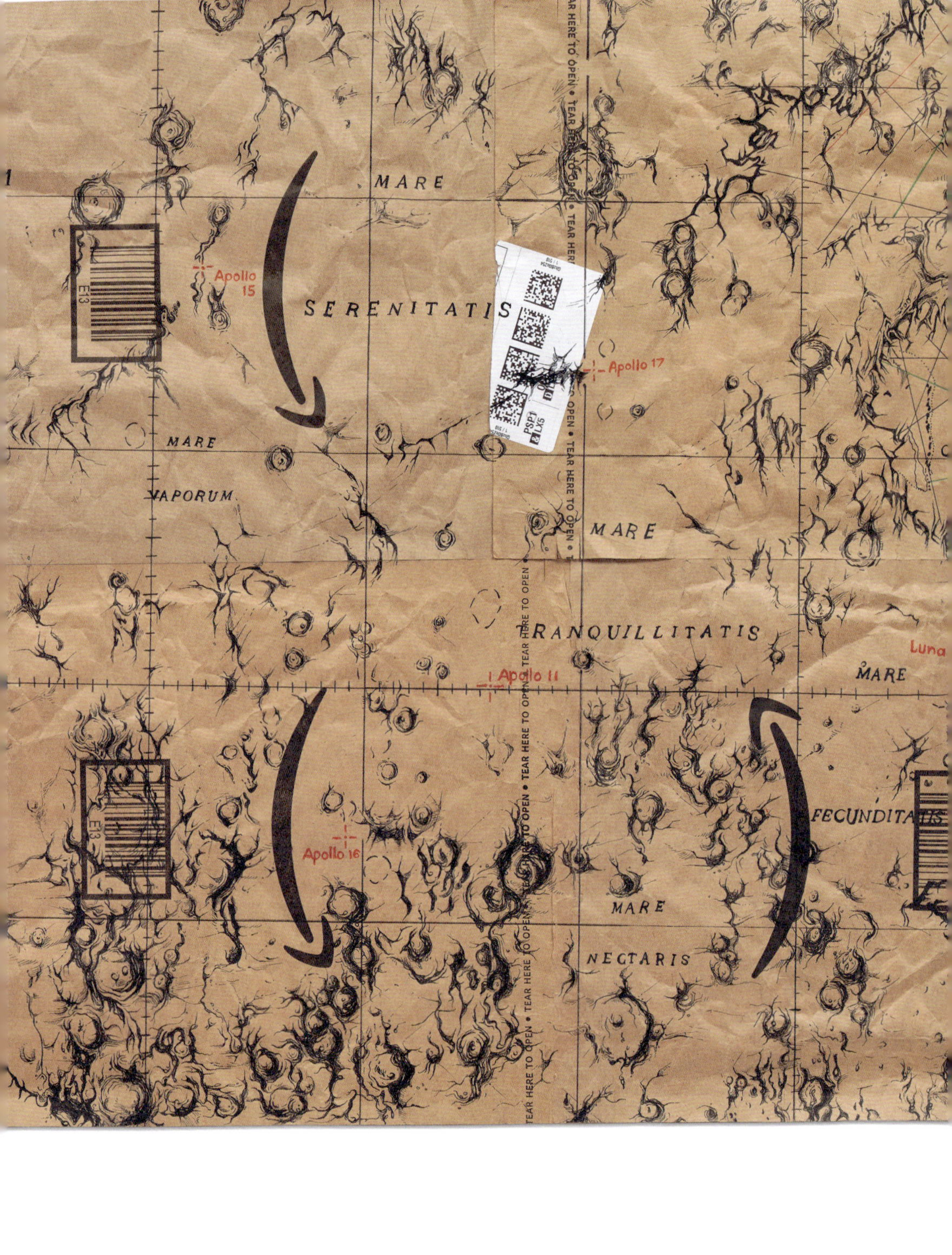

MARE
SERENITATIS
Apollo 15
MARE
VAPORUM
Apollo 17
MARE
TRANQUILLITATIS
Apollo 11
Luna
MARE
FECUNDITATIS
Apollo 16
MARE
NECTARIS
TEAR HERE TO OPEN
E13

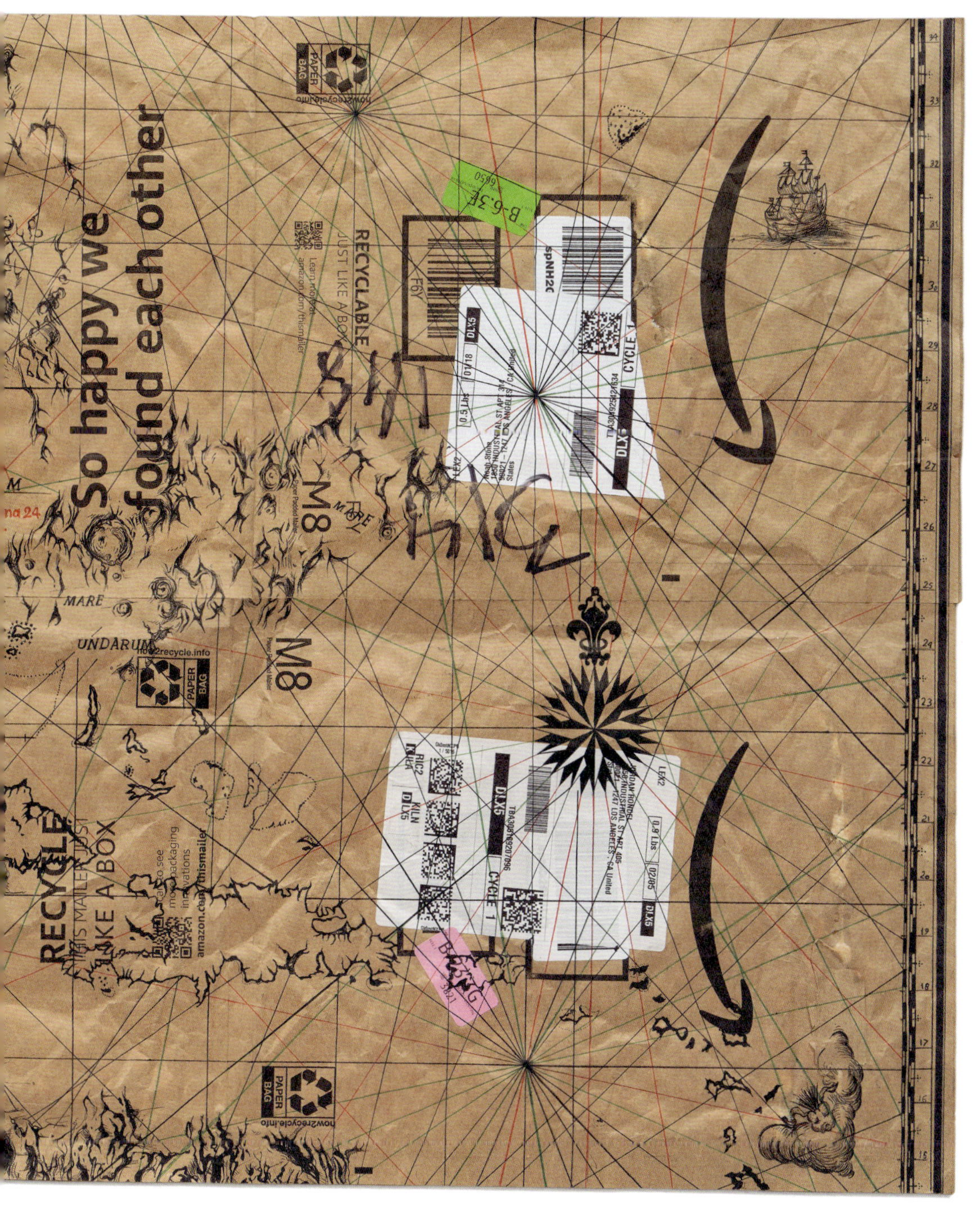

Plate 32
Maritime Arrivals, 2023. Archival ink on used Amazon.com delivery envelopes. 23¾ × 61¾ in. Commissioned by the Frye Art Museum. Courtesy of the artist, Galeria Luisa Strina, São Paulo, and Commonwealth and Council, Los Angeles. Photo: Brica Wilcox

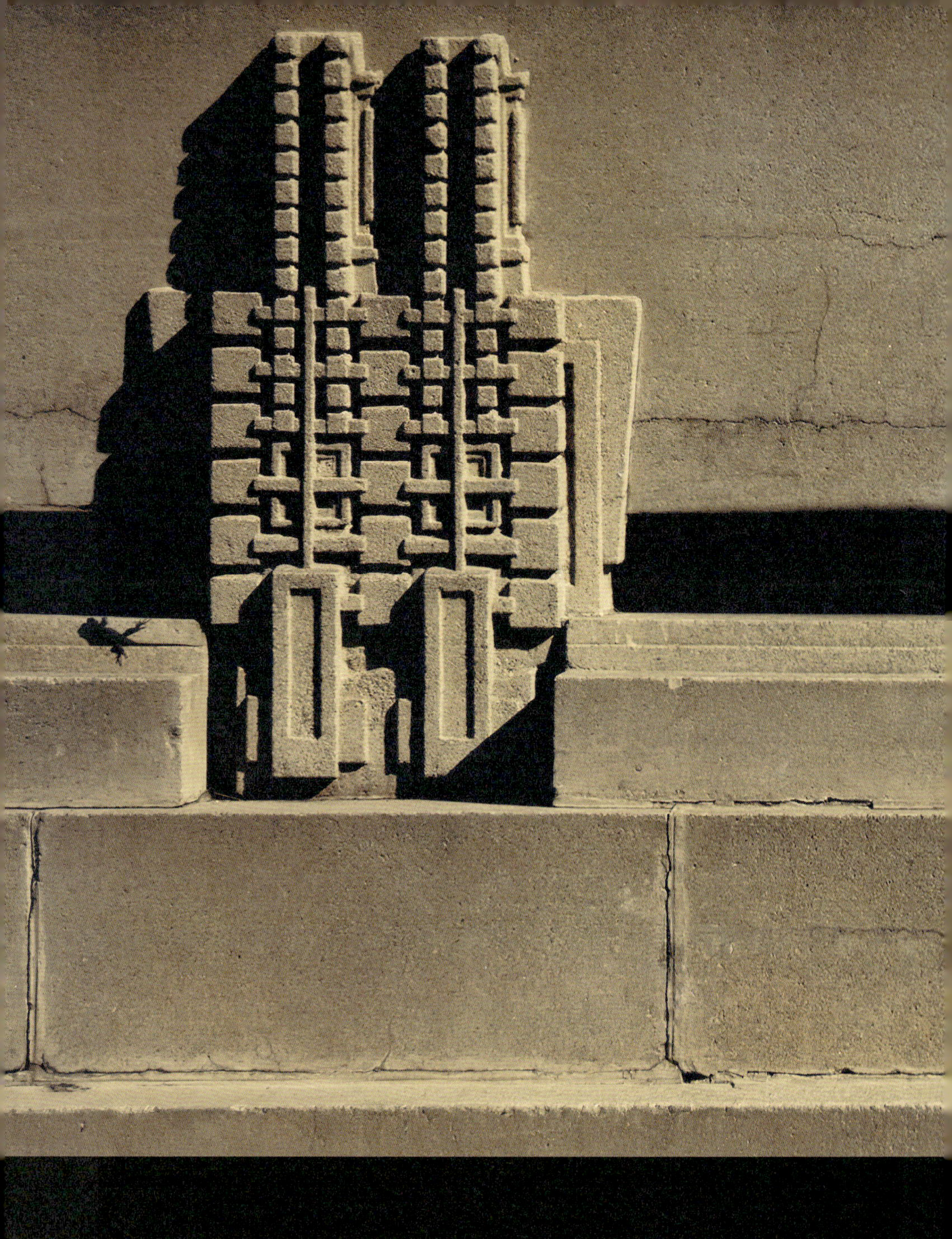

Plates 33–36
Ch'u Mayaa (stills), 2017. Digital video (color, sound); 17:56 min. Commissioned by the City of Los Angeles Department of Cultural Affairs for the exhibition *Condemned to be Modern* as part of the Getty Foundation's *Pacific Standard Time:LA/LA*. Choreographer/Performer: Crystal Sepúlveda. Courtesy of the artist, Galeria Luisa Strina, São Paulo, and Commonwealth and Council, Los Angeles

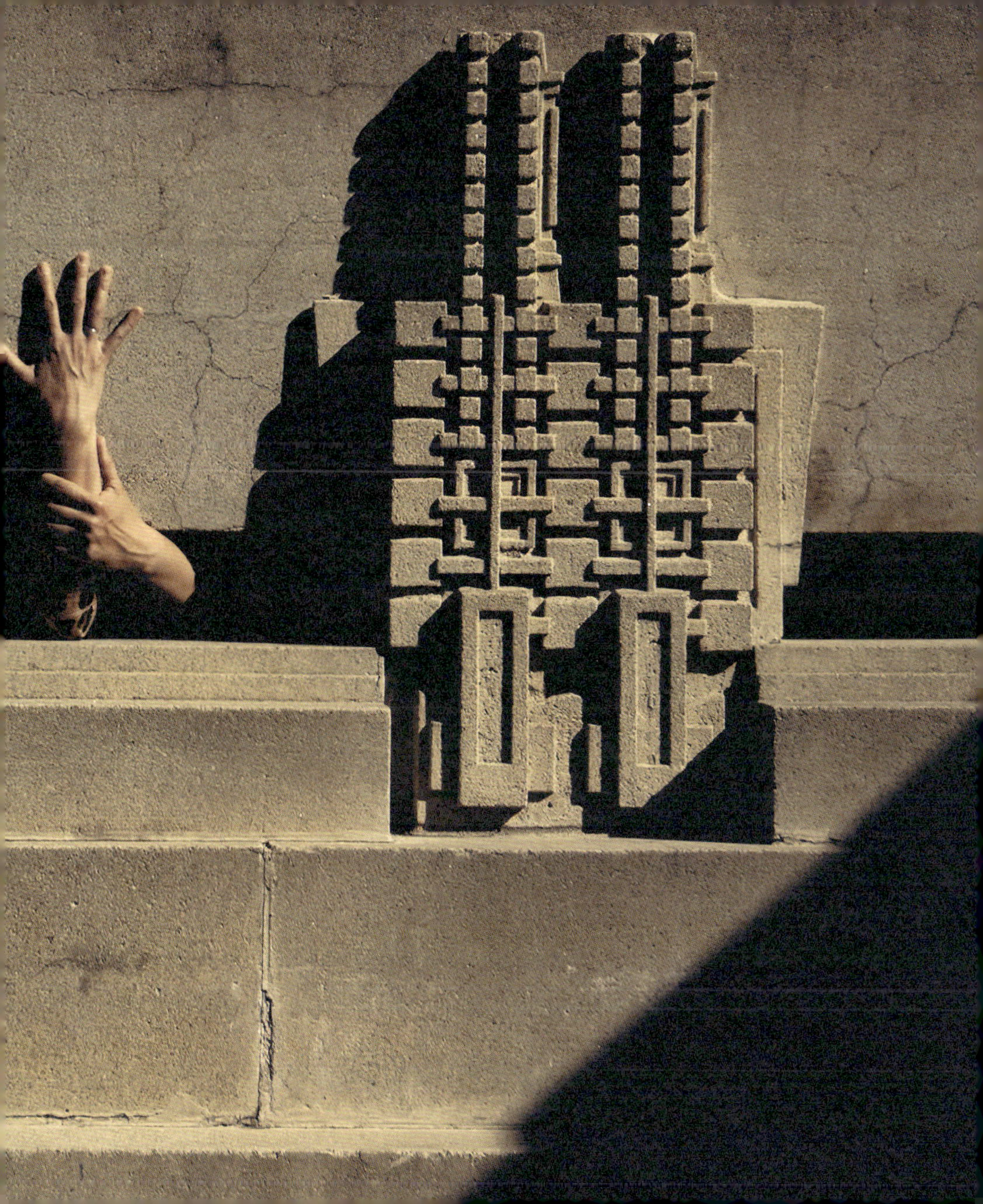

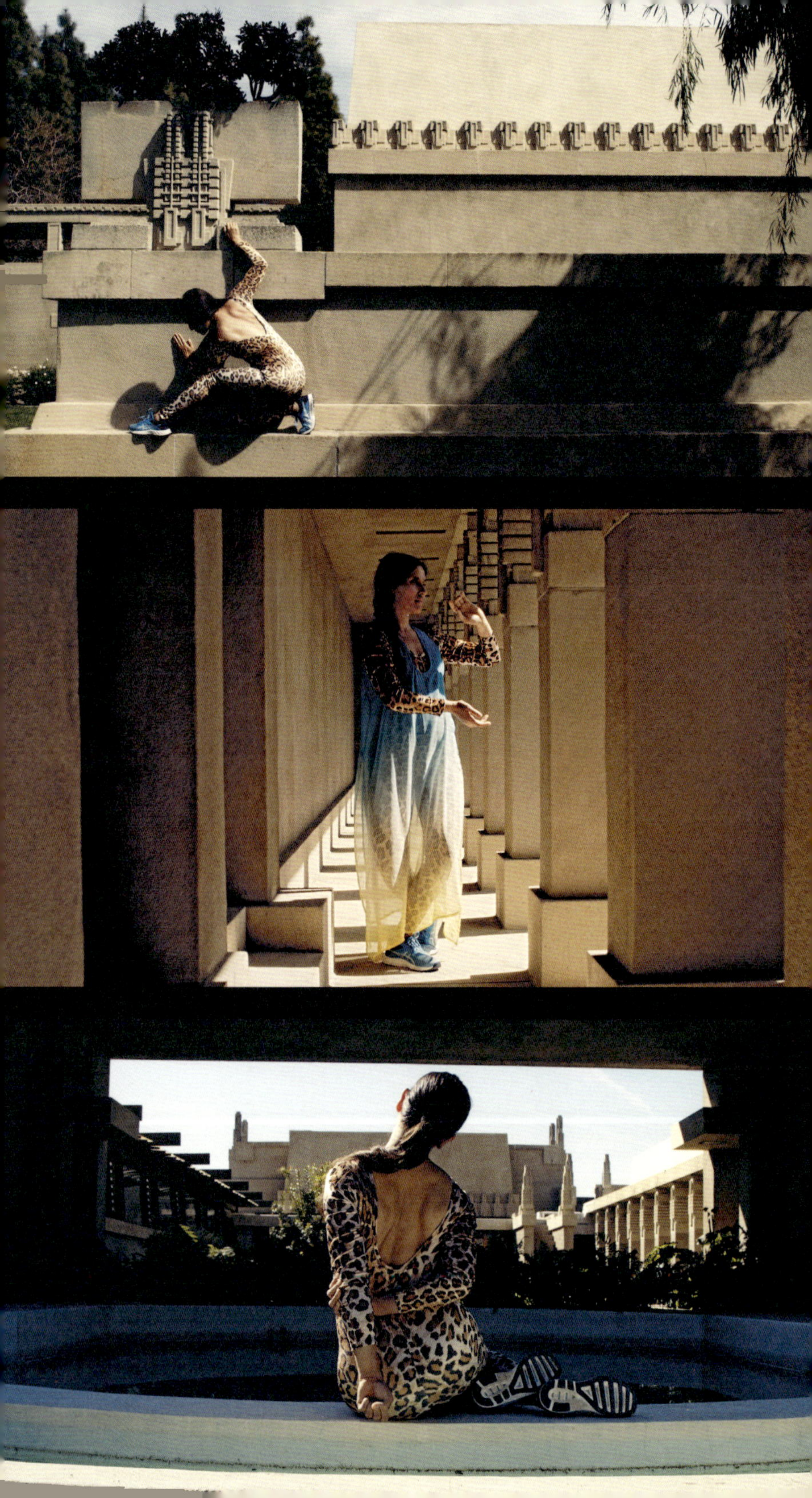

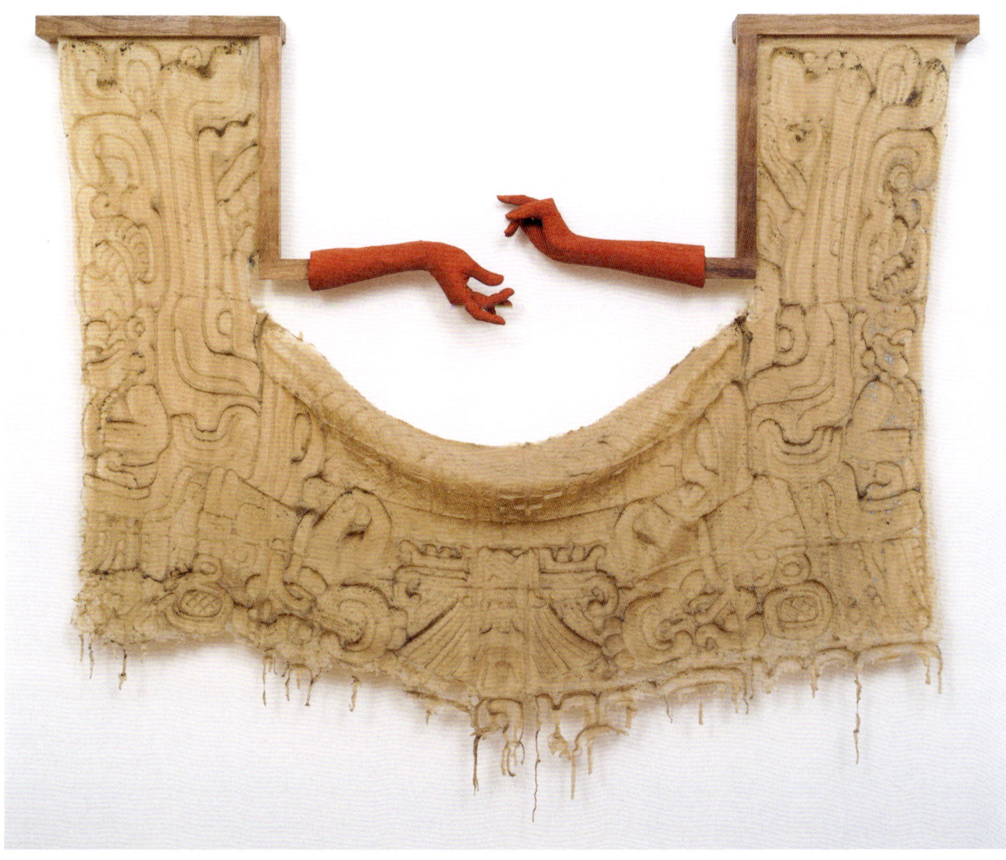

Plate 37 (above)
A two-headed serpent held in the arms of human beings, or, Ticket Window, from *The Mayan*, 2017. Silicone, walnut, faux terracotta (dyed plaster). 46 × 53½ × 5 in. Whitney Museum of American Art, New York; purchase, with funds from the Painting and Sculpture Committee, 2019.37a-c. Installation view, *The Mayan*, Commonwealth and Council, Los Angeles, September 9–October 21, 2017. Courtesy of the artist and Commonwealth and Council. Photo: Ruben Diaz

Plate 38 (next page)
From left to right: *A cycle of time we don't understand (reversed, invented, and rearranged)*, from *The Mayan*, 2017. Silicone, walnut, faux terracotta (dyed plaster). Whitney Museum of American Art, New York; purchase with funds from the Painting and Sculpture Committee 2019.35a-e; *xojowisaj ja (to make the building dance)*, from *The Mayan*, 2017. Silicone, walnut, jaguar faux fur, faux terracotta (dyed plaster). Courtesy of the artist and Galeria Luisa Strina, São Paulo. Installation view, *Pacha, Llaqta, Wasichay: Indigenous Space, Modern Architecture, New Art*, Whitney Museum of American Art, New York, July 13–September 30, 2018. Photo: Argenis Apolinario

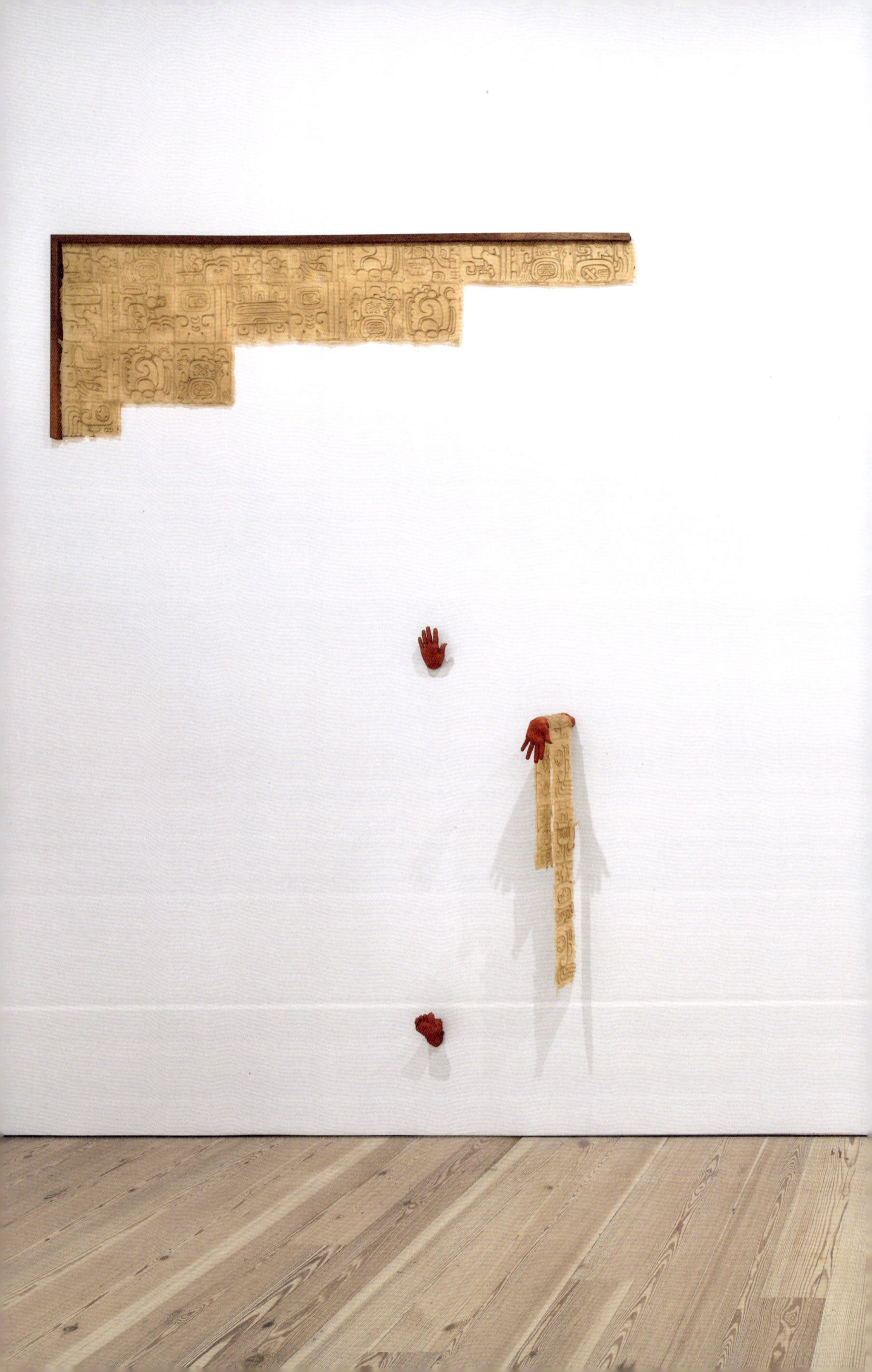

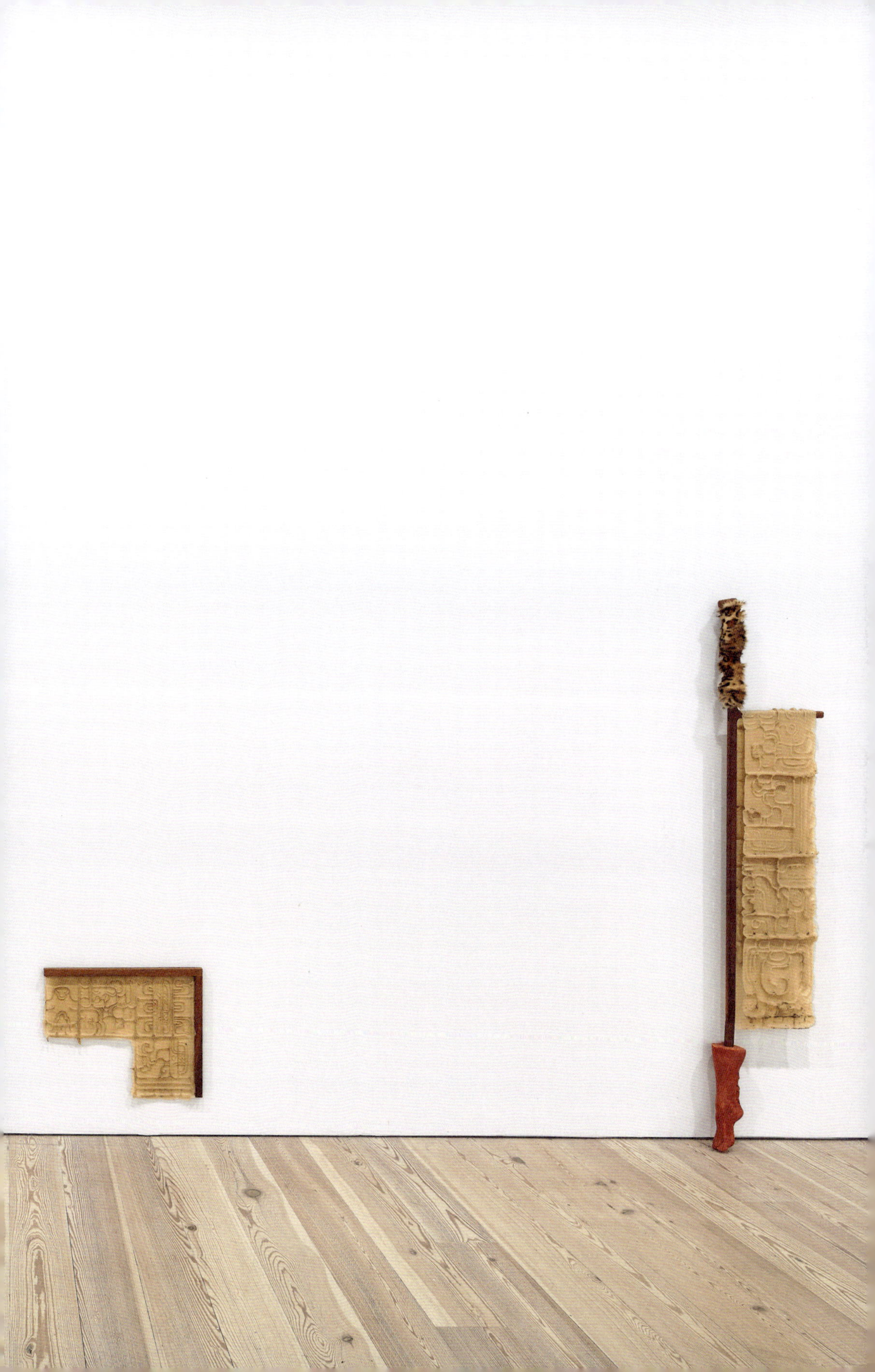

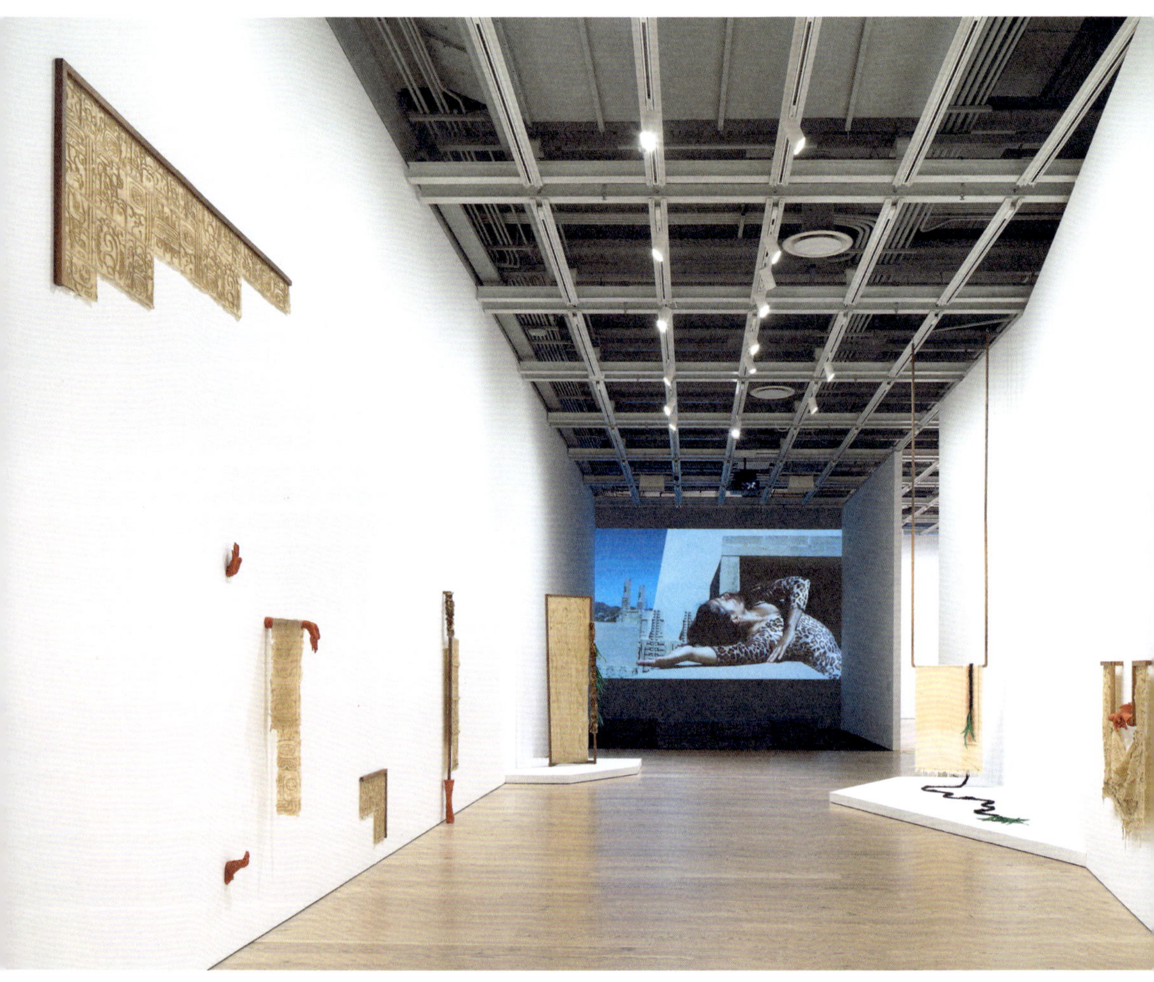

Plate 39
From left to right: *A cycle of time we don't understand (reversed, invented, and rearranged)*, 2017; *xojowisaj ja (to make the building dance)*, 2017; *Ha' K'in Xook, from Piedras Negras to Hill Street*, 2017; *Ch'u Mayaa*, 2017; *Yaxchilán Lintel 25 (feathered serpent)*, 2017; *A two-headed serpent held in the arms of human beings, or, Ticket Window*, 2017. Installation view, *Pacha, Llaqta, Wasichay: Indigenous Space, Modern Architecture, New Art*, Whitney Museum of American Art, New York, July 13–September 30, 2018. Courtesy of the Whitney Museum of American Art. Photo: Ron Amstutz

Plate 40
Yaxchilán Lintel 25 (feathered serpent), 2017. Silicone, walnut, faux serpent skin, synthetic hair, quetzal faux feather (dyed rooster feather). Dimensions variable. Whitney Museum of American Art, New York; purchase, with funds from the Painting and Sculpture Committee and Sonia and Gaurav Kapadia, 2019.36a-d. Photo: Argenis Apolinario

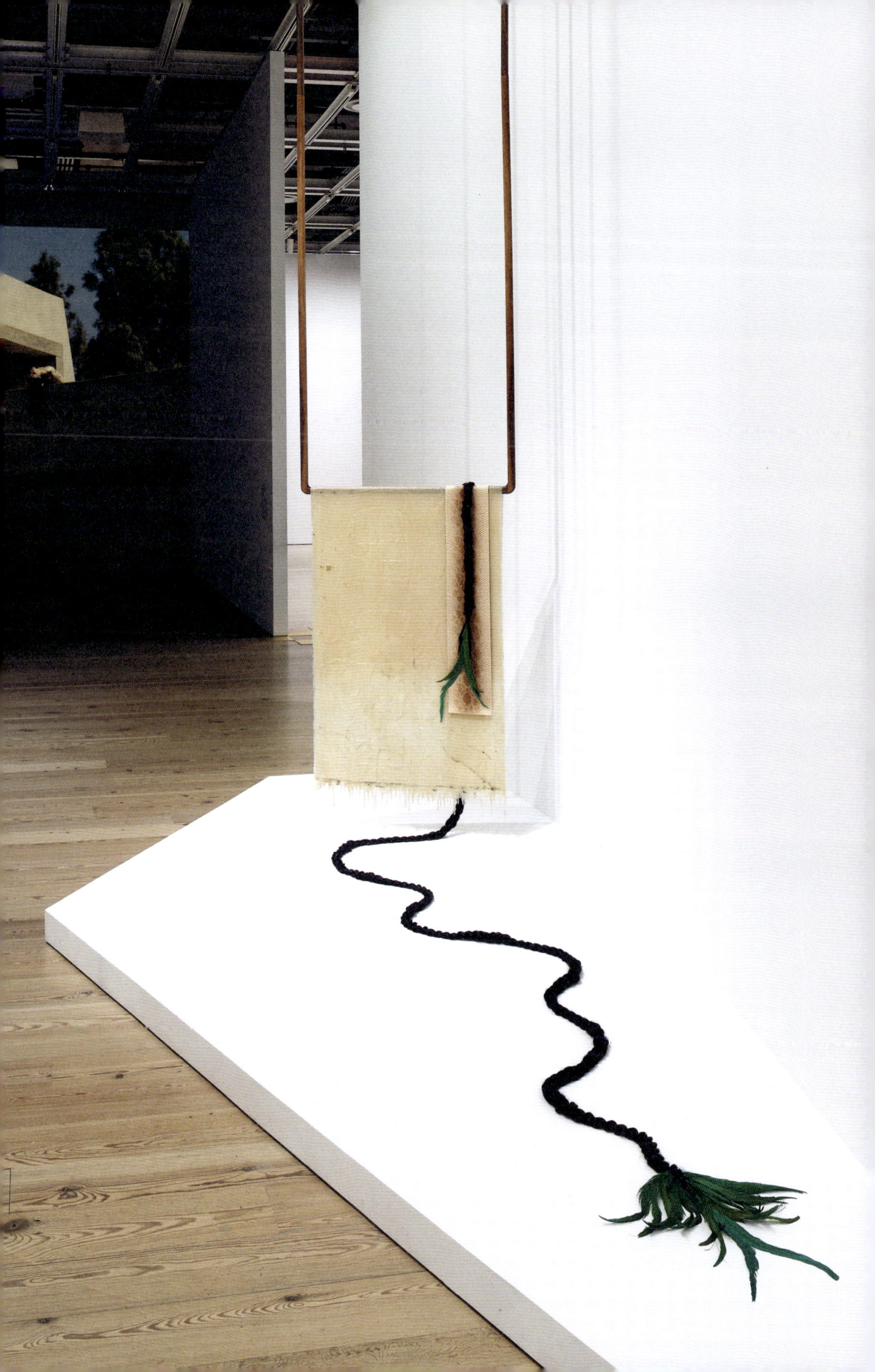

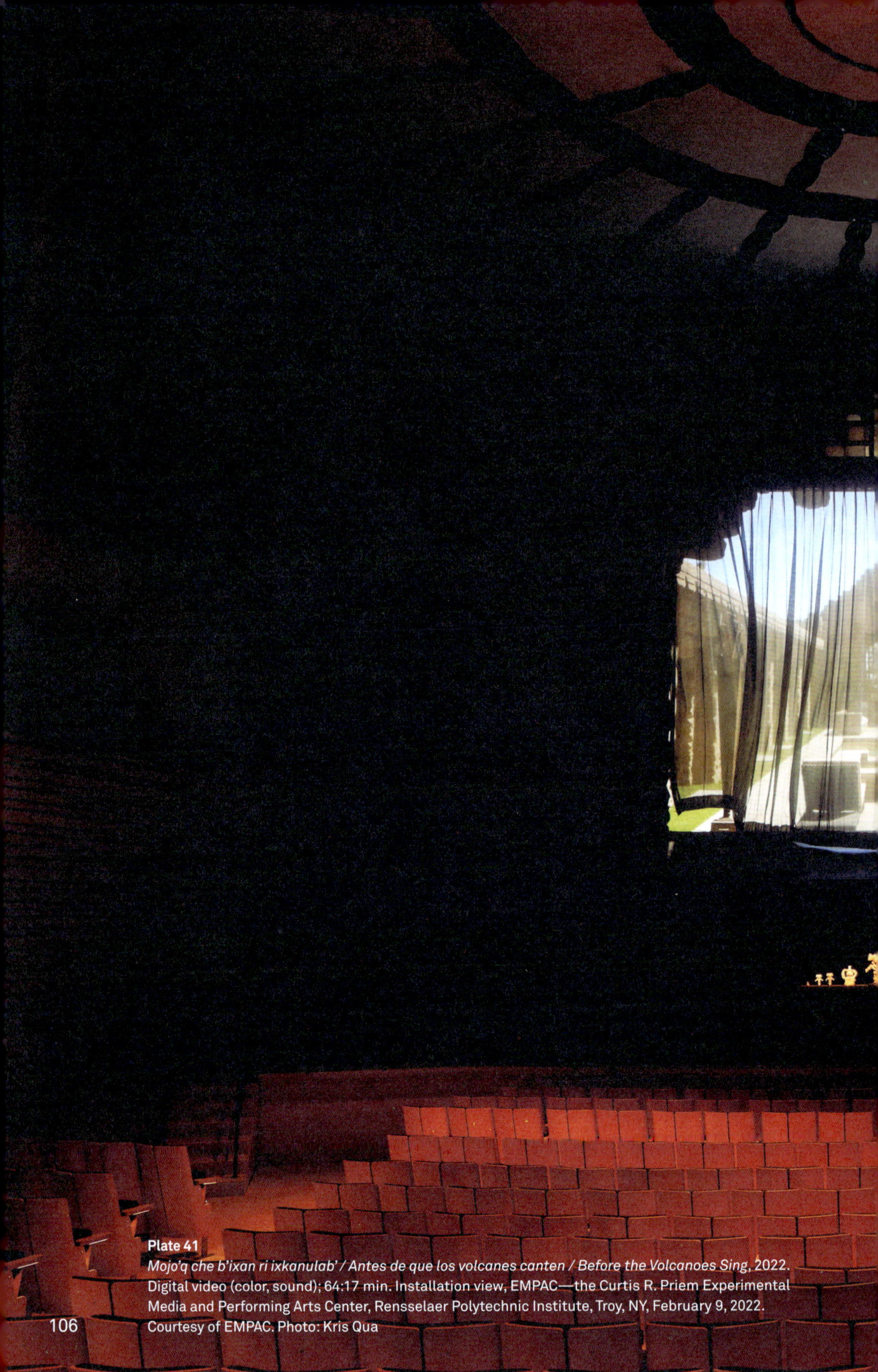

Plate 41
Mojo'q che b'ixan ri ixkanulab' / Antes de que los volcanes canten / Before the Volcanoes Sing, 2022. Digital video (color, sound); 64:17 min. Installation view, EMPAC—the Curtis R. Priem Experimental Media and Performing Arts Center, Rensselaer Polytechnic Institute, Troy, NY, February 9, 2022. Courtesy of EMPAC. Photo: Kris Qua

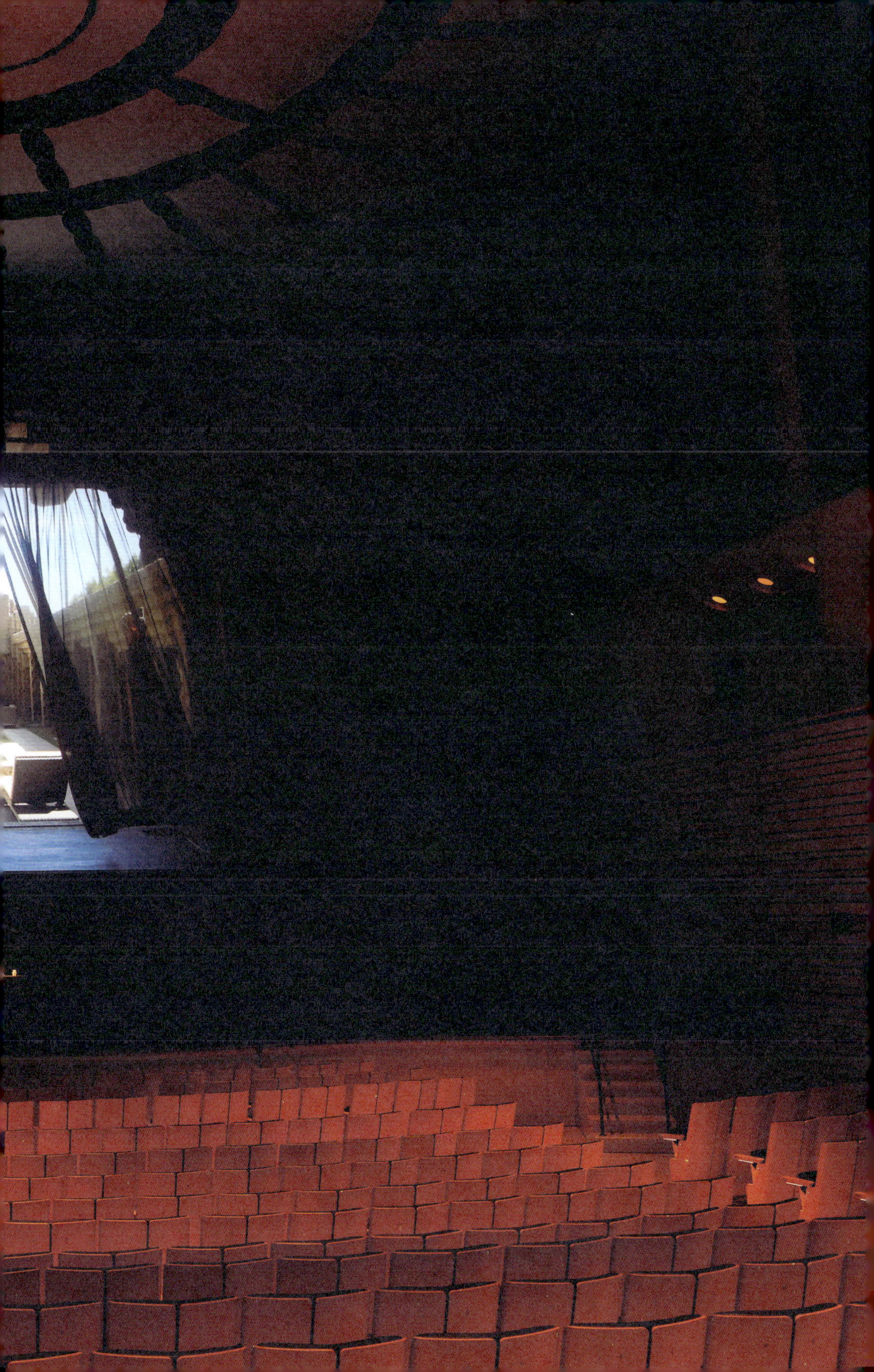

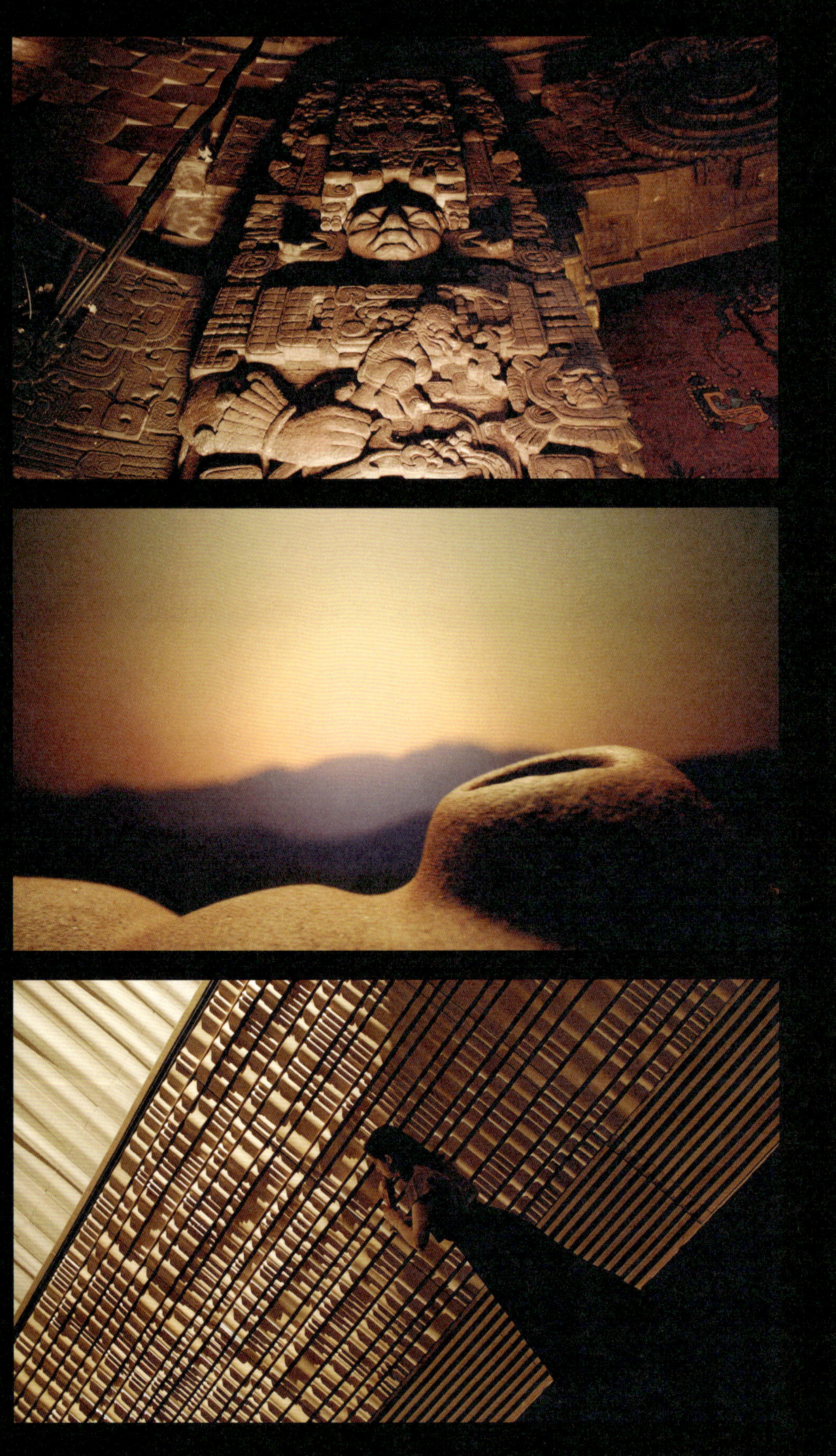

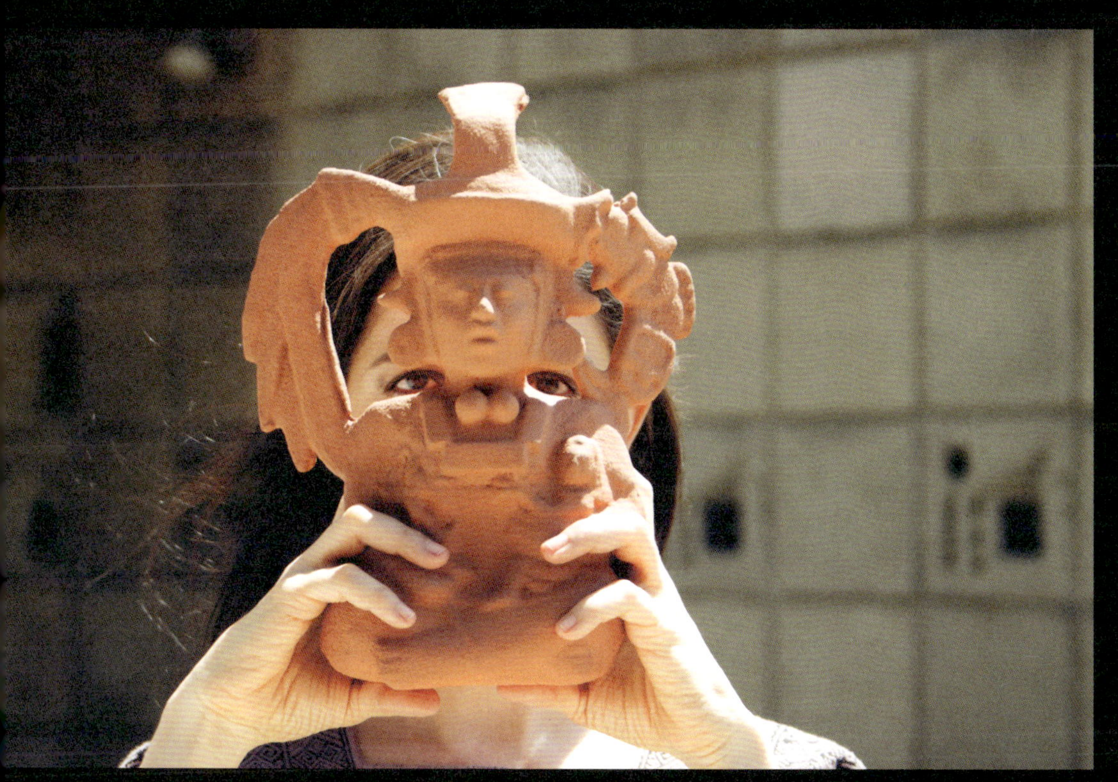

Plates 42–45
Mojo'q che b'ixan ri ixkanulab' / Antes de que los volcanes canten / Before the Volcanoes Sing (stills), 2022. Digital video (color, sound); 64:17 min. Courtesy of the artist, Galeria Luisa Strina, São Paulo, and Commonwealth and Council, Los Angeles

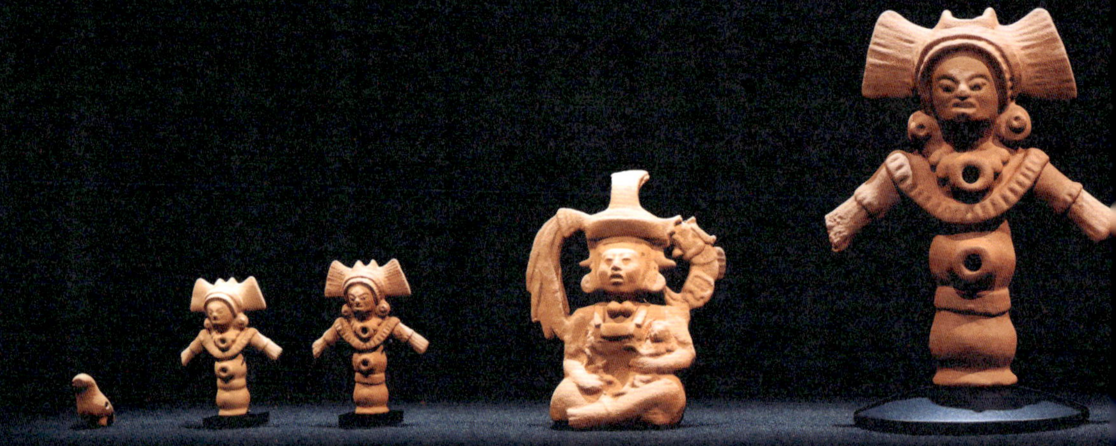

Plate 46
3D-printed replicas of Maya wind instruments played in *Mojo'q che b'ixan ri ixkanulab' / Antes de que los volcanes canten / Before the Volcanoes Sing*, 2022. Installation view, EMPAC—the Curtis R. Priem Experimental Media and Performing Arts Center, Rensselaer Polytechnic Institute, Troy, NY, February 9, 2022. Courtesy of EMPAC. Photo: Kris Qua

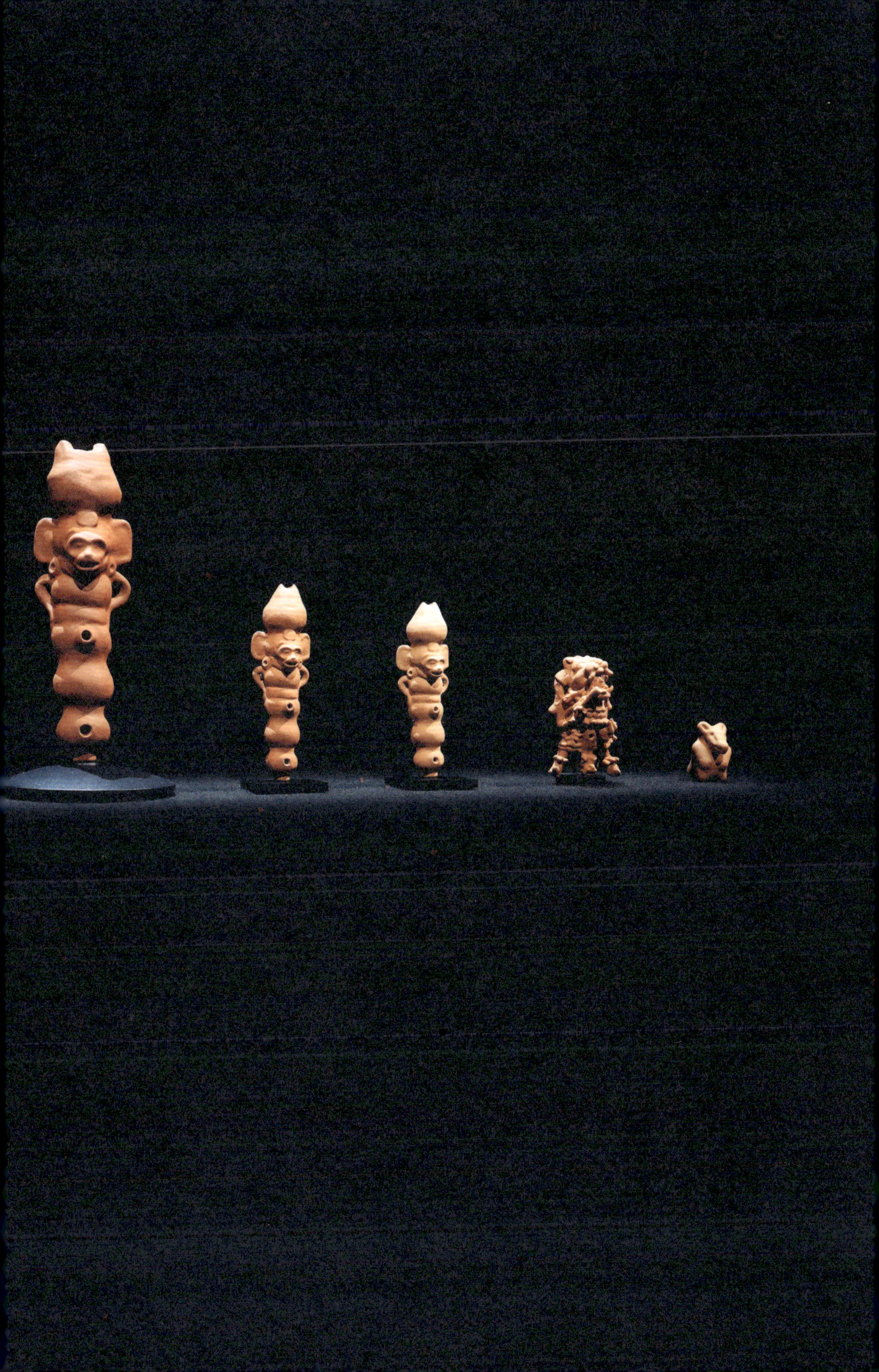

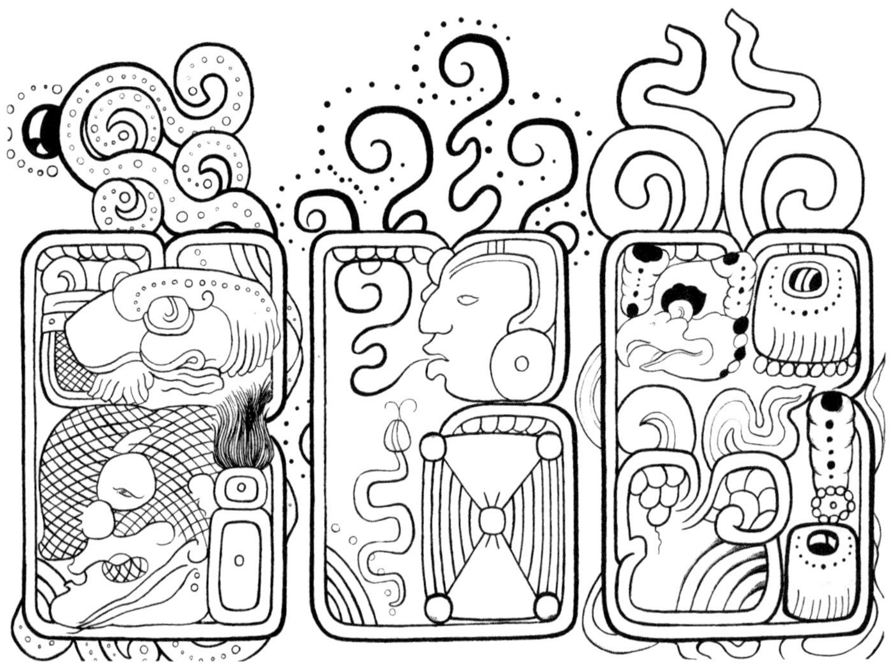

Mojo'q che b'ixan ri ixkanulab'
Antes de que los volcanes canten
Before the Volcanoes Sing

Plate 47
Classic Maya hieroglyphs Tohil Fidel Brito Bernal created for the film, which translate as "Before the Volcanoes Sing." Courtesy of the artist and Tohil Fidel Brito Bernal

Plates 48–50
Mojo'q che b'ixan ri ixkanulab' / Antes de que los volcanes canten / Before the Volcanoes Sing (stills), 2022. Digital video (color, sound); 64:17 min. Courtesy of the artist, Galeria Luisa Strina, São Paulo, and Commonwealth and Council, Los Angeles

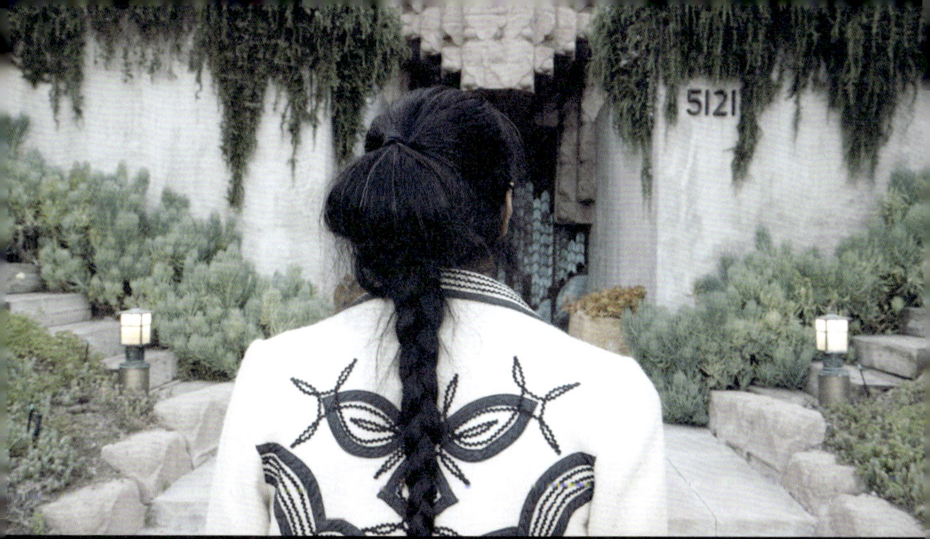

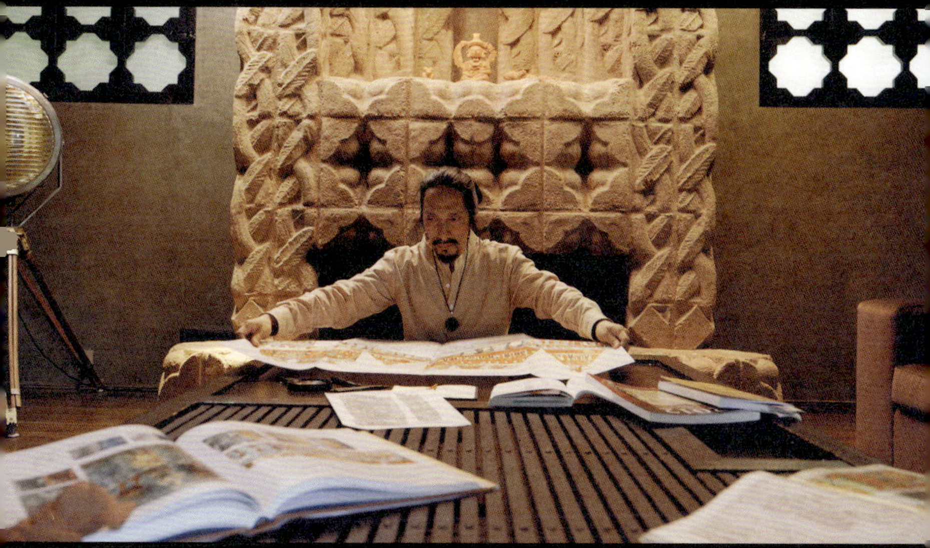

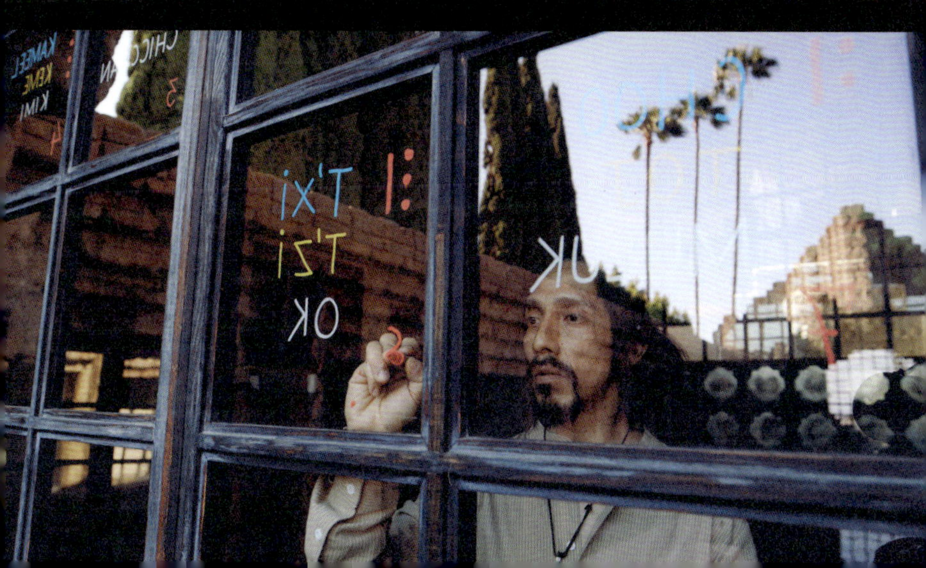

Dame permiso espíritu del camino

Dame permiso espíritu del camino
regalame permiso
para caminar
por este sendero de cemento
que abrieron en tú ombligo
por esta autopista de viento
que corta el silencio
permiso también a ustedes
pájaros que rompen el tímpano del acero
permiso piedras
permiso plantas
permiso animales que resisten en la neblina.
Dejame pasar camino
deja que esta rabia que desorbita mis ojos
se me salga en palabras dulces,
palabras finas, zarandeadas, reventadas,
dejame pasar
que mi voluntad no se pierda
dejame cruzar el barranco, la hondonada,
dejame por favor regresar a mi casa
antes de que los volcanes canten
antes de que el discurso de los cerros
escupa en nuestras bocas.

Rosa Chávez
"Dame permiso espíritu del camino"

K'iche' translation by Vianna González Ajiataz
English translation by Gabriela Ramirez-Chavez

Chaya'a b'e chwech rajawal ri b'e

Chaya'a b'e chwech rajawal ri b'e
Chaya'a b'e kinq'ax na
Kinb'in na apan chi upam ri
Ab'aja b'e
Ri xq'ajow ri amuxu'x
Pa we kaqiq'alaj b'e
Ri ktz'apin uchi' ri tz'ininem
Kinta toq'ob' che alaq xuquje'
laj taq tz'ikin ri kkixilij ri ko'alaj ch'ich'
kinq'ax na laj taq ab'aj
kinq'ax na laj taq che'
kinq'ax na laj taq awaj ri kkikoch' ri sutz'.
Xa kinq'ax na nub'e
Chaya'a b'e chi we ch'u'jarik ri kurech' ri nuwach
Kel lo chwe pa taq ki' taq tzij,
Ch'uch'uj taq tzij, e xojowsam, e paq'inaq,
Chya' alaq nub'e
Mat b'a chja'r ri nuch'uq'ab'
Chya'a la b'e chwe kinq'axej ri siwan, ri jomojik,
Chaya'a la b'e chwe kintzalij chi uwach wachoch
Mojo'q che b'ixan ri ixkanulab'
Mojo'q chi ri kitzijonik ri taq juyub' chechub'an
ulo pa ri qachi'.

Give me permission spirit of the path

Give me permission spirit of the path
grant me permission
to walk
along this cement trail
they carved into your navel
along this wind highway
cutting off silence
I ask your permission, too
birds that break the steel eardrum
permission, stones,
permission, plants,
permission, animals fighting the fog.
Let me pass through
let this eye-gouging rage
come out as sweet words,
words delicate, shaken, exploded
let me pass through
so I don't lose my will
let me cross the ravine, the hollow,
let me please return home
before the volcanoes sing,
before the hills speak,
spit into our mouths.

Plates 51–53
Mojo'q che b'ixan ri ixkanulab' / Antes de que los volcanes canten / Before the Volcanoes Sing, 2022 (stills). Digital video (color, sound); 64:17 min. Courtesy of the artist, Galeria Luisa Strina, São Paulo, and Commonwealth and Council, Los Angeles

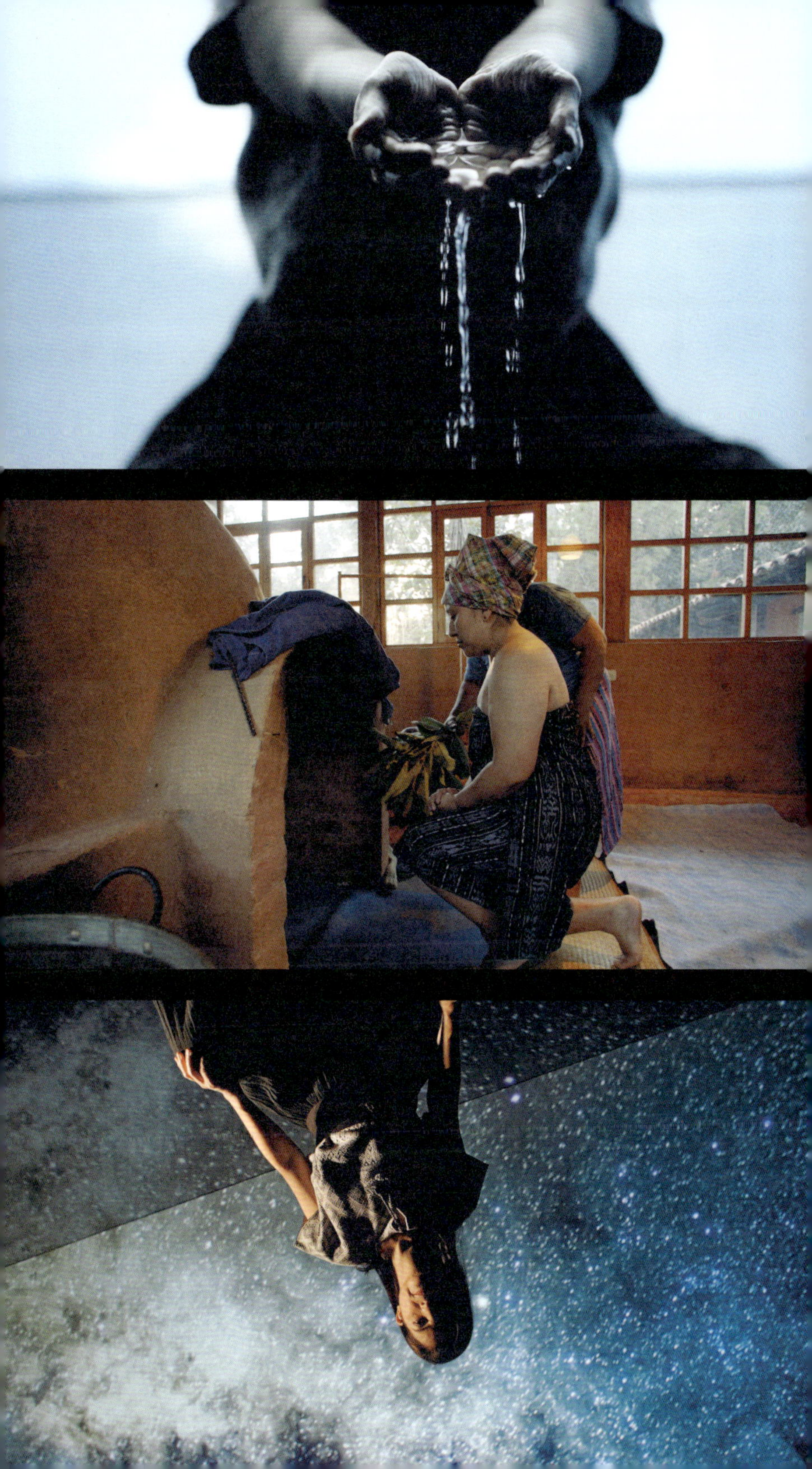

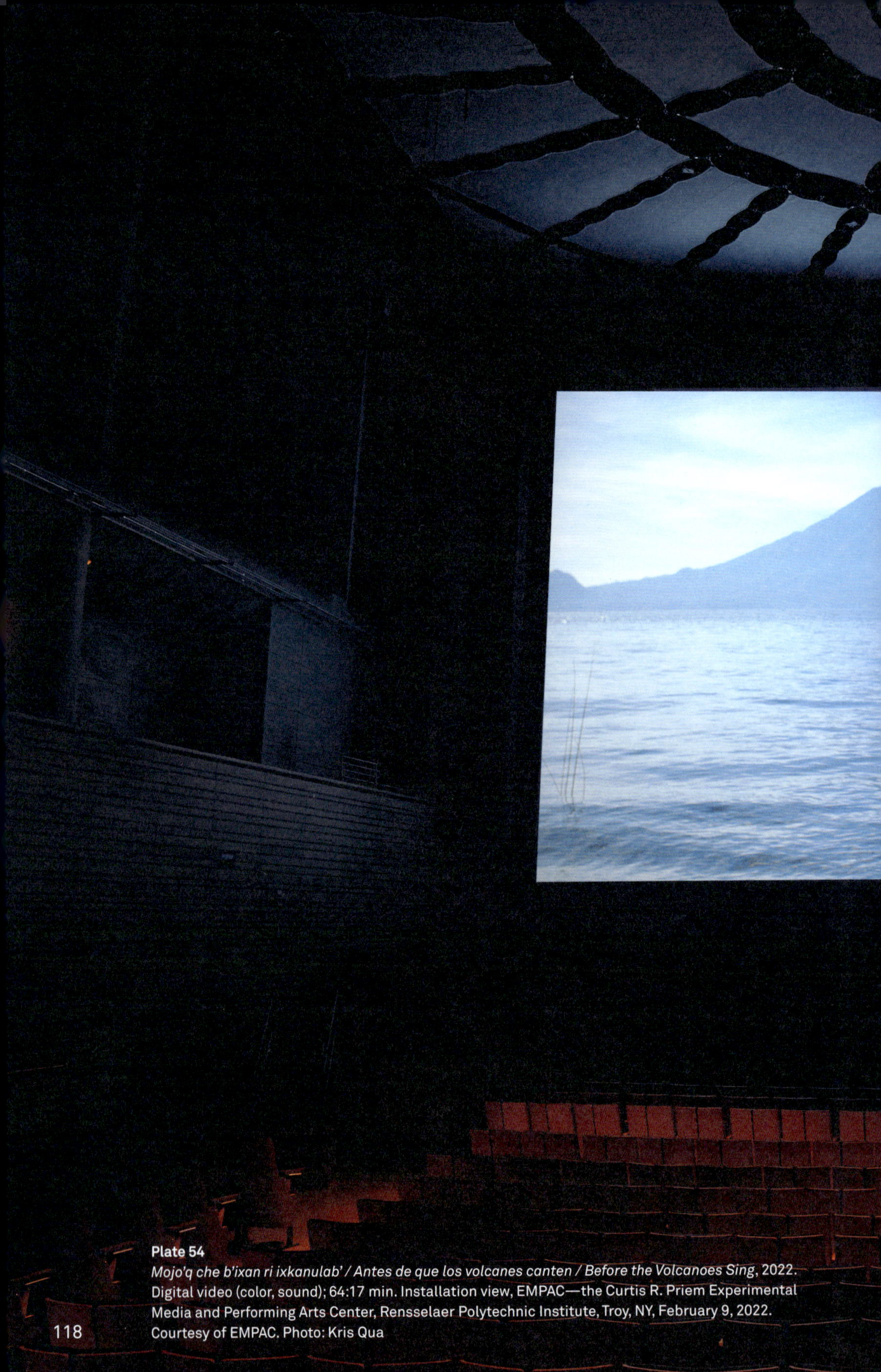

Plate 54
Mojo'q che b'ixan ri ixkanulab' / Antes de que los volcanes canten / Before the Volcanoes Sing, 2022. Digital video (color, sound); 64:17 min. Installation view, EMPAC—the Curtis R. Priem Experimental Media and Performing Arts Center, Rensselaer Polytechnic Institute, Troy, NY, February 9, 2022. Courtesy of EMPAC. Photo: Kris Qua

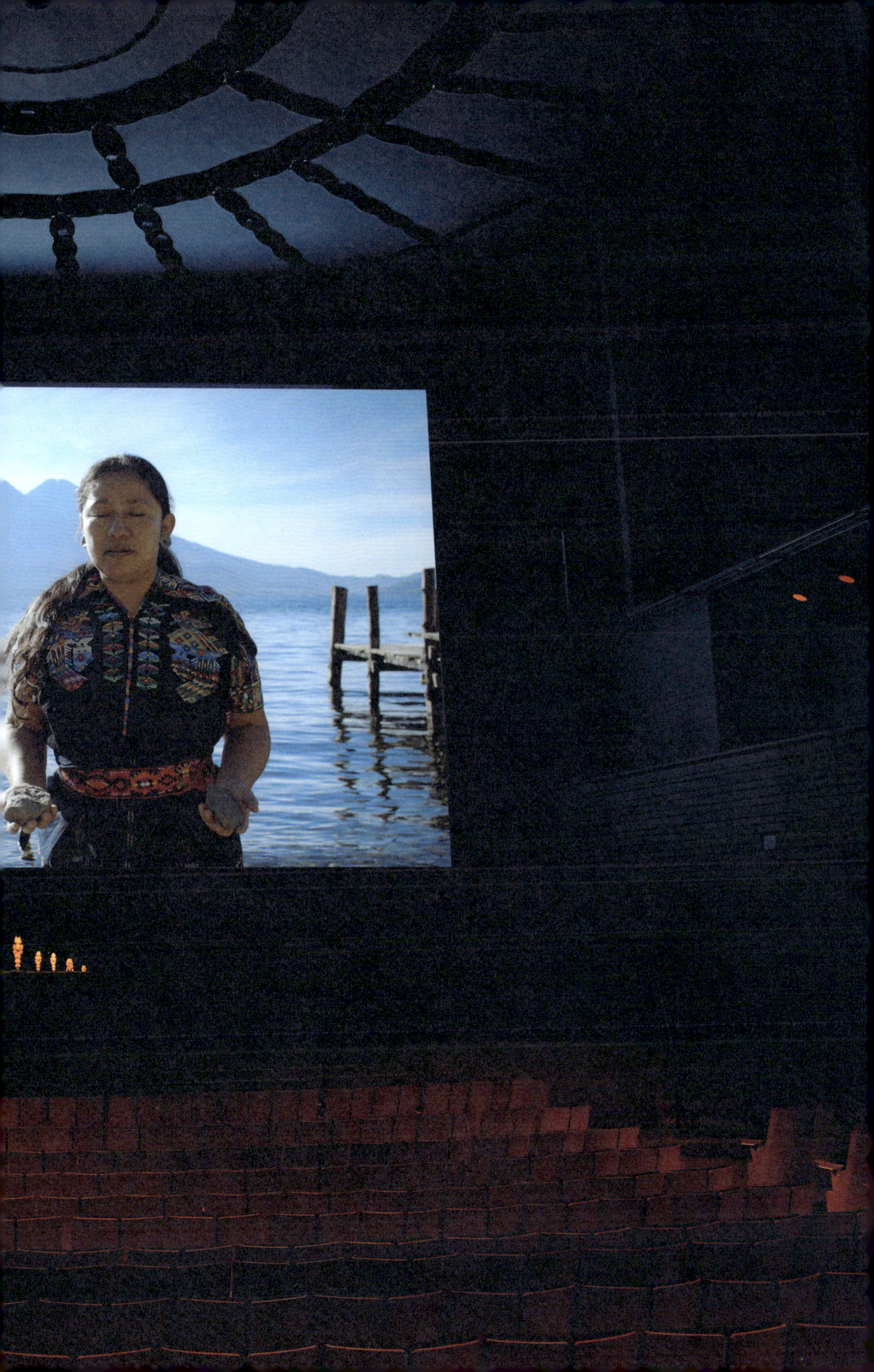

Artist Biography and Exhibition History

Born 1973, Porto Alegre, Brazil
Lives and works in Los Angeles

Selected Solo Exhibitions

2023 *to take root among the stars*, Frye Art Museum, Seattle
Vulneravelmente Humano, Galeria Luisa Strina, São Paulo, Brazil

2022 *Falling From Earth*, Museum of Contemporary Art Denver
Disorientation Towards Collapse, Commonwealth and Council, Los Angeles

2021 *Circumnavigation Towards Exhaustion*, La Kunstalle Mulhouse, France
The 8th Continent, Raymond and Susan Brochstein Pavilion, Moody Center for the Arts at Rice University, Houston

2019 *Future Fossil*, Harvard Radcliffe Institute for Advanced Study, Johnson-Kulukundis Family Gallery, Harvard University, Cambridge, MA
21st Century Wisdom: Healing Frank Lloyd Wright's Textile Block Houses, 18th Street Arts Center, Santa Monica

2018 *Azul Maia*, Galeria Luisa Strina, São Paulo, Brazil
Encontro das Águas, Blanton Museum of Art, University of Texas at Austin

2017 *The Mayan*, Commonwealth and Council, Los Angeles
Stereoscopic Vision, Ezra and Cecile Zilkha Gallery, Center for the Arts, Wesleyan University, Middletown, CT

2016 *Meeting of Waters*, JOAN, Los Angeles

2015 *Streamlined: Belterra, Amazônia / Alberta, Michigan*, Museum of Latin American Art, Long Beach, CA
Brasília Teimosa, Galeria Baobá, Fundação Joaquim Nabuco, Recife, Brazil
How does it travel?, Samuel Freeman Gallery, Los Angeles

2014 *Transplantado (VW Brasília)*, Galeria Luisa Strina, São Paulo, Brazil

2013 *Brasília, Cars, Pools and Other Modernities*, Artpace, San Antonio
Blind Spot, Blaffer Art Museum, University of Houston
Study for a Landscape, Sicardi Gallery, Houston

2011 *Gasto*, Galeria Luisa Strina, São Paulo, Brazil

Selected Solo Screenings

2023 *Ch'u Mayaa*, Video Art Program, High Line, New York
Mojo'q che b'ixan ri ixkanulab' / Antes de que los volcanes canten / Before the Volcanoes Sing, Museum of Contemporary Art Denver
Mojo'q che b'ixan ri ixkanulab' / Antes de que los volcanes canten / Before the Volcanoes Sing, Museum of Contemporary Art, Los Angeles

2022 *Mojo'q che b'ixan ri ixkanulab' / Antes de que los volcanes canten / Before the Volcanoes Sing*, EMPAC—the Curtis R. Priem Experimental Media and Performing Arts Center, Rensselaer Polytechnic Institute, Troy, NY
White Marble Everyday, Museum of Fine Arts, Houston
Ch'u Mayaa, Utah Museum of Fine Arts, University of Utah, Salt Lake City

2020 *Light and Space*, The Broad, Los Angeles (online)

2019 *Ch'u Mayaa*, Saint Louis Art Museum
Ch'u Mayaa, Smith College Museum of Art, Northampton, MA
Ch'u Mayaa, EMPAC—the Curtis R. Priem Experimental Media and Performing Arts Center, Rensselaer Polytechnic Institute, Troy, NY

2018 *When the Land Speaks*, Eli and Edythe Broad Art Museum, Michigan State University, East Lansing

Selected Group Exhibitions

2024 *Whitney Biennial*, Whitney Museum of American Art, New York (forthcoming)

2023 *The Inheritance: Selections from the Whitney's Collection, 1971–2022*, Whitney Museum of American Art, New York

2022 *Mountain/Time*, Aspen Art Museum

2021 *ReVisión: Art in the Americas*, Denver Art Museum
Born in Flames: Feminist Futures, Bronx Museum of the Arts
Por um Sopro de Fúria e Esperança, MuBE (Museu Brasileiro da Escultura e da Ecologia), São Paulo, Brazil

2020 *Mending the Sky*, New Orleans Museum of Art
Kissing Through a Curtain, MASS MoCA, North Adams, MA
Farsa, língua, fratura, ficção: Brasil-Portugal, Sesc Pompéia, São Paulo, Brazil
InterStates of Mind: Rewriting the Map of the United States in the Age of the Automobile, Eli and Edythe Broad Art Museum, Michigan State University, East Lansing
Seismic Movements: Dhaka Art Summit, Bangladesh Shilpakala Academy, Dhaka, Bangladesh

2019 *Crossing Lines, Constructing Home: Displacement and Belonging in Contemporary Art*, Harvard Art Museums, Cambridge, MA
garcía, Raina, Shore, Tossin, Luhring Augustine, New York

2018 *Pacha, Llaqta, Wasichay: Indigenous Space, Modern Architecture, New Art*, Whitney Museum of American Art, New York
12th Gwangju Biennial: Imagined Nations/ Modern Utopias, Gwangju, South Korea
Other Walks, Other Lines, San José Museum of Art
Mon Nord est Ton Sud, Kunsthalle Mulhouse, France
The House Imaginary, San José Museum of Art
Emerald City, K11 Art Foundation, Hong Kong

2017 *Mundos Alternos: Art and Science Fiction in the Americas*, California Museum of Photography, University of California, Riverside (traveling exhibition)
Condemned to Be Modern, Los Angeles Municipal Gallery
Baggage Claims, Orlando Museum of Art (traveling exhibition)
99 Cents or Less, Museum of Contemporary Art Detroit
Lives Between, KADIST, San Francisco, and Center for Contemporary Art, Tel Aviv, Israel
Between Words and Silence: The Work of Translation, Armory Center for the Arts, Pasadena

2016 *TransAMERICAS: a sign, a situation, a concept*, Museum London, Canada
Customizing Language, Los Angeles Contemporary Exhibitions

2015 *United States of Latin America*, Museum of Contemporary Art Detroit
After Landscape. Copied Cities, Fabra i Coats: Centre d'Art Contemporani de Barcelona, Spain
MetaModern, Scottsdale Museum of Contemporary Art (traveling exhibition)

2014 *Made in L.A. 2014*, Hammer Museum, Los Angeles
Unsettled Landscapes, SITE Santa Fe
Bringing the World into the World, Queens Museum, New York
Liberdade em movimento, Fundação Iberê Camargo, Porto Alegre, Brazil

2013 *Southern Panoramas—18º Festival Internacional de Arte Contemporânea Sesc_ Videobrasil*, SESC Pompéia, São Paulo, Brazil
La Elipsis Arquitectónica, Centro Cultural Universitario Tlatelolco, Mexico City

2012 *When Attitudes Became Form Become Attitudes*, CCA Wattis Institute for Contemporary Arts, San Francisco (traveling exhibition)
Dallas Biennale, Dallas Contemporary
2012 Core Exhibition, Glassell School of Art, Museum of Fine Arts, Houston

2011 *Nowhere Near Here*, Houston Center for Photography
Building Arts, Sicardi Gallery, Houston
Young Latino Artists 16: Thought Cloud, Mexic-Arte Museum, Austin

Selected Grants, Awards, Fellowships, and Residencies

2023 Video Commission from the City of Los Angeles for LAX Art Program

2020 Graham Foundation for Advanced Studies in the Fine Arts, Chicago
Video Commission from EMPAC—the Curtis R. Priem Experimental Media and Performing Arts Center, Rensselaer Polytechnic Institute, Troy, NY
Video Commission from The Broad, Los Angeles

2019 Foundation for Contemporary Arts Grants to Artists Award, New York
Fellows of Contemporary Art Fellowship, Los Angeles
Artist Lab Residency, 18th Street Arts Center, Santa Monica
Juméx Foundation Research Grant, Mexico City
LABVERDE, Manaus, Brazil

2018 Los Angeles Artadia Awards

2017 Harvard Radcliffe Institute for Advanced Study Fellowship, Harvard University (ended 2018)

2016 Video Commission from the City of Los Angeles Department of Cultural Affairs for the exhibition *Condemned to Be Modern* as part of the Getty Foundation's *Pacific Standard Time: LA/LA* exhibition

2015 Residency Fellowship, Fundação Joaquim Nabuco, Recife, Brazil

2014 Emerging Artist Fellowship, California Community Foundation

2013 Artpace San Antonio International Artist-in-Residence
ARC Grant, Center for Cultural Innovation

2012 Artistic Innovation Grant, Center for Cultural Innovation
VI Concurso de Videoarte Grant, Fundação Joaquim Nabuco

2011 SOMA Residency, Mexico City

2010 Core Program Fellowship, Museum of Fine Arts, Houston (ended 2012)

2009 Skowhegan School of Painting & Sculpture

Public Collections

Art Institute of Chicago
Eli and Edythe Broad Art Museum, Michigan State University, East Lansing
Casa Niemeyer, Universidade de Brasília, Brazil
Frye Art Museum, Seattle
Hammer Museum, Los Angeles
Harvard Art Museums, Cambridge, MA
Instituto Inhotim Collection, Brumadinho, Brazil
Kadist Art Foundation, San Francisco
Los Angeles County Museum of Art
New Orleans Museum of Art
Museum of Fine Arts, Houston
Seattle Art Museum
Smith College Museum of Art, Northampton, MA
Whitney Museum of American Art, New York

Education

2009 MFA, California Institute of the Arts, Valencia, CA

2000 BFA, Fundação Armando Álvares Penteado, São Paulo

Exhibition Checklist

Unmapping the World, 2011
Ink on tracing paper
Four drawings, 33 × 46 in. each; one balled-up drawing, 6 × 7 × 6 in. (approx.)
Courtesy of the artist, Galeria Luisa Strina, São Paulo, and Commonwealth and Council, Los Angeles
Plate 31

Nova gramática de formas #2 (New Grammar of Forms #2), 2018
Terracotta, baskets woven from used Amazon.com delivery boxes and archival inkjet prints, thread, wood
Dimensions variable
Collection of Janice Niemi and Dennis Braddock, Seattle; Promised gift to the Seattle Art Museum
Plate 21

Future Fossil, 2018
Cedar tree trunk, rocks, roots, leaves, bark, soil, sand, plaster, cement, silicone, foam, resin, aluminum foil, electronic waste, recycled plastics (PET, HDPE, LDPE, PP, and PS)
14 × 240 × 17 in.
Los Angeles County Museum of Art, Purchased with funds provided by AHAN: Studio Forum, 2019 Art Here and Now purchase
Plates 25–26

#AmazonisPlanitia2, 2018
Archival inkjet prints on glossy photo paper, recycled plastic from artist's own waste
20¾ × 29⅞ in. and 11¼ × 19⅝ in.
Courtesy of the artist and Commonwealth and Council, Los Angeles
Plate 28

The Only Lasting Truth Is Change, 2019
Plaster, cement, foam, urethane, silicone, aluminum foil
12 in. diam.
Courtesy of the artist and Commonwealth and Council, Los Angeles
Plate 27

Disorientation Towards Collapse, 2020
Used Amazon.com delivery boxes, wood
60 × 84 × 1½ in.
The Mohn Family Trust
Plates 17–18

Becoming Mineral, 2021
Porcelain
8 × 6 × 1½ in.
Frye Art Museum, Purchased with funds provided by the Contemporary Council, 2023.005.02
Plates 3–4

Rising Temperature Casualty (Prunus persica var. nucipersica, home garden, Los Angeles), 2021
Silicone, black pigment, tree bark
44 × 115 × 4 in. (approx.)
Courtesy of the artist and Commonwealth and Council, Los Angeles
Plates 6–7

Rising Temperature Casualty (Prunus persica, home garden, Los Angeles), 2022
Silicone, black pigment, tree roots
126 × 48 × 58 in. (approx.)
Frye Art Museum, Purchased with funds provided by the Contemporary Council, 2023.005.01
Plate 10

Valuable Element, 2022
Archival inkjet print, inkjet dust, glass vial
34 × 34 × 1½ in.
Courtesy of the artist and Commonwealth and Council, Los Angeles
Plate 30

Mojo'q che b'ixan ri ixkanulab' / Antes de que los volcanes canten / Before the Volcanoes Sing, 2022
Digital video (color, sound); 64:17 min.
Commissioned by EMPAC—the Curtis R. Priem Experimental Media and Performing Arts Center, Rensselaer Polytechnic Institute. Courtesy of the artist, Galeria Luisa Strina, São Paulo, and Commonwealth and Council, Los Angeles
Plates 41–54

Replicas of Maya wind instruments played in *Mojo'q che b'ixan ri ixkanulab'*
All courtesy of the artist, Galeria Luisa Strina, São Paulo, and Commonwealth and Council, Los Angeles
Plate 46

Human Figure, 2019
3D-printed terracotta replica of a Pre-Columbian Maya globular flute (Guatemalan Highlands, 300–900 CE) in the Vical Museum of Pre-Columbian Art and Modern Glass, Antigua, Guatemala
6 × 4¾ × 2½ in.

Monkey, 2019
3D-printed terracotta replica of a Pre-Columbian Maya globular flute (Guatemalan Highlands, 300–900 CE) in the Vical Museum of Pre-Columbian Art and Modern Glass, Antigua, Guatemala
11 × 3½ × 3⅛ in.

Bird, 2019
3D-printed terracotta replica of a Pre-Columbian Maya ocarina (Ceibal, Guatemala, n.d.) in the collection of the Ceibal Laboratory, Guatemala
1¾ × 1⅝ × 1¼ in.

Opossum, 2019
3D-printed terracotta replica of a Pre-Columbian Maya ocarina (Playa de los Muertos, Ulúa Valley, Yoro, Honduras, n.d.) in the Peabody Museum of Archaeology and Ethnology, Harvard University, Cambridge, Massachusetts
3½ × 2½ × 2¾ in.

Figure in Jaguar Costume with Blowgun, 2021
3D-printed terracotta replica of a Pre-Columbian Maya globular flute (Guatemalan Highlands, ca. 500 CE) in the Denver Art Museum
7 × 4½ × 3¾ in.

Seated Female Figure with Monkey and Child, 2021
3D-printed terracotta replica of a Pre-Columbian Maya ocarina (Guatemalan Highlands, Alta Verapaz region, 550–950 CE) in the Denver Art Museum
14¼ × 8½ × 4¼ in.

Future Geography: The Five Galaxies of Stephan's Quintet, 2022
Used Amazon.com delivery boxes, archival inkjet print on photo paper with lamination, wood
66 × 79½ × 1½ in.
Commissioned by the Frye Art Museum. Courtesy of the artist, Galeria Luisa Strina, São Paulo, and Commonwealth and Council, Los Angeles
Plate 11

Future Geography: Cosmic Cliffs, 2023
Used Amazon.com delivery boxes, archival inkjet print on photo paper with lamination, walnut
60 × 71½ × 1 in.
Commissioned by the Frye Art Museum. Courtesy of the artist, Galeria Luisa Strina, São Paulo, and Commonwealth and Council, Los Angeles
Plates 12–13

Future Geography: Small Magellanic Cloud, 2023
Used Amazon.com delivery boxes, archival inkjet print on photo paper with lamination, wood
72 × 45 × 1½ in.
Commissioned by the Frye Art Museum. Courtesy of the artist, Galeria Luisa Strina, São Paulo, and Commonwealth and Council, Los Angeles

Future Geography: Tapestry of Blazing Starbirth, 2023
Used Amazon.com delivery boxes, archival inkjet print on photo paper with lamination, wood
60 × 72 × 1½ in.
Commissioned by the Frye Art Museum. Courtesy of the artist, Galeria Luisa Strina, São Paulo, and Commonwealth and Council, Los Angeles

Maritime Arrivals, 2023
Archival ink on used Amazon.com delivery envelopes
23¾ × 61¾ in.
Commissioned by the Frye Art Museum. Courtesy of the artist, Galeria Luisa Strina, São Paulo, and Commonwealth and Council, Los Angeles
Plate 32

Corso del fiume delle Amazzoni fino a Marte (Course of the Amazon River to Mars), 2023
Archival ink on used Amazon.com delivery envelopes
23½ × 20½ in.
Commissioned by the Frye Art Museum. Courtesy of the artist, Galeria Luisa Strina, São Paulo, and Commonwealth and Council, Los Angeles

Facsímil de la disputada carta portulana de Cristóbal Colón, Mappa Mundi, siglo XV (Facsimile of Christopher Columbus's Disputed Portolan Chart, World Map, Fifteenth Century), 2023
Archival ink on used Amazon.com delivery envelopes
38¼ × 52½ in.
Commissioned by the Frye Art Museum. Courtesy of the artist, Galeria Luisa Strina, São Paulo, and Commonwealth and Council, Los Angeles

Planisphere Celeste Septentrional; Planisphere Celeste Meridional, Paris, 1705 (Northern Celestial Planisphere; Southern Celestial Planisphere, Paris, 1705), 2023
Archival ink on used Amazon.com delivery envelopes
32¼ × 46¼ in.
Commissioned by the Frye Art Museum. Courtesy of the artist, Galeria Luisa Strina, São Paulo, and Commonwealth and Council, Los Angeles

Contributors

Tohil Fidel Brito Bernal
Multidisciplinary Ixil artist Tohil Fidel Brito Bernal studied archaeology at the University of San Carlos in Guatemala. Exile marked his way of perceiving time-space, leading him to explore temporalities of Maya philosophies. In engravings, sculptures, texts, performances, and exploratory symbolic language, he alludes to fire as a means of communication and as an entity. Mesoamerican epigraphy and iconography foster an aesthetic and political dialogue in his work. Through collaboration, he generates dynamics that foster new nuances in his work.

Vic Brooks
Vic Brooks is associate director of arts and senior curator of time-based visual art at EMPAC—the Curtis R. Priem Experimental Media and Performing Arts Center at Rensselaer Polytechnic Institute. She is also on the visiting faculty at the Center for Curatorial Studies Bard and serves on the board of Atelier Calder. Brooks is a recipient of the Warhol Foundation's Curatorial Research Fellowship and writes on the infrastructures and production of time-based art.

Rosa Chávez
Rosa Chávez is a poet, artist, activist, and educator of K'iche'-Kaqchikel Maya origin. Alongside work for theater, performance, and video, Chávez has published the poetry collections *Casa Solitaria* (2005), *Piedra Abaj'* (2009/2019), *El corazón de la piedra* (2010), *Quitapenas* (2010), *AWAS secretos para curar* (2014), and *Fanzine Abya Yala* (2017). Her work appears in various magazines, plays, memoirs, and poetry anthologies in Latin America, Europe, and the United States.

Leslie Dick
Leslie Dick is a writer currently living in Connecticut. She taught in the Art Program at CalArts (the California Institute of the Arts) from 1992 to 2021 and has been a visiting critic at Yale School of Art for the last ten years. Her writing on art includes essays on Marisa Merz, Paul Thek, Sarah Charlesworth, Walid Raad, Fiona Connor, and Kang Seung Lee, among others.

Georgia Erger
Georgia Erger is associate curator at the Frye Art Museum. Previously, she was assistant curator at the Eli and Edythe Broad Art Museum at Michigan State University, where she organized exhibitions ranging from the thematic survey *InterStates of Mind: Rewriting the Map of the United States in the Age of the Automobile* (2020) to solo presentations including *Caroline Monnet: Bridging Distance* (2021) and *John Lucas and Claudia Rankine: Situations* (2020).

Frye Art Museum

Staff

Curatorial and Exhibitions
Amanda Donnan
Georgia Erger
Ken Kelly
Laura Landau
Erin Langner
Shane Montgomery
Alexis L. Silva

Collection Management and Registration
Nives Meštrović

Exhibition Installers
Timothy Brown
Sarah Crouse
Dan Gurney
Claire Johnson
Robert Kunz
Leo Mayberry
Tyna Ontko
Dave Proscia
Chris Sheridan
Kristin Schimik
Tamara Twa
Sihan Wang

Communications
Runyon Colie
Kristin Galioto
Ingrid Langston
Lexi McCauley
Rachel Townsend

Development and Membership
Victoria Boles
Annick Garcia
Stephen Jackson
Becky Kowals
amanda mead
Micah Nemerever
Anatol San Jose Steck

Education
Lynda Belt
Anna Buxton
Yazmin Cojulun
Kelsey Donahue
Connie Fu
Samantha Sanders
Lila Thomas

Facilities
ChanMakara Ken
Chanphalla Ken
Adam Porter
Sopheap Rany

Finance and Accounting
Lanie Bolieu
Dana Forhan
Tom Mitchell
Heather Ratcliff

Director's Office
Roxanne Hadfield
Jamilee Lacy

Human Resources
Nathanael Elongo

Security
Johnny Banchero
Kurt Burghardt
Garrett Clark
Zack Conklin
Lydia Gerard
Thomas Hanchett
Sandra Huezo-Menjivar
Stephen Kelley
Ilan Levine
Cam Lipham
Ben Moreau
Jeremy Pierson
Kassie Procopio
Lila Thomas
Suzann Vaughn
Andrew Wonders
Alex Wong

Store
Rachael Lang
Elissa Maxwell

This book is published in conjunction with the exhibition *Clarissa Tossin: to take root among the stars*, organized by the Frye Art Museum, Seattle, curated by Associate Curator Georgia Erger, and presented at the Frye, October 7, 2023–January 7, 2024.

The exhibition and publication are made possible with generous support from the Frye Foundation and Frye Members. Media sponsorship provided by Encore Media Group.

FRYE
/Foundation

encore

Library of Congress Cataloging-in-Publication Data
Names: Erger, Georgia, editor. | Charles and Emma Frye Art Museum, organizer, host institution.
Title: Clarissa Tossin : to take root among the stars / edited by Georgia Erger.
Description: Seattle, WA : Frye Art Museum, 2023. | "This book is published in conjunction with the exhibition Clarissa Tossin: to take root among the stars, organized by the Frye Art Museum, Seattle, curated by Associate Curator Georgia Erger, and presented at the Frye, October 7, 2023–January 7, 2024"—Colophon. | Includes bibliographical references.
Identifiers: LCCN 2023024642 | ISBN 9781646570355 (paperback)
Subjects: LCSH: Tossin, Clarissa, 1973-—Exibitions. | Human ecology in art—Exhibitions.
Classification: LCC NX533.Z9 T672 2023 | DDC 709.2–dc23/eng/20230609
LC record available at https://lccn.loc.gov/2023024642

Designed by Purtill Family Business
Layout by Thomas Eykemans
Copyedited by Kathleen Garrett
Proofread by Janice Lee
Typeset in Akkurat Pro by Maggie Lee
Color separations by I/O Color, Seattle
Produced by Marquand Books, Seattle
www.marquandbooks.com
Printed and bound by Artron Art Group, China

Cover: *Rising Temperature Casualty (Persea americana, home garden, Los Angeles)* (detail), 2021. Silicone, bark, roots. 126 × 48 × 58 in. Courtesy of the artist and Galeria Luisa Strina, São Paulo. Photo: Edouard Fraipont
Back cover: *Death by Heat Wave (Acer pseudoplatanus, Mulhouse Forest)* (detail), 2021. Silicone, black pigment, bark. 62¼ × 36 ft. Courtesy of the artist and Commonwealth and Council, Los Angeles
Inside front and back covers: *Future Geography: Cosmic Cliffs* (detail), 2023. Used Amazon.com delivery boxes, archival inkjet print on photo paper with lamination, walnut. 60 × 71½ × 1 in. Commissioned by the Frye Art Museum. Courtesy of the artist, Galeria Luisa Strina, São Paulo, and Commonwealth and Council, Los Angeles. Photo: Brica Wilcox

Frye Art Museum
704 Terry Avenue
Seattle, WA 98104
USA
www.fryemuseum.org

Available through:
ARTBOOK | D.A.P.
75 Broad Street, Suite 630
New York, NY 10004
USA
www.artbook.com